MAKE YOUR HOUSE DO THE HOUSEWORK

By Don Aslett
and Laura Aslett Simons

Illustrated by Craig LaGory

Writer's Digest Books

Cincinnati, Ohio

Library of Congress Cataloging-in-Publication Data

Aslett, Don, 1935-
  Make your house do the housework.

  Includes index.
  1. House cleaning. 2. House furnishings. 3. House construction. I. Simons, Laura
Aslett, 1958—
TX324.A7583   1986   648'.5   86-24541
ISBN 0-89879-227-4

*Design by Carole Winters and Craig LaGory. Additional illustrations by
Lawrence Goodridge.*

Quality Paperback Book Club ® offers recording on compact
discs, cassettes and records. For information and catalog
write to QPB Recordings, Dept. 902, Camp Hill, PA 17012.

Make Your House Do the Housework is dedicated to all of you brilliant women who for years (make that centuries) have thought up and planned out ways to design and build housework out of your lives, but were ignored and put down by builders, architects, and financial institutions. You made sense to us, so here are your ideas and ours for ways we can all spend less time on the housework and more on the truly important things in life.

Acknowledgments

Book work, like housework, involves more than one person. Thanks to those who made *Make Your House Do the Housework* work!

Nancy Everson
Carol Cartaino
Mark Browning
Craig LaGory
Marylyn Alexander
Beth Franks
Linda Sanders
David Lewis
Jo Hoff

Also, thanks to Russell and Mary Wright, for their inspiring book, *Guide to Easier Living*.

Contents

*A **house with most of the housework and
chores designed, built, and decorated out?
Is there . . . could there . . . be such a thing?***

Certainly!
There should have been one a long time ago.

Why hasn't a maintenance-free house appeared before now? Ask any homemaker. The answer is simple. MEN build houses, but men, for the most part, don't do housework (cleaning, cooking, laundry, child care). So they don't think much about the time and labor it takes to keep a house up. Only a minute percentage of the homemaker's work-saving ideas ever get implemented in structure or furnishings. Yet most cleaning and maintenance chores can be minimized if not eliminated entirely from your house.

This book is intended to show and share with you all the possibilities . . . for cutting the maintenance problems out of your house and your life.

All you need is some ingenuity, a little effort, and a modest amount of money . . . and you can do most of your housework with a hammer. It's been your idea all along. Here is how *we* got involved—began to pick up on your ideas and launch our study of maintenance-free design and construction.

About the Authors:

Who We Are
and
Why We Wrote This Book

Don Aslett

Laura Aslett Simons

Don Aslett

Thirty years of professional cleaning, both homes and businesses, has required lots of sleepless nights, personal commitment, and an enormous shoulder. Why the enormous shoulder? To push mops, carry ladders, and handle huge cleaning machines? Nope, it was for home and building owners to cry on.

A professional cleaner and painter gets a concentrated view of house problems. Homeowners express and confide their house design displeasures to "the professional" more than they would even to a friend or psychiatrist.

"Someone ought to . . ."

"Things would be a lot easier if . . ."

"That's the last time I'll ever . . ."

"Wouldn't it be nice if . . ."

"When will they stop making . . ."

"In my new house I'm going to . . ."

2

This book is my answer to those complaints—and my effort to rescue the homemaker.

Thirty years ago I left a remote Idaho farm, enrolled at Idaho State University, and started a housecleaning business to pay for my education. Earning my way as a professional cleaner, I developed skills and techniques that reduced some common cleaning chores up to 75 percent. I expanded my business into other states and added services such as home repair, floor refinishing, paperhanging, painting, rebuilding after fire loss and water damage, and even landscaping. By graduation, I'd handled almost every conceivable home maintenance problem.

During our school years my wife, Barbara, and I worked on plans for a house for ourselves and our six children, ages one to eight. Remembering the cleaning woes of the thousands of homes we'd cleaned by then, we designed *out* some of the time-takers and designed *in* low-maintenance, easy living, and safety. We finished the plans, got the permits, and started building the 5,000-square-foot ranch home ourselves. We poured concrete, bricked, roofed, plumbed, and wired most of the house, where we still live today.

By the time we'd finished the house, my cleaning business was rapidly growing into one of the major cleaning firms in the country. In a short while, a growth opportunity required that we move to the resort town of Sun Valley, Idaho. Since the contract called for a five-year stay, we decided to build another house.

It took three months to find a ten-acre piece of land in the pines by a creek, a month to design the house, and two years to build it. Again we built it ourselves—we even put in the road, built the fireplace, and laid the carpets—

this time we did it all! And in our second house I incorporated even more of the maintenance-freeing ideas I'd collected from homemakers whose homes I'd cleaned over the years.

By the time we returned to our original ranch home, I was writing and consulting on ways to cut cleaning costs in homes and commercial buildings. I was hired to design "cleaning prevention" into a new 2.3-million-square-foot Southern Bell headquarters building in Atlanta, Georgia. This design job was an excellent chance to use more of the maintenance-free design and building ideas I'd garnered in my years of professional cleaning. **I helped Southern Bell eliminate unneeded equipment, reduce energy costs, and make the operation safer, as well as save millions of dollars' worth of unnecessary cleaning.**

At the same time I was expanding my efforts to free homemakers of unnecessary drudgery. My first book, *Is There Life After Housework?*, was devoted to teaching people the best and easiest ways to do housework. It had a short chapter on preventing housework through maintenance-free design and construction. That chapter resulted in hundreds of letters asking for ideas to save cleaning time and money. I decided to take all those ideas and concepts and put them into a book.

To round out my practical experience in this area I decided to design and build a model maintenance-free house as I worked on the book. We love Idaho but building and pouring concrete are slowed down by the cold weather there. So we vowed to build our next house in a more temperate area—the most beautiful place we'd ever seen—the Island of Kauai, Hawaii. A friend hunted up a piece of property, we acquired it and spent four years (still collecting maintenance-

free ideas) planning the design of the building and landscaping. It became a huge project involving many people . . . trying to build a house that you didn't have to be rich to afford, a house that called for a minimum of cleaning yet still had the spark of warmth and personality.

Meanwhile, as soon as I announced the topic of this book, I was flooded with requests for the book and for information. Major women's magazines and architectural design firms called; people who were building houses begged me to come show them how to make their homes "easy to clean." I was doing hundreds of media appearances a year by now to promote my other books, but no matter how hard I tried to keep the subject on the fine points of housecleaning or clutter control (or whatever the topic of the book I was currently promoting), everyone wanted to talk about cutting chores by building them OUT! The needs—and how well existing materials and designs met those needs—were reported by letter, TV call-in, evaluation cards, and during on-the-spot visits to homes with problems.

Feeling the need for help in pulling all this information together (and realizing that the feminine touch on this book would be a great advantage), I asked my daughter Laura, an interior designer and mother of three, to jump in and join the project.

Laura Aslett Simons

Laura is the oldest of our six children, and she had a head start on most interior designers. At age twelve, she was keeping books, doing maid work, cleaning, and helping to run the family motel in

Sun Valley. From the age of fourteen to seventeen she ran one of the regular routes for my janitorial company—cleaning buildings, banks, condominiums, and hotels. Painting, carpet laying, and wallpapering were not strange tasks to Laura either.

When she left for college, her interest (besides skiing) was in interior design. She completed her degree and then married a classmate. While he finished his degree, Laura worked as a designer in a custom kitchen and bath cabinet shop. She worked with people who were building their dream homes, remodeling their present dwellings, or building first homes; almost all of them had one objective for their new home or kitchen (and they expressed it with great gusto and persistence): "IT MUST BE EASY TO CLEAN" as well as beautiful to look at. Either of these tasks is fairly easy to accomplish by itself, but to design a lovely kitchen which is also step-saving and easy-to-clean takes a special talent. But Laura understood housecleaning. Her firsthand knowledge of the working problems combined with her professional training enabled her to design simple, workable, low-maintenance kitchens and baths.

During the four years we worked on this book, Laura analyzed the "comment cards" we handed out to the more than 100,000 women and men I taught at cleaning seminars. We sent out questionnaires, contacted manufacturing firms and decorating specialists, and sought out all the information we could find. **We compiled, assembled, weeded, condensed, and simplified and found lots of good ideas. We're going to share a few hundred of these work-saving ideas with you, many of which you may have imagined or dreamed about but never quite got around to incorporating into your house.** You'll learn not only how to minimize cleaning, but how to *prevent* it in the first place.

Do Your Housework With a Hammer

Your home takes a good slice of your life, and it does give you some comfort, shelter, and dignity in return . . . but you really pay for this.

- It costs you to buy it . . . (seems like forever!)

- It costs you to insure it . . . (forever!)

- You have to pay taxes and utilities . . . (forever!)

- It costs you to repair and replace everything that wears out . . . (forever!)

- It costs you care and cleaning . . . (forever!)

We know you can get more for your money. You can get your house to earn some of its way in life. **We're going to show you how you can get your house to do lots of the cleaning and maintenance all by itself.**

Time is the most valuable commodity we have. We don't want to use it all up cleaning, caring for, or earning a way to pay for a dwelling. So we need to make our homes as maintenance-free, as expense-free, and as mind-freeing as possible. Fast, easy, orderly, and *less* daily upkeep for the entire house, inside and out, will take pressure off the entire family and give you time to enjoy life again!

We've concentrated here on exactly how you can alter your dwelling to cut your maintenance time. The material in this book is something you can actually use, and we hope you'll be motivated to put it into practice. But no, this book doesn't give you complete plans for a trash chute or blueprints for how to put a floor grate in to put an end to sweeping for-

By designing, decorating, and building your home and its furnishings to be low-maintenance, you *can* do your housework with a hammer.

4

ever. Some things—however badly needed and wanted—aren't practical yet, and we couldn't tell you in a book this size how to perform every step of every project. There are already many fine books that will tell you how to do every kind of construction and installation, and if we tried to do it here, we'd end up with a 12,000-page book.

But although we couldn't put complete instructions for every idea in these pages, we've tried to give *enough* guidance so that anyone with a desire for household freedom can proceed from here to get the rest of the materials and advice they need to make their house do the housework. The Source List on page 198 provides specific references for anything that's not readily available at hardware or building supply centers.

There are thousands of new ideas published every month in books, magazines, and pamphlets, plus manufacturers come out almost weekly with something new. Keep your eyes open—much of it

is being geared to cut maintenance time in your house. If it works and will cut your time—grab it—your time is worth it! We have faith that if you see and like an idea, it will spark your own ingenuity and ambition to seek out and find a way to get it done exactly the way YOU like it.

You'll notice that this book is opinionated—sometimes very much so. That's because working firsthand with the problems and materials discussed in these pages for a combined total of forty-five years now, we do have some strong opinions about what things are best or how they should be done. We'd like you to consider some of the ways we, and others, have relieved ourselves of maintenance burdens, but in the end, you should have it *your* way.

Your house exists for you and should be tailored to the enjoyment of your family and friends. We realize that you may want to adapt some of the ideas in this book to suit your taste, and that

pleases us, too, because your house designed to clean itself should be what *you* feel comfortable with—not us. We only want to help you eliminate all the chore work that keeps you living for a house instead of in it.

If we give you even one great time-reducing principle in this book, or trigger just one of your own ideas and motivate you to pull it off—then we've succeeded. We hope we give you at least one million-dollar idea for your $9.95.

We don't claim to have all the answers, we realize these are only a fraction of what is out there. If you have something more or better, please share it—call us, write us, or visit us. Anything that can cut the financial and emotional burden of housekeeping is worth the effort—let's spread the word, the gospel of easier, better living. Let's all get together to reduce the time and agony of cleaning chores, so we'll have the freedom in our lives to enjoy some "Life After Housework"!

Chapter 1

Any House Can Help Out With the Housework

In 1985, *Statistical Abstract* placed the average cost of a new home at $79,900. That's bad enough, but when you add the interest, taxes, insurance, utilities, maintenance, repair, and upkeep costs that you pay over the thirty years you're paying off the mortgage, the total cost is staggering—over $400,000.

Acquiring a home of your own is a milestone. You don't want it to end up a grindstone or a gravestone, but the demands of ownership and upkeep could do just that. Many of us don't fully enjoy our homes because we pay the bills *not* just with money, as we may think, but with our lives.

We often groan and laugh about the inconvenience of the olden-day style of living and doing things, but when it comes to

making a home easier to clean and freeing the homemaker from chores, we haven't really changed very much in the last hundred years. We all need freedom from chores, but our home demands are always growing, and the time for them is always shrinking.

This may be the age of disposables, but you can't cast your dwelling in the trash or alongside the road. The solution is to fix the house so it takes care of itself.

Preventive Maintenance

A recent national medical fact-finding committee produced a statement on health care that parallels our concept of a maintenance-free house perfectly. In essence they said: "We spend most of the medical money, research, and time trying to repair injuries and extend or prolong the life of the afflicted for weeks or months, and almost nothing up front to prevent the problem. A little preventive medicine might add fifteen years to a life, but most of the efforts and publicity are focused on the last breath. Somehow we don't have the wisdom to see the dramatic difference between adding fifteen years to life and improving a few suffering minutes at the end."

Housework is like that, too: Most of the money is spent treating the problem and almost none preventing it. Lots of things demand our money, but housework also asks for our lifeblood, our time. You can replace money, but never time.

Maintenance-freedom is achieved by applying some smarts at the beginning, when you're planning and building—instead of at the end, when you've been frustrated by it all for years.

Don't stifle your excitement for a maintenance-free house and say, "Yeah, but I'm stuck with this house I have for now—and maybe forever. . . ." Keep your excitement. You probably won't be moving from your old house to a magnificent new one, at least not anytime in the near future. So you have to do something with what you have. *Any* house can be changed—some rather easily—to reduce the cleaning, repair, and chore time.

You don't have to make major structural changes to cut out unnecessary maintenance in your home. Many changes can be done immediately, some in a few weeks or months, some over the next couple years; others you can toss in your long-range project file for when the kids leave, or when you retire. And lots of maintenance-freeing is simple elimination—no changing or adding of anything. Surely you can do that (and man, will it be fun)!

And don't think, because you have an apartment or rent your home, that you can't apply these ideas to make living easier and kick cleaning into the minor league of your life. A lot of maintenance-freeing ideas can be moved—you *can* take them with you!

So whether you're renting or simply can't afford a major structural change, there are lots of things you can do. For some time now, you may have been trying to improve your home—replacing carpets, building shelves, adding storage or solar modifications, and all sorts of things. The do-it-yourself publications are thriving and you're probably doing and paying for things that will alter your home.

In the next few months and the next few years, you may be changing, or redoing your:

Carpets

Faucets and fixtures

Appliances

Lamps and lighting

Drapes

Cabinets

Furniture

Decor

Windows

Floor covering

Walls

Ceilings

Landscaping

All of the things that wear out regularly are being replaced regularly by you, so regardless of where your house is located, or what kind it is, you can take advantage of much of the material in this book.

Existing Homes

Every room in your home can be changed to cut some need for cleaning. When furniture and fixtures wear out, or walls, floors, and ceilings need repainting or recovering, use low-maintenance materials. Many things can be "designed into" existing structures, and you can do most of it yourself. You don't have to undertake a giant rebuilding or remodeling job. Some lifetime regrets and dreams can be changed or realized. A few nails and a gallon of paint or a can of texture mud will save a lot of time in your home or rental.

New Homes

Where major or minor remodeling plans or a new house is definitely in your future, a small effort to change a few old "traditional" building methods and materials can save you literally thousands of wasted chore hours, limit damage and depreciation, and provide a safer, more enjoyable home. There's no great magic involved, just deciding to bring to reality the things you always wanted to do, but didn't because you were too timid to question building codes, FHA, banks, or contractors. Remember, it's *your* future. Now is the time for a change, for better planning.

Dream Homes

From age seven to ninety-seven we all have our dream house, a special home that, someday, we want to have. Dream-home planning is the seed that all special and spectacular real-life houses sprout from. If you don't have a dream home, mentally build it now, so when the opportunity arises you'll be ready for it. We hope this book provides some "dream fuel" that you'll use and enjoy. And before you dream in problems, time, and money-consumers (which can make any dream home a nightmare) read this book.

No matter where you live, you can make improvements that will free up your time for other pursuits. The key is thinking through and planning the things that will make things better around the house for *you*—and then carrying them out.

It doesn't matter if you have $30 or $30,000 to spend. You have to start somewhere—and you can. Even a small step towards freeing your life from cleaning is worth taking.

Let the Buyer Beware

Walking through the mall one day, you spot a cashmere coat on display. The style and cut shout "Buy me," so you walk in, point to the coat and say, "Wrap it up." Later, as you attempt to wear it, you discover the sleeves lap over your fingernails and the waist has a six-inch pucker. But you say, "Oh well, it's a good, expensive coat. That's the way it was made, so I'll keep it until it wears out and someday I'll get one that fits." Sound a little unlikely that you'd settle for this? It is.

You would never buy something as expensive as a coat without making sure the cut is right for you. After all, you may wear that coat 300 times over the next three years. What misery it would be to fight a pinching, hanging, or unattractive piece of apparel. Yet your *dwelling,* where you live for maybe forty years—too often *is* left to misfortune and chance.

Very Few People Really Get Their Way

Most people acquire their homes just like buying that coat in the window. They saw something they liked about it and bought it. But it didn't really fit their family's size or lifestyle, and they never did get it to fit. They're so particular about clothes, autos, and entertainment, so why not about their homes?

When it comes to where we live, we generally take what we get. Maybe because a house or dwelling is so "permanent," it's awesome or intimidating to us. So we back off from our dreams and ideas for changing for the better and accept what we have.

The User Knows Best

We know a woman 6'5" who has hunched over all her kitchen activities for twenty years. For about a hundred dollars, a taller base could have been installed and the counter level raised. But it wasn't—because it wasn't "the standard." The standard says kitchen appliances and cupboards are thirty-six inches high.

We also have a friend 4'4" who has had to work at standard counters and cupboards for twelve years. She hangs over the sink on her elbows, and needs a stool to get the salt down. The standard, again, does her no service.

Don't accept things the way they are if you hate them and they make your life miserable. Don't accept them because some designer says they are "in" or because you see them applauded in *House Glamorous* magazine (that's not the real world). If something is too high, too short, too big, or too little, *change it!* Standards in buildings and furnishing are just that—standard—made to fit the average. I'm not average in every way and neither are you.

We've discussed this subject of designing and building a house for speed and efficiency of housework with many people, and they all had the ideas, dreams, and enthusiasm to make their existing or future home much better. So why didn't they? Here are some of the reasons:

"I didn't know how to go about it."

"I've learned to live with it."

"The contractor said 'No one does that.' "

"The architect said 'Special things cost more.' "

"The bank said 'We don't finance weirdo ideas.' "

All of these excuses are way off base. What's important is *you*—your life, time, comfort, and relationships. Since much of your life centers in and around the home, why not design for your needs and design out problems?

What usually happens to all those clever, brilliant, life- and time-saving ideas for changing and building things around the house? What happens to all those truly workable shortcuts, those new and better structures and furnishings, those revolutionary ideas for walls and floors?

Most of them are given up! And you, the surrenderer, are usually saying to yourself: "Well maybe someday a brilliant young architect will come along and devise a home to make life easier." We have faith in heavenly visions, but little in architects of any age—we've seen few who were concerned with the mundane matter of housework, or with making life easier for homeowners. Often designers and architects are more concerned with the "statement" their structure makes (how it

Wrong

Wrong

Right

looks), than with how easy it is to care for.

Don't be intimidated by architects, contractors, bankers, neighbors, or relatives. When it comes to maintenance-free ideas, go for it! No one else has the inside track or all the secret answers of maintenance-free living. You the user can think up as many good ideas and implement them as well as the builder or contractor.

Don't back off from your best ideas, either. Remember, nothing is a failure or silly in design if it enhances your lifestyle. We can't overstress how stress-free your life will be when you bring your dwelling around to fit your living needs!

You know better than anyone else what fits you, what doesn't, what wastes your time, what you need.

The threatening mountain of potential maintenance problems about to be inflicted on us is not only a reality, but they aren't going to go away. We must eliminate them or live with them as an eternal adversary.

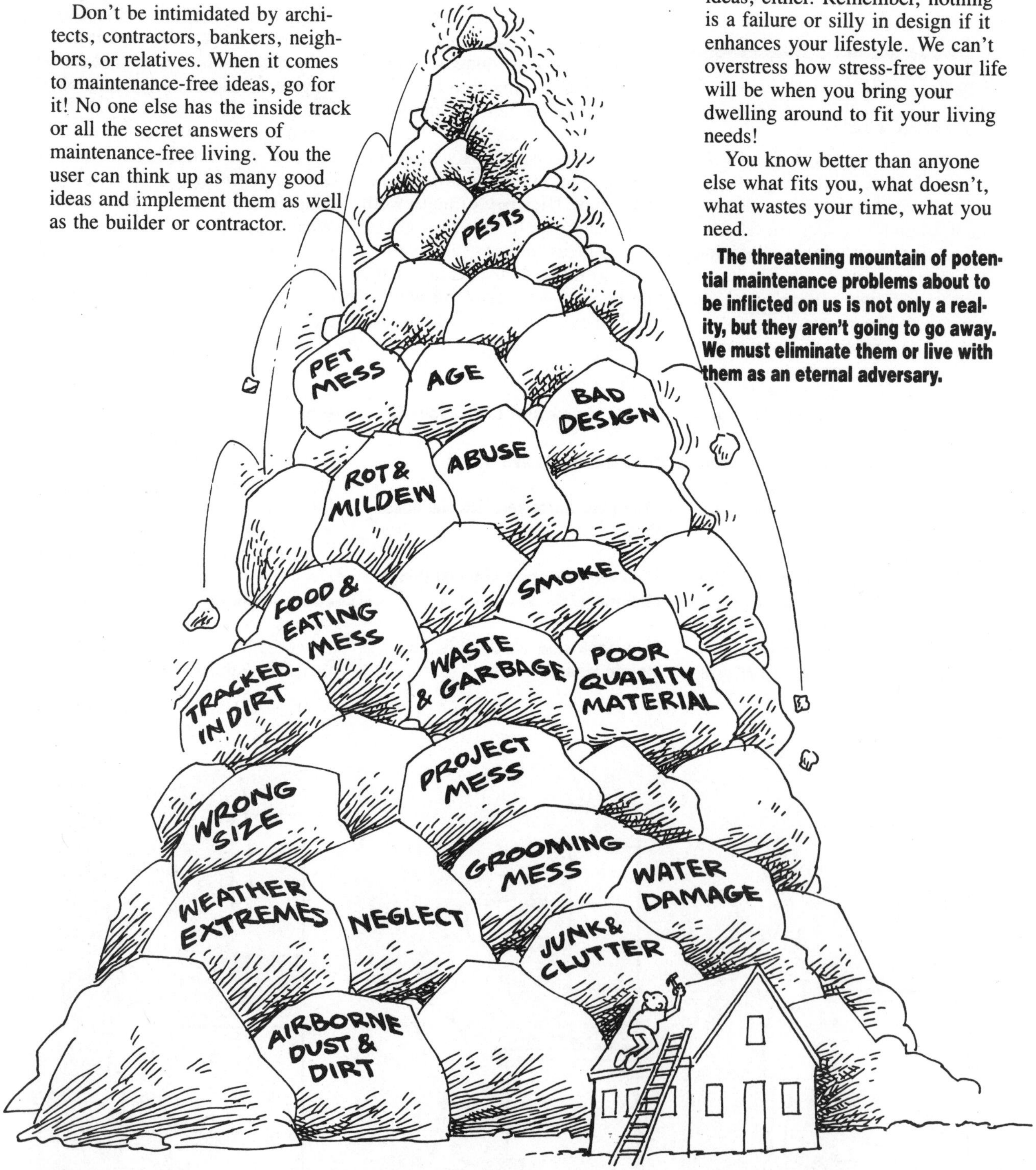

PESTS

PET MESS   AGE   BAD DESIGN

ROT & MILDEW   ABUSE

FOOD & EATING MESS   SMOKE

TRACKED-IN DIRT   WASTE & GARBAGE   POOR QUALITY MATERIAL

PROJECT MESS

WRONG SIZE

GROOMING MESS   WATER DAMAGE

WEATHER EXTREMES   NEGLECT   JUNK & CLUTTER

AIRBORNE DUST & DIRT

With a little determination, you can turn the mountain of maintenance problems that threatens the enjoyment and usefulness of your home into a molehill.

Chapter 2

The Basic Principles of Maintenance Freedom

Once you're convinced that even *your* home can be made easier to clean—and you're resolved to start working toward that end—you may not at first know how to proceed. What in fact are maintenance-free items?, you ask. Is my kitchen floor good or bad? Should I buy a new couch?

First, don't automatically accept the decorating ideas you see in magazines and books. Seventy-five percent of those ideas compound housework rather than diminish it. Decorators and architects—like fashion and car designers—have many things to concern themselves with besides mere utility. Things like how to be different from last year, how to manage to use the latest materials, and whether their fellow designers will be impressed.

Later we'll get into the nitty-gritty of designing out housework, but first let's consider some general guidelines to get you thinking along the right lines. Here are the seven basic principles of maintenance freedom:

Start by simplifying

Avoid high-maintenance materials

Multiple surfaces multiply the work

Camouflage wherever you can

Concentrate the cleaning

Take convenience into account

Keep things compatible

Keep these basic principles in mind.

Start by Simplifying

For looks and glamour human beings have suffered, surrendered, compromised, and endured the torture of confining corsets, oppressively ornate white-powdered wigs, arch-aching high heels, enormous ear-lobe anchors, and suffocatingly tight jeans. We've embraced anything and everything we thought would enhance our image, and function, if considered at all, came in a very sad second.

Somewhere we need relief, an escape to a place where we're not always sacrificing comfort and function simply for *looks*. Our home should be it.

Yet too often people assume that simple means sterile. I've spent five years planning this book and building the house that will clean itself, and every time I mention the word "maintenance-free," the first response is a big sigh or wistful look, followed by flared nostrils and a snort of "fat chance." Then, inevitably, a sober wrinkle of the nose and forehead and the remark, "Oh, but it would be so cold and heartless. . . ."

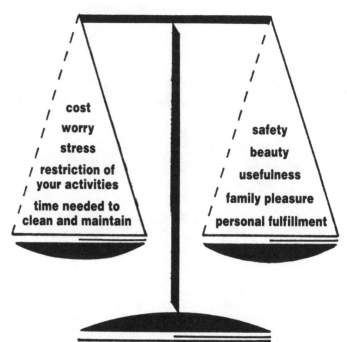

When you're buying or building anything for your home, take time to weight the advantages against the disadvantages to make sure the pleasure you get from it is worth the work it requires.

Almost everyone translates simplifying into eliminating all comfort, luxury, and decoration.

Simple *doesn't* mean sterile. And maintenance-free doesn't mean that a sprinkler lowers from the ceiling and washes the whole house down.

Most of the time, *less is really more*. Which room makes you feel more comfortable, more able to concentrate on the book, person, or activity at hand? Not the one dripping and crowded with stuff, with pounds and piles of extras.

Simple doesn't have to mean sterile—for example, you can have the beauty of flowers without the trouble by choosing a floral pattern in your drapes. The effect is much the same.

What Extra Maintenance *Really* Costs You!

An Extra		In one year		In a lifetime
5 minutes 2 times a day	*equals*	61 hours	*equals*	3,650 hours (or 22 weeks)
½ hour 2 times a week	*equals*	52 hours	*equals*	3,120 hours (or 19 weeks)
2 extra hours a week	*equals*	104 hours	*equals*	6,240 hours (or 37 weeks)

Too much ruins everything: Clothes, conversation, food . . . and yes, homes.

The same goes for decorating. A well-decorated room is simple. It has one focal point. If you have too many, you ruin even the nicest room. More *isn't* better in cleaning and decorating, so don't let the quest for more make you a slave. Fifteen vases on a table doesn't show any of them off—it just looks like a junk pile. If there's one vase on the table it will be noticed and appreciated for its beauty.

Simplicity and a sense of order are better than plushness. When home ownership amounts to tending a tabernacle, you're in trouble. You have the opposite of a maintenance-free environment.

Good Living—By Design

Architects address a similar issue when they talk about the eternal struggle of "form" vs. "function." One or the other is easy to achieve, but both at the same time is the essence of good design.

Most of the time you can make the two meet. But sometimes in trying to achieve both you'll have to compromise a little on one or the other. One example is the bathroom—most people say it's worth the extra cleaning time to have two bathrooms in a house.

One bath would make the house easier to clean, but two makes the house more convenient. It's your choice. Is the luxury or comfort of something truly worth it to *you?* If it is, then put it in. If it's not, get rid of it!

If you can't stand the looks of something even though it's easy to clean, don't buy it. You just won't be happy with it. The goal is to have things you can enjoy and use but don't have to mollycoddle every day to keep them nice. There are plenty of wallcoverings, for example, that are both beautiful and easy to clean, as well as many handsome low-maintenance furniture styles. Things used every day can't be designed like a trophy that only goes on display, they have to be able to *take* it.

Why do you have dishes for every day and another set for "special occasions"? Because your "everyday" dishes are plain and durable—easy to use and clean. On special occasions you're willing to tolerate the inconvenience of carefully hand-washing the crystal, using extra mild soap on the fine china, and polishing the silver. You realize that if you went through this ordeal daily, it would take a large chunk of your time—and so you don't. Things

that are used over and over every day *have* to be low maintenance, because no one wants to spend endless hours cleaning.

Avoid High-Maintenance Materials

You have things you clean several times a day, things you clean several times a week, once a week, once a month, once a year, etc. The key to using the right materials is using the hardiest ones where they're most needed and indulging yourself where it will cost you the least. So classify your cleaning chores into these categories:

High Maintenance/Constant Cleaning: These are the things you deal with at least daily, or even hourly—kitchen tables and countertops, stovetops, kitchen floors, kitchen sinks, beds, playrooms, the garbage. These are the things to change first; it's essential to use materials here that are easy to clean. An hour a day wasted on hard-to-clean things is a lot of time over a year . . . or a lifetime.

Medium Maintenance/ Frequent Cleaning: Things you clean every week or a couple of times a week—the outside of appliances and kitchen cabinets, the laundry, tubs, showers, toilets, bathroom sinks, furniture tops, entranceways, living room and bedroom floors, active storage, the yard.

Frequently cleaned things are almost as important to change because many of them, with only minor changes, can become infrequent cleaning items—be changed from a weekly to a monthly or yearly chore. Some can even be eliminated completely.

Low Maintenance/Infrequent Cleaning: These are things that you clean once a month or so or maybe only once or twice a year. Seasonal storage, baseboards, bedroom walls, the exterior of the house, windows, draperies—these items should be as low-maintenance as possible, but a small splurge here and there won't kill you.

Multiple Surfaces Multiply the Work

We seem to take quality items (even beautiful, expensive building materials), then pile, almost cram, them onto a structure—trying to give it life or looks or "atmosphere." Once while sitting in a lecture hall of a large university, I noticed to my amazement that the walls were made of ten different types of material: glass, wood paneling, carpet, stainless steel, tile, paint, fabric wallcovering, vinyl wallcovering, brick facing, and plastic laminate. That room not only lacked the beauty of simplicity, but because of the many variations in surface material and texture, taking care of the walls required an extra janitor, ten different sets of cleaning tools and supplies, and a cleaning cart the size of a foreign car (which skinned up the facilities as it moved around). The facts are actually *worse* than that, because it's tricky to clean different materials that butt up against each other.

The amount of time saved by simplicity is phenomenal. Whenever we try to crowd in too much, we pay a toll in "taking care of"—and the bottom line is less time for living.

A room that uses only two different surfaces—an attractive carpet and a wall painted in one (or maybe even two) colors would not only look 100 percent better than a room that uses six, it would also be much easier to maintain.

For example: Brass trim by carpet is guaranteed trouble. How can you polish brass without getting the carpet soiled? You can't. Or mirrors with oak frames. The ammonia in glass cleaners will quickly deteriorate the wood.

A single surface on the floor needs only one type of equipment

Materials to Avoid

Many a maintenance problem results from using hard-to-clean materials to create a striking showplace or reception area. Here is a list of the prime offenders:

High-Maintenance Materials

Soft woods such as pine and fir

Raw, unfinished wood

Flocked or uncoated wallpaper

Soft, easily scratched plastics

Cotton velvets

Paint that won't hold up to cleaning

Solid, dark-colored fabrics

Porous countertops

Deep craggy textures

Cheap carpeting

Light-colored carpet

Excessively long-napped carpet

Floor coverings with little indentations in the surface

Intricate handles and hardware

Brass

Chrome

Shower enclosures

Crystal chandeliers

Fancy lamps & light fixtures

Elaborate lampshades

Ornate furniture or cabinets

Decorative pillows

Cottage cheese ceilings

Cathedral ceilings

Louvers or blinds

Thin metal siding

These are things that can't be maintained and cleaned by normal humans . . . you want to check them *out*, not in.

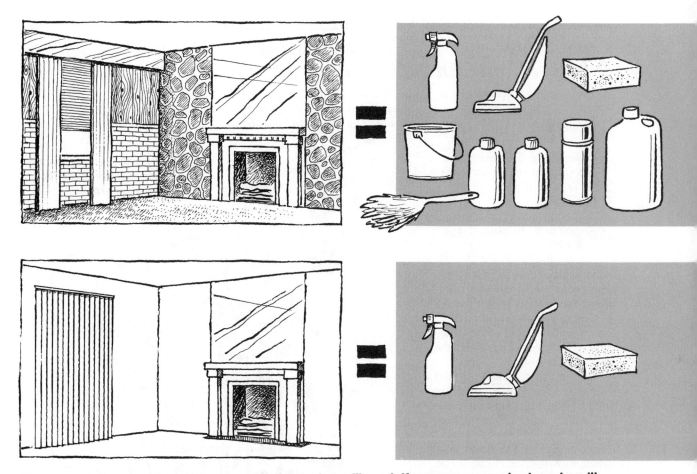

The more surfaces you have, the more cleaning tools you'll need. Keep your rooms simple and you'll keep your cleaning simple, too.

to maintain it. If you just can't live without the frills, get a wall-to-wall carpet with a border of a contrasting color around it. It gives a decorative effect with only half the cleaning.

Minimize Surface Maintenance

Your house doesn't have to be a museum of everything that was available in the DIY (Do-It-Yourself) store. One ceiling type is all you need in a house. Then once you've learned the fastest and best way to maintain it, your job will be easy. You won't need

to use one process and set of equipment for the living room ceiling, one for the kitchen, and another for the bedroom. The same with the walls—if you use the same kind of paint throughout the house (perhaps in different colors), you can maintain it with ease. For a change of color or design in a room, an "accent wall" can be painted a different color. If you've chosen a single dominant paint color or wallcovering pattern, you're sure to be ready with what you need to repair dents, chips, or scratches. If you have twenty colors of paint in your house, you're a lot more likely to

be running to the store to match the color.

Simplicity is the key to a maintenance-free house. Too many materials and surfaces intensify the demands on you for cleaning and maintenance. Choose a good attractive, durable surface and then stick with it. It'll not only save a lot of cleaning, it'll give you a psychological lift, too. If there isn't a dominant color or pattern in a room it will look disheveled, no matter how many handsome things are in it. **Half the battle of cleaning is how clean the room looks.**

15

Camouflage Wherever You Can

You clean for three basic reasons:

- Health: To kill germs and bugs

- Preservation: To prevent depreciation and preserve the value of your walls, floors, furnishings

- Appearance: To make things look good

Anything you can do in a home to improve appearance without sacrificing the goals of health and appearance, you should! It doesn't hurt to enlist a little optical illusion when it comes to one of the biggest indicators of "clean."

A solid white, yellow, or gold carpet in a family room or dining area isn't exactly camouflage—but one with a pattern in colors like gravy brown, stringbean green, or carrot orange is. You could spill a whole taco salad in the center of the room and no one would notice.

Camouflage isn't cheating, it's simply reducing the bad visual impact that can cause you to be forever servicing an area or object that's going to get use and abuse anyway!

Pattern and design hide wear, tear, and imperfections because they are visually distracting, while solid colors hide very little. **A pattern in the vinyl flooring of your kitchen that camouflages crumbs and itty-bitty droppings until you get them swept up will free you from a lot of anxiety.** And in many living rooms a striped couch beats a pink velvet one—twenty to one!

We'll be offering specific suggestions throughout the book for building materials and furnishings that are "camouflage conscious." Meanwhile, think camouflage.

Concentrate the Cleaning

You want to concentrate the cleaning every place you can in a house. The idea is to have the

Camouflaging can cut down on one of the main reasons for cleaning—appearance.

16

main mess generators together—the garbage can, storage shelves, tissue boxes, paper rack, hooks for quick hanging. That spot will get pretty messy but the rest of the room will stay cleaner. It's easier to clean one small, very dirty area than a huge somewhat dirty area; you can concentrate on that spot and go lightly over the rest of the room. Otherwise, you clean up moderate messes all over the room and cleaning takes longer. The various control centers we describe elsewhere in this book apply this theory: keeping the most-used and messiest things together. In the control center system, too, everything has its place and everyone knows where it is—so a lot less time is spent hunting for lost items.

Plants are a good example of how you can concentrate cleaning. Houseplants are wonderful—they look exotic and they blend into every decor. But they shed leaves, tip over and spill soil, attract bugs, have to be watered, and do need to be trimmed and manicured from time to time. Don't put them in twenty-two different places around the house—it'll be a full-time job just keeping up with them. Concentrate them in a central area—an atrium, greenhouse window, or multishelved plant rack—where you can enjoy their beauty and yet care and cleanup will be fast and easy because they're all in one place.

Think Like a Traffic Cop

In essence: You only have to treat where people tread. The more you contain the treading area, the less you have to clean. I cleaned the operator's lounge in a big telephone building once; the ladies' room had so many stalls it looked like the starting gates at Santa Anita. It had twenty sinks, and even when only ten women worked one shift, they managed to use all the stalls and all the sinks, which meant I had to clean them all. I couldn't leave toilet paper out of any of the stalls to limit that traffic, but I could do something with the sinks, so I put a bar of lovely fragrant soap on one sink. They all used that one, and I saved cleaning nineteen sinks a night. That's called traffic control or direction.

Applying traffic savvy to maintenance-free design is easy; simply direct the traffic the best you can and use the most maintenance-free surfaces and equipment in the highest use areas.

If there is a place that is used a hundred times a day, that traffic pattern dictates the selection of floor. Ever notice how some people seldom use their front door? Their traffic pattern is the side or back door. There's a lovely concrete walk leading to the front door, but just a worn-down grass path to the back. The *back* door is where to shore up, double mat, and toughen up to hold the abuse level down. (We'll give you more ideas for how to handle high traffic areas in later chapters.)

Blow the whistle on cleaning time with traffic control.

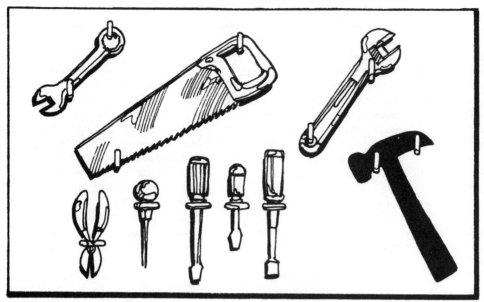

Outlining the tools' shape with paint or permanent marker makes sure they end up back where they belong. Who could resist putting tools away in a shop like this?

Take Convenience Into Account

Whether or not most people will do something depends more on convenience than on training or fear. They like things easy and convenient. Why does *everyone* clean up at McDonald's? It's easy and convenient! Why do people cut across the lawn? Because it's the easiest way to get there.

- People will set things on the nearest surface, not the intended one. This goes for everything from glasses and keys to galoshes and groceries.

- People will sit on anything available (not necessarily something comfortable or meant to be sat on) when a conversation starts.

- If it's too high, people won't reach for it. If it's too low or too heavy, they'll leave it or step over it.

The Most Predictable Human Response is Convenience!

Checkout-counter impulse buys should convince anyone of the human response to convenience—if it's there, available, people will buy it, eat it, photograph it, even take it home and store and clean it!

In your design, it makes a lot more sense to work with the irresistible pull of convenience than to try to fight it.

Almost any of us will replace something or put it away if it's in easy reach or "on the way" and we don't have to fight a crowded closet or overstuffed bookcase, or rumble all the way down to the basement to dispose of it.

Keep Things Compatible

The upkeep of a home gets pretty complicated when you have scores of different kinds of light fixtures, plumbing fixtures, door-knobs, locks, hinges, etc. If every wall and every surface requires a different cleaning or repair approach, it's almost impossible to deal with anything efficiently.

Take for example faucets—the average home has seven of them and there are at least seven different faucet makers. If all of your faucets were the same, you'd have simplified maintenance—you'd always have parts "in stock" and the know-how to replace them and care for them.

Chapter 3

The Discipline of Structure:
Make Mess-Making Impossible

You can design the structure of your home to encourage the kinds of uses and activities you desire, and discourage or eliminate the undesirable ones.

After her three-year-old lost her mittens for the fourteenth time, some mother somewhere said to herself: "This is dumb, finding or buying new mittens over and over again—I have better things to do than muddle around with mittens." So she went to the sewing drawer, got a strong piece of string, and attached the mittens to her son's coat sleeves. And from then on the mittens, used or not, always came home with the kid. Her hunting and worrying days were over.

A teller in a bank somewhere, sometime, got a little string and tied the pen to the counter. In this single stroke she freed herself from endless replacing of pens and the complaints about nothing to write with.

A homeowner had to step up on a stool every time she turned on the ceiling light in the basement (most old basement lights were wired to a pull switch with a short chain). After banging her shins once too often, she got a piece of shoelace and tied it on the end of the pull chain and after that she could turn on the light in a second.

These strings are an example of what we call structure. Structure is simply any tangible thing that directs and controls the actions of human beings. It can discourage or encourage an activity without you even being around. It works by itself.

People will struggle with problems and their fallout for months and years, when one simple change or addition to the structure could take care of them.

Dad returned home from town with a little black spring (28 cents) and installed it on the screen door. We now had no chance to leave the door open. The structure took care of itself . . . and the flies . . . and the problem. Whether it be a doorstop to keep a doorknob from puncturing a Sheetrock wall, carpet protectors to keep furniture from marking the rugs, or a mat that will knock the dirt off your shoes before you enter the house, this is a structure discipline. Anything you can build, invent, or install that doesn't allow the mess or the problem to happen in the first place.

A car that won't start until the door is closed—that's structure discipline. If you don't want people to sit down, don't provide a chair. It's that simple—structure discipline.

Another simple example of the

discipline of structure: I once did a job for a big shopping mall where a store was opened before the newly laid asphalt was striped for parking. Cars were parking all sorts of ways, and before 200 cars fit in there, the whole lot was full. The next day, after we did nothing more than put down $80 worth of yellow paint, over 400 cars could park there easily.

In public places, structure solves problems that even signs and p.a. systems can't. Amusement parks, airports, and other commercial establishments invest a few dollars for little chains, a post or two, a rail or pipe and suddenly people know what to do and do it, on their own. No one has to be the bad guy and shout orders or direct traffic. The structure is self-disciplining. It's cheaper and more effective than any other method.

It Kept the Flies Out

Would you believe, for example, that 28 cents could save hours of running back and forth, as well as emotional distress and potential health problems?

The old farmhouse where I grew up was very active one hot afternoon. Mother was feeding the threshers and canning at the same time. The sugar was a prime draw for all the flies emanating from the barnyards. If the screen door stayed open even a second, the flies would slip in, and even one or two caused Mother great distress trying to keep them off the fruit. How many times does a parent ask kids to close the door? And how many times do they remember? That door was causing lost tempers, lost time, and lots of tension. It was time for some structure discipline.

The structure discipline of a self-closing door kept the flies out and tempers cool.

Motels are good examples of structure discipline at work.

In the home, structure, all by itself, can take care of a surprising number of things. Structure can prevent cleaning, maintenance, repairs, tension, and unhappiness.

For example, you can control the traffic in a house by adding or taking out a wall. Walls are an obvious structure discipline. Furniture can serve this purpose, too. By arranging furniture, you can define and control traffic in certain areas and discourage it in others. (We'll discuss built-in and suspended furniture as prime self-disciplining structures in Chapter 13.)

Structural Smarts

A homeowner, after reaching clear to the back of the cabinet again to get a can of tomato paste, decided a lazy Susan would put things she needed only occasionally up front when she needed them and in back the rest of the time. So she installed them in all her corner cabinets—instant order!

Another homeowner, tired of a messy tabletop in the entryway, removed the table—there was no handy place to set junk.

Structure discipline is as simple as mounting a phone or knife holder just a few inches higher to take it out of the reach of children. If they can't reach it, they won't get into it.

And if they can't move it, you won't have to move it back to where it was to begin with. If pictures are hanging on the wall instead of sitting on a table, they won't have to be maintained—straightened, dusted around, worried about, picked up after they fall, etc.

Structure discipline is not an option for a maintenance-free environment, it's a necessity. It not only controls actions and prevents unnecessary maintenance, it does so whether you are around or not. This is important, because a lot of rooms get cleaned up and things put away when you are standing over them; it's when your back is turned that things fall apart.

Structure discipline arranges things so that people can use but not abuse them.

Have you ever noticed, when you stay in a hotel or motel, how neat things seem to be, and stay—and how relaxed and comfortable you feel? Why is that? Take a look around the room next time—it isn't only because someone else is responsible for the cleaning.

Modern hotels and motels are great examples of structure discipline. Everything is durable, streamlined, and orderly. There are no knickknacks or unnecessary clutter so anything out of place really stands out—encouraging the guest to help keep things shipshape. The lamps are hanging or attached, the bedside tables are suspended, and the bed is built in, as is the tissue dispenser. This isn't just so the customers won't steal them—it's to minimize the work necessary for daily upkeep. If the maid has to straighten the lamps every day, for example, it takes extra time—and motel owners realize that the maid's time is their money. We aren't suggesting that you limit yourself to motel decor, but you can apply these *principles* to your own home.

Is It Tough Enough?

The very appearance of some materials seems to forbid damage. In a school hall in Fort Greely, Alaska, one wall was smooth, expensive wallcovering. The opposite wall was concrete block with a rough texture and epoxy finish. All of the damage, dirt, marks, and writing were on the lovely wallcovering. The concrete wall was immaculate, untouched. (Because it said "Leave me alone, I'm here to support the roof and keep you warm, not to write on.")

Anything loose, like grass cloth, invites children (and adults) to pick at it until fibers are hanging loose and frayed. Smooth, hard surfaces, like glass, discourage meddling. There are no edges to get a fingernail under, no interest in poking or pulling at it—so people leave it alone. That's why plain old semigloss enamel paint can often be a great structural improvement.

Structure discipline can be applied to simple things like the door handles and hardware in a home—brushed surfaces hide use marks, shiny surfaces magnify them.

All through this book, we're going to give examples of using structure instead of your back and biceps to care for your house. But our goal is to get you thinking up your own ways to improve your home and grounds.

What About the Shape, Size, and Height of Your House?

Does this make a difference? Of course it does. The handful of rebel designers who pursued the "round house" style have their hands full. Rectangles are four times easier to build mechanically, and when it comes to cleaning, most round houses still seem to have corners.

Big houses take more time to clean than small houses, and if a house is truly too big for you, you'll be doing a lot of unnecessary cleaning. The basic space needed in a house or apartment to make it comfortable for two adults is 1,200 square feet—you then add approximately 200 square feet per child and 300 per adult, usually as a bedroom or bath. The square footage can vary, but this is a guideline. Also, as you add occupants, the kitchen and living areas need a little extra space—about 10 to 15 square feet per person out of the 200 or 300 should be given to the main living area.

No matter how low-maintenance it is, square footage still has to be vacuumed, swept, dusted, painted, furnished, etc. Human beings can only *use* so much space, no matter how much they'd like to have just to look at. But being cramped can add to cleaning, too—because rooms and spaces tightly packed with furniture and stuff take a lot longer to clean (and never look clean even when they are).

Rough-textured concrete and stone walls discourage marks and meddling.

Too much in either direction, big or small, is a cleaning handicap. A small house is jammed and cluttered with too much on the floor, the shelves, the closets, etc. A large house needs additional furnishings (which must be maintained and cleaned) to fill it up, plus it has extra windows to wash and floors to mop. Every square foot has to be maintained—if it's used, it's worth it; if it's not used, it's just unnecessary work.

In addition, larger homes tend to be more than one story. In a multilevel house the upstairs and basement are not only farther away, but those stairs are difficult to clean and tiresome to climb. And a multistory house usually doubles or triples window maintenance and exterior painting.

One-story homes are by far the easiest to clean. You only need live in a mobile home a little while to realize how a one-level rectangle lessens cleaning time. Stairs, distance, and hallways add a lot of effort. Less-used rooms such as bedrooms are always on the end of a rectangular-shaped house or mobile home. A well-designed low-maintenance home condenses the kitchen and living room into a handy area central to all other areas.

The kitchen is the perfect place for your home control center.

Open Planning

Open planning is a modern concept—in fact most new houses today use this design. Basically, it eliminates the doors and walls between major rooms—the kitchen and family room are "open" to each other and entries and living rooms are "open" to each other. Unlike the designs of older houses—where every room was enclosed and had a door—open planning makes small rooms seem larger because the eye can extend into other areas instead of being confined to the bounds of a single room. Open planning lowers maintenance simply because there are fewer walls and doors to maintain and clean; houses of open design can be smaller without the rooms feeling—or being—cramped. Fewer halls are needed so there's more living space in the rooms. And open spaces are lighter, so you need fewer fixtures and less energy. Light from outdoors can also be dispersed more easily throughout the house—there are no walls in the way.

Create a Control Center

It often takes as much organization to get a bunch of kids and adults off to work or play on time as it does to get a rocket launched.

NASA has a control center, a nerve center to coordinate and direct all traffic and activity. Why not do the same in a house? We've never seen a house (and that includes the newest and best designed) that actually designated an area to monitor, store, and distribute the paraphernalia of daily function in a home—keys, mail, papers, lost and found, grocery lists, freshly arrived photos, messages, etc., etc. Most of this is stuck on the refrigerator, stuffed in between the toaster and can opener, crammed in a top drawer, or piled somewhere on or around the kitchen or the phone table in the hall. Who knows how many family fights and last-minute schedule snafus have been produced by this approach?

A control center will help you concentrate the cleaning. You might want to put a control center in each room, or at least the most heavily used ones. Put all the oft-needed and much-used items (such as the garbage can, a bookshelf, built-in tissue dispenser, a junk drawer, the clothes hamper, and miscellaneous storage) together in one part of the room. Instead of having to clean the entire room, you've got most of the mess right in one place, so it can be dealt with in one stop. Plus everyone will always know where these things are.

For example, a bedroom control center "controls" the bedroom clutter. Locate it in a central area, such as between bed and closet, so it's handy. Dump your wallet and empty your pockets here instead of all over the room—the garbage is right here, too. You can slip your shoes off and hang up your sweater on the handy hooks. You can grab a tissue; the dispenser is built in so it isn't kicking all over the house and you always know where it is. Then when you clean, all the most intensive cleaning is in one place.

Other great places for control centers are the kitchen (see the illustration shown on page 23) and the bathroom (see page 61).

"Zoning" Makes Your Home More Maintenance-Free

You have three main living zones:

1. Work: Kitchen, utility room, recreation room, entryways, garage—informal areas that get hard and heavy use

2. Formal: Living room, dining room—"public" areas that are more luxuriously finished and furnished

3. Private: Sleeping areas and bedrooms, bathrooms—private and quiet

Locate the "luxury" zones in the rear of the house so dirt isn't constantly tracked through them.

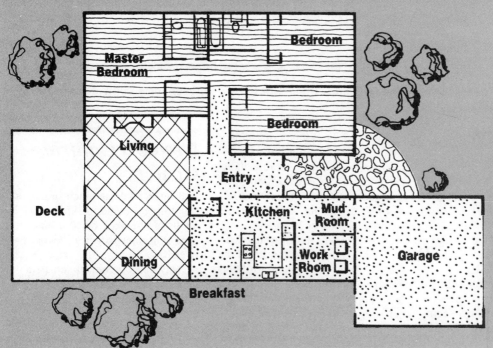

In a "zoned" home, the kitchen, utility room, entryway, and garage are located so that the toughest cleaning is concentrated in one area. The bedrooms and living areas are in back, where dirt won't get tracked through them.

Chapter 4

Maintenance-Free Starts With What It's Made Of

It's a shame that we have to be dead to finally acquire a low-maintenance structure. That granite tombstone is great—wind and rain pelt it, heat and cold punish it, birds drop on it, but it still sparkles year after year. Had we jumped the gun a little and installed a granite or marble floor or countertop, we might have delayed our need for that granite marker.

Can you imagine a Sheetrock marker, or a tin or particle board one? How about a no-wax tombstone to mark that final resting place? That would enrage us, even dead. Why, then, while we're still living and trying to enjoy life, do we build and bear with materials that need constant attention from the moment we acquire or install them? It doesn't make sense. Why can't we enjoy low-maintenance

while we live—now, today, every day?

Fifty, even twenty-five years ago, people like us didn't have much choice in materials. Today there's no excuse. Not only do the materials abound, but so do the engineering and information as to how, why, where, and when to use them. Your climate, location, budget, taste, and the nature and limitations of your present house will of course

25

IT COSTS LESS TO GO FIRST CLASS

	COST NEW	2 years	4 years	6 years	8 years	10 years	True cost over 10 years
Kitchen Cabinets							
Solid-Core Birch	$4,000				Refinish $200		$4,200
Vinyl-Clad Particle Board	$2,500		Repair 4 broken drawers $100	Vinyl $75 spot repair	Replace 3 doors $150	Replace all cabinets $2,500	$5,325
Washing Machine							
Good Heavy-Duty Maytag, Sears, or Whirlpool Model	$600			Replace belt $75		Replace pump $125	$800
El Cheapo Model	$400		Replace timer $100	Replace belt & rebuild gear box $150	Replace motor $125	Replace washer $400	$1,175
Kitchen Faucet							
Good Quality Faucet	$40			Cylinder repair $6			$46
El Cheapo Special	$25	Repair Kit $5	Replace $25		Replace $25		$80
Carpet							
Good Antron Nylon Treated with Soil Retardant	$600	Clean $40	Clean $40	Clean $40	Clean $40	Clean $40	$800
Cheap Untreated Carpet	$400	Clean $40	Repair $140	Replace $500	Clean $40	Clean $40	$1,120

influence your choice of materials for inside and outside your home. But the secret is to choose the materials that will give you the quality of life you want . . . which means fewer of your precious hours spent on cleaning, repair, and upkeep.

Many cheap, flimsy materials seem like good choices at first—they are inexpensive, convenient, and even attractive when new. So we don't look at the long-term consequences and often end up with homes full of thin, vinyl-clad paneling, paperboard siding, Sheetrock, particle board, etc.

It Costs Less to Go First Class!

Sometimes upfront costs shock and numb our economic good sense. Even though we know how quickly a cheap item wears out, needs replacing, and ultimately

You'll live with the decisions you make about your home for a long time.

exceeds the cost of a better quality item that is initially more expensive, sometimes we just can't see beyond this month's bank balance.

The first commandment of maintenance-free living is *do it right the first time*. Your house's structure and basic furnishings are going to be with you a long time.

In the long run, it costs less to buy the best.

The money saved is just one advantage. Good quality also means dramatically improved function, comfort, safety, and even looks. But the most important savings are in your personal time and labor. The time and energy you invest in unnecessary cleaning, tearing out, and replacing can't be recovered—it's part of your life gone. If you pay a little more to get the best, you'll have more free time—which is the most precious

and expensive commodity of all.

Maintenance-freedom isn't an *abstract* concept; it's a tangible value.

Think Twice Before You Buy or Build

You have the freedom to make things the way you like them. Just remember as you plan and design that no matter *how* much something pleases the eye, if the muscles and might needed to sustain it take up too much of your time, your life, your resources, you'll grow to hate it. And if you make the wrong choice in the very structure of your home, you'll have to live with it. So take your time and make good decisions.

The Masked Maintenance-Free Marauders

Some materials and surfaces are sold as lifetime, indestructible, never-care, non-maintenance items. Check these materials out carefully (read *all* the literature the manufacturer provides) before you buy them for a particular use. While they may be good for certain purposes, they aren't recommended for general use. Materials that can be foolers include:

Plexiglas

No-wax flooring

Aluminum siding

Fiberglass and plastic (bath fixtures)

One-inch tile

Three-section storm windows

Take a Lesson From Commercial Builders

I'm about to ask you to shed some prejudices and misconceptions about certain materials. You may be accustomed to seeing some of these things in large commercial buildings. But why do you suppose big, high-use businesses and offices use lots of masonry, steel, glass, and hardwood? How are they achieving a more inviting look that's actually much easier to clean? The secret is in the materials, and they can work the same for you.

Before you buy, find out if it will:

☑ **ROT**

☑ **RUST**

☑ **FADE**

☑ **SOIL**

☑ **STAIN**

☑ **CRACK**

☑ **PEEL**

☑ **SPLINTER**

☑ **DENT**

☑ **DEPRECIATE**

☑ **SCRATCH**

☑ **SHRINK**

☑ **WEAR OUT**

☑ **OUTDATE**

☑ **DETERIORATE**

Masonry

Masonry is basically anything constructed of stone, brick, or earth tile that is held together with mortar. It also includes plaster and concrete construction. For the most part masonry is hard, dense, heavy, and fireproof. Some examples: your brick fireplace, the floor tile in many shopping centers, the cinder blocks in your foundation, the stone fence down the road.

So you'll grow to appreciate masonry products, let's take a glance at how masonry can help you achieve your goal of maintenance-free (and stress-free) living.

1. It won't burn.

2. It won't rot.

3. It's waterproof.

4. It won't deteriorate in your lifetime.

5. It reduces insurance costs.

6. It projects not just a feeling but the reality of strength and permanence.

7. It's inexpensive over the long haul.

8. It's easy to build with and install.

9. It practically eliminates replacement costs.

10. It's tough to steal or vandalize.

Most of us, over our lifetimes, will have one or more insurance claims for damage to our homes. During my college contracting days, restoration of insurance losses in homes was one of my more frequent jobs; a fire, flood, or windstorm would damage a home and we would come in and repair, rebuild, clean, and paint it back to its original condition. After four years of this I noticed that the surfaces with brick, block, or other masonry finishes were always easy and inexpensive to fix; for that matter, they were seldom damaged by the elements—not even by humans. **Nothing compares with masonry for durability and ease of maintenance and it can be used in all kinds of ways to get thousands of decorator effects.**

Masonry comes in cast blocks, pre-cast slabs, decorative veneers, and prefabricated units such as steps, lawn edgers, etc.

Beauty Is in the Promise of Function

The Case for Concrete

You say you're not sure about the aesthetics—the *looks* of masonry? If masonry is ugly, why do people travel to Greece, Egypt, and Italy to see masonry ruins? How would Mt. Rushmore look in

Some of the world's most enduring—and beautiful—structures are made of masonry.

fiberglass? Or the pyramids in pine wood?

Take a good look at the structures you most enjoy and admire. You'll discover that many of them are masonry or concrete. Concrete, for example, can be tinted almost any color you want; it can even be made to look just like wood.

Stone, for another example, is art in itself. The structure *is* the design. It's strong, impressive, and beautiful, and its luster is perpetual. It gives you the feeling of closeness to nature, strength, security, and comfort. It won't dent or buckle, and you won't have to adjust or repair it and it's too heavy for most thieves to carry away.

The most beautiful buildings, castles, and, yes, homes in this world are masonry. It comes in many types and styles that can be fashioned to suit any architectural taste. Those Mexican hacienda hotels are concrete block faced with stucco, and they last forever. Some of Frank Lloyd Wright's most beautiful home designs are of masonry block. But once a few farmers found out the advantages

of masonry and built barns and a couple of chicken coops out of it, the Van Snoots didn't want a home out of the same stuff, so masonry homes never made it big. I wouldn't live in anything but a masonry house. They look good and feel good, are soundproof, safe, and economical.

Masonry isn't just for sidewalks, driveways, temples, towers, and tunnels—masonry is for your home.

The main types of masonry are:

Concrete

Concrete Block

Decorative Block

Uncoursed Stone

Coursed or Quarried Stone

Brick

Uncoursed stone is irregular-shaped rocks laid in a random pattern, as opposed to coursed or quarried stone, where stone is cut into rectangular blocks and laid in neat rows.

Glass

The second most overlooked and underused maintenance-freeing material in the home is glass.

You're probably muttering that we're wrong, glass is a *high*-maintenance material. Lots of people think window cleaning is a big job, but the average person only cleans windows once a year for a total of about 1½ hours. **Glass is one of the quickest and easiest surfaces to clean.** I've taught multitudes of people to clean windows 80 percent faster (if you missed out, read my book, *Is There Life After Housework?*). Cleaned with the right tool—a squeegee—glass takes even less time than you're spending on it now. In fact, it's hardly cleaning—it's a few-minute job any wimp can do, just a pleasant excuse to look out a window at a lovely landscape and presto, it's clean!

Inch for inch, glass is the lowest-maintenance surface in your home:

1. You never have to paint, sand, or seal it.

2. It doesn't rot, fade, peel, or blister.

3. It doesn't rust.

4. It can't be easily scratched.

5. It doesn't wear out.

6. Kids can't write on it.

7. It doesn't burn.

8. You don't have to hang pictures on it or decorate it.

9. It's easy and inexpensive to install.

10. It matches anything.

11. It doesn't go out of style.

12. It reflects light and is cheerful.

13. It's psychologically clean even when it's dirty.

Glass projects a constant image of clean.

Glass can be used almost anywhere. I remember how awestruck we all were when someone suggested glass basketball backboards—now look, we have glass tabletops, partition walls, and whole building exteriors and the glass only makes the products superior.

Windows and mirrors aren't the only possible uses of glass in a house. Call or visit a glass dealer—you'll be amazed what they know and have. You can have glass:

Shelves

Ceiling panels

Partitions

Tabletops

Skylights

Sliding doors

Mirrored tiles

Lighting fixtures

Glass can be used for easy-to-clean walls, furniture, ceilings, and much more.

Stained glass can make an artful, decorative addition to a room, and a stained-glass window doesn't show soil or require drapes, curtains, blinds, or other window treatment.

There are almost as many ways to use glass as there are types of glass to choose from. Frosted glass, for example, is attractive, practical, and almost never needs cleaning.

Shatter Your Illusions About Glass

Most people suffer from some "paneful" misconceptions about glass. One is that glass windows increase energy costs. Though they're definitely not as good an insulator as regular insulation-filled walls, glass windows do make a contribution to energy conservation. They let you use daylight instead of electric lighting, and the passive solar heat gained through windows in winter probably offsets the loss from their lower insulation value.

Using double-glazed windows helps a lot, and some window treatments can protect your interiors from direct summer sun—and cut cooling costs dramatically. (More on this in Chapter 18.)

Glass isn't dangerous, either—when chosen properly for the purpose. There are different types of glass for different uses, and some are designed to withstand anything you can throw at them. Tempered glass, like that used in a car windshield, is almost impossible to break. And if it *does*, it breaks into thousands of tiny cubes instead of jagged shards. You may want to use glass blocks or occluded glass for partitions and other places where seeing the glass is as important as seeing through it.

Class Up with Glass

For years I used 6'8" glass doors. I liked them because they eliminated a wall, gave a sense of openness, and were a cinch to maintain. Then, while visiting a California contractor's home, I felt an even greater sense of openness and light, and when I commented on this, he said, "It's the eight-foot slider door." I'd never seen one before. It was just like my doors, only it extended clear to the ceiling. The extra sixteen inches at the top allowed a lot more light in and eliminated that strip of wall along the top to clean.

The drapery rods were mounted on the ceiling, and that flushed the curtains right to the ceiling, which looked superb—no gap!

Another good use of glass is mirrors—they have such potential I cry when I see how sparsely they're used. They require almost no maintenance, have a built-in protection system (seven years bad luck if you break one, you know!), and can make any room appear larger.

My wife and I installed designer mirror tile on our bedroom wall. It's beautiful and super restful and I haven't touched it for years! It's inexpensive and easy to use and the veined pattern in the surface hides soiling. However, don't use mirrors or mirror tile in the playroom or other handprint-prone areas such as near doors or light switches.

Mirrored sliding closet doors are a little heavier but beat the alternatives (such as bi-fold louvered doors) by 100 percent!

Porcelain and Ceramics

Applied as a liquid coating and fired in a kiln to a smooth, glassy finish, porcelain and ceramics make superior maintenance-free materials. Harder than steel, these vitreous coatings are extremely scratch-resistant and impervious to staining and chemical action. In the home we find ceramics used on glazed floor and wall tiles, cabinet handles, cooktops, cookware, and furnishings. Porcelainized steel and cast iron are used extensively for kitchen sinks, lavatories, bathtubs, washer and dryer tops, stovetops, and cookware.

If you have a choice between porcelain and baked enamel on something like a washer or dryer top, take the porcelain every time—it's far more durable than paint. The only real drawback to porcelain is that it will chip if something hard is dropped on it (remember: it *is* glass). For plumbing fixtures, porcelainized cast iron is much superior to porcelainized steel, because the rigid heavy cast iron reduces flexing (and thus chipping) of the porcelain coating. Solid vitreous china bathroom fixtures are extremely durable and long-lasting, but you have to be careful not to drop anything hard and heavy onto them because they will break.

Plastic Laminate

Plastic laminate is probably the most familiar maintenance-free material. Most to us refer to this as Formica, though that is the name of just one brand. There are a number of other brands of laminate besides Formica, such as Textolite and Wilson Art.

Usually, we only associate this hard, slick, easy-care surface with countertops, but look around. It's also a great low-maintenance covering for walls, ceilings, shelves, cabinet fronts, furniture, tabletops, windowsills, and doors.

Plastic laminate can give you a beautiful and trouble-free surface. The convenience of having a surface so easy to clean that is also water-resistant and durable more than makes up for the difference in cost over a painted surface. And it's priced within most people's price range.

There's no end to the things you can do with laminate, and if you're fairly handy, you can handle most laminate applications with simple woodworking tools. Your local DIY store can supply the materials and give you helpful advice on applying it.

When you're choosing laminates, bear in mind that the shiny or semishiny types are easiest to clean. The suede or matte finishes have a rich, low-luster look, but are still quite cleanable. Beware the heavily textured (such as "slate") finishes. They won't be easy to clean.

Color also plays a role—stick with neutrals. Dark browns, reds, and blues show every speck of dust. And stark white shows every drop of grape juice. **A bit of a pattern (flowers, wood grain, leaves, geometrics) will help hide the little specks and make the counter look clean.**

Corian

Du Pont's Corian is great stuff. It's resilient, nonporous, and resistant to abuse and chemicals. Unlike plastic laminates, it can be formed into almost any shape, such as a sink unit. That means you have one unbroken surface to clean, without seams to collect dirt and soap scum. You can sand out most any damage it sustains and it's almost impossible to chip.

It's the ultimate material for countertops, tub surrounds, etc. But it costs two to three times as much as plastic laminate.

Plastic

Some associate plastic only with the cheap, brittle plastic used to make dimestore toys—the kind you break trying to get out of the bubble pack. But there are high-tech, space-age plastics developed for specific uses in industry and the military that are incredibly strong and durable. The Lexan plastic originally developed for jet fighter canopies, for example, has been adapted to many other uses, including consumer products.

Plastic is a coming thing so do keep an open mind about it. There are now toolboxes and wheelbarrows and furniture and storage containers made of plastic which are just as strong, good-looking, and hard-wearing as wood or metal—but they'll never need painting and they'll never rust or be damaged by water, and if they do scuff against something, they're much less likely to be damaged. And plastic is lighter and more portable.

Children's furniture and outdoor patio furniture made of plastic are especially worth considering. They're often cheaper—manufacturers can mold and make products out of plastic for less than they can be assembled out of other materials such as wood or metal.

Plastic can also be made to look *just like* wood or leather or metal,

and the only way to tell it's not is to touch it. It makes sense to consider quality plastic items for the recreation room, child's bedroom, and other high-use or casual areas.

Usually price is a good indicator of quality in plastic; the better materials, which will hold up over time, are generally found in the higher-priced items. If the price of a plastic product looks too good to be true, it probably is.

Vinyl

The word may conjure up images of cheap inflatable beach toys and wading pools, but vinyl is used to manufacture a number of excellent low-maintenance items for the home.

Flooring—Vinyl has become the standard for hard-surface flooring, and is available both in sheet goods and in tiles. Vinyl provides a good balance between the various criteria we use in selecting an all-around resilient hard flooring: affordable price, ease of installation, durability, maintainability, and a wide range of colors and patterns. Vinyl has become the hard flooring of choice.

Wallcovering—Vinyl is also used to produce some of the most attractive and easily maintained wallcoverings used in homes and commercial buildings. **Quality vinyl wallcovering can lend a rich, interesting look to a wall that cannot be achieved with paint, and vinyl is far superior to paint in durability and in its ability to camouflage soil and small surface irregularities.**

Nylon

An excellent maintenance-free material, nylon is very good for "hardware" uses where metal would rust or corrode (toilet seat anchor bolts, shower head diffusers, plumbing washers, ballcocks, drawer glides, and many appliance parts). It makes strong, long-lasting rope and cord, and it is the overwhelming favorite carpet fiber for strength and cleanability.

Wood

That handsome grain that makes wood so endearing isn't just appealing—it hides a multitude of sins. **Wood is uniquely repairable, restorable, and refinishable. Many nicks and marks simply blend in with the grain, to become unnoticeable or actually make the surface more attractive.** I remember once seeing a carpenter install a massive wood beam; it was so smooth and handsome. Then suddenly two burly carpenters attacked it with hammers and beat dents, nicks, and gouges into it. My heart almost stopped beating until I saw it finished and stained. Totally rustic and rugged, it would camouflage anything.

Fifteen years ago I paneled our kitchen dining area with plain old weathered barn wood, some nails and old tarpaper still on it. The room had instant atmosphere and in fifteen years I haven't had to touch it ever. The more abuse it gets, the barnier it looks.

Good close-grained woods are very easy to care for. Paneling, for example, if made of a true hardwood like oak with a good surface protectant, requires almost no care.

Lighter finishes on wood are lower maintenance, because scratches and nicks won't show. Light to medium-colored woods hide a lot.

Solid wood is the best for paneling or furniture, but depending on the type of wood, it can be expensive. Solid wood can be sanded and repainted forever, whereas veneers can be gouged or scratched clear through. But there isn't really a great deal of difference in durability and "camouflage"ability between a good thick hardwood veneer and solid wood. If a protective finish is applied, all either will need is an occasional cleaning with vegetable oil soap.

When it comes to paneling, you'll pay about $1.50 and up per square foot for 1-inch-thick panels of such prized hardwoods as walnut, oak, cherry, and certain exotic imported woods. A few handsome hardwoods such as pecan and elm may be priced even higher, because they are scarcer or harder to process. Prices drop to as low as twenty cents to thirty cents a square foot for softwood paneling. Redwood, western red cedar (which are both termite- and rot-resistant), fir, and knotty pine can all be used attractively, but all soft woods are prone to damage. **All wood needs some kind of finish to seal and protect it. The best is a nonpermeable film like urethane.** It comes in a variety of glosses, is easy to apply, and protects better than "oiled" or "waxed" finishes. Once a good protective film has been applied, you can wash and scrub wood just like any other cleanable surface.

Wood is the basic material for doors, trim, cabinets, and much of the furniture in most homes, and can be used for more than decoration on ceilings, walls, and floors.

Aluminum

Aluminum is widely used in window framing and storm windows and doors. It is lightweight, rustfree, and can be coated with a protective film (anodized) in several attractive colors. It's also used in home construction for siding and roofing, as well as in many decorating and furnishing items, such as blinds or cookware.

Stainless Steel

Stainless steel is also a low-maintenance material, if you buy the better grades. Cheap stainless tends to streak and stain quite readily, but the good grades can be kept quite attractive. **Best left in a "brushed," low-luster finish, stainless won't have the gleaming sparkle of chrome, but it won't show every water spot or mark, either.** It requires only periodic wiping down to stay good-looking for years. Commonly used for sinks, cooktops, appliance doors, and bathroom hardware.

Chapter 5

Clear Out the Clutter First!

Before you pick up a hammer or draw up a single floor plan, there is one important thing you must remember: The first rule of housework is *prevent it*. Clutter is one of the greatest enemies of efficiency and stealers of time. Junk makes every job harder and makes cleaning take forever. Any project will be slowed, dampened, and diluted if you constantly have to fight your way to it through a mountain of clutter. First—declutter.

About half of housework is caused by junk, litter, and clutter—having things around that we don't need and never use. We're a nation of junkers, we have mounds and rooms and drawers and bookcases and trunks and closets and attics and basements and sheds full of stuff we don't use or need. But we keep it, and it ends up keeping *us* in perpetual motion, cleaning and rearranging it and working to pay for it and maintain it.

If you want to take a giant step toward reducing cleaning and maintenance and cutting down on arguments and utility bills, not to mention insurance costs . . . then do a simple thing called decluttering. Clean out all the excess

and unwanted, then chuck it. When it's gone, so is the need to clean and maintain it. Only then will you really know where to start building and changing things to create your maintenance-free house.

You can hardly overestimate the importance of decluttering. If you had a totally maintenance-free house and you loaded it with clutter, it wouldn't be maintenance-free any more.

Too much decoration on the walls is clutter, too many ornaments sitting on the fireplace mantle is clutter. Clutter is having

scads of gadgets and appliances (kitchens are very prone to this) that you must store and keep track of. Clutter is basically having too much of anything. Too much yard, too many clothes, too many toys, too many couches, chairs, or tables, too many windows, walls, light fixtures, sinks, etc. You can even have too many tools, many that just do one very specific thing; you could spend all your time hauling and taking care of your tools and never do anything with them.

Before you start building it in—toss some of it out!

Laura says her eyes were opened the summer she lived in a camp trailer with her two small children. To fit into the trailer and have room to function, she realized she'd have to eliminate a few "conveniences" the family was used to. So she went through the kitchen cupboards and faced the fact that in the five years she'd been married, she'd only made muffins once and although "everyone" has a set of muffin tins she really didn't need to shuffle them around in that small space.

"I also took only a week's worth of clothes for everyone—

you wash every week anyway! We didn't miss the others at all," Laura says. "I selected only the books we really used and what a difference! The bookshelf had fifteen books instead of a hundred. I had the kids pick their favorite toys and games—and at the end of the day we only picked ten up instead of an entire room full and they were just as happy." She also eliminated quite a few other things and discovered she was just as well off without them—with less junk to shuffle and thus more time.

Often eliminating, reducing, or removing something is the best, cheapest, and easiest way to go. Almost everyone has too many things, more furniture and junk (and sometimes even *room*) than they need. Because it's there it has to be cleaned, whether they use it or not. How many times have you gone into a home, noticed a huge piano, and asked who plays the piano? There is silence . . . then someone finally says "No one," or "Sue used to and she's hoping to get back to it someday," or "We hope maybe one of the children will." In the meantime it takes up prime space and costs time and money.

Don't think that just because you don't have junk the size of a grand piano you don't have to declutter. What about all those newspapers and magazines you're saving for the sake of one recipe or that guide to the best restaurants in Bangkok? Cut out the article you want and trash the rest. Or that collection of bottle caps you started when you were eleven? Pick your favorites, mount them in a display for the game room, and you'll have the memories without the mess. You're saving that battered old bathroom faucet because you might need the washers someday? Take out the washers and throw out the rest of it.

Declutter the Decorations, Too

Wrong

It takes a lot of doing to clean a table cluttered with picture frames, books, vases, and knick-knacks. You have to pick up each little picture frame to dust it. You have many more places for dust to collect and cobwebs to form, and nothing is shown off to its best advantage. If every table in your house has a swarm of curios on it, it may take one morning a week just to dust them all.

Right

With the small photos combined in one or two larger frames, the lamp suspended, and the books on a suspended shelf, you can dust the tabletop with a few quick swipes and be done with it. You don't have to worry about something getting knocked over every time you touch the table.

If you need more guidance on dejunking, my book *Clutter's Last Stand* will give you all the inspiration you'll need—it's guaranteed to help. Read it and you'll be well on the way to maintenance-free living.

Yes, there should be a place in your house for everything you do need and use (or desperately want to keep, even if you don't use it), because if there's a place for everything, things stay neater, cleaning is easier, and you don't spend a lot of time chasing lost things. It's the rest of the stuff that you want to get rid of, rather than find or create a place for.

Chapter 6

Conquering the Kitchen

You don't have to be told where you spend most of your cleaning time every day. It's the kitchen—where maintenance never ends. **You spend more time working in and cleaning your kitchen than any other room in the house. The average homemaker will spend a total of fifteen years there.**

When people remodel, they remodel the kitchen more often than any other room in the house. Everyone realizes this is the most used and thus the most maintained room in the house. Everyone is looking for an easier-to-clean kitchen.

So the kitchen is the first place to tackle in planning a house that will do its own housework. The main objectives in a low-maintenance kitchen are to eliminate cracks and corners that will collect dirt buildup and to simplify this area you clean so often. **There should be *nothing* in the kitchen that isn't readily cleanable.** This is the last place you want curtains that have to be dry-cleaned, flocked wallcovering, or-

nate hardware—things that take hours to maintain but will still never look good in the high-use environment of a kitchen.

If you're starting from scratch, eliminate ledges, crevices, corners, curves, and moldings everywhere you can. If you like frills and fancies, put them in the pattern of your curtain fabric or your tough vinyl wall and floor coverings. The kitchen will be just as eye-catching and will save you a lot of time to spend enjoying the good things of life.

Function—The Number One Objective

When Laura worked as a kitchen designer, many clients came to her almost at the point of hysterics about what they wanted in the kitchens of their new homes. Most of them had been in their older homes for at least ten years and they *knew* how much time and energy a poorly designed or substandard kitchen could waste. They were willing to spend hours working out every last little detail so that their new kitchen would be *perfect*.

We each have our own "dream kitchen," and no two are the same. So very individual preferences as well as important practical questions should be considered when designing *your* ideal low-maintenance kitchen.

Start by asking yourself:

1. How many people will be using it? What are their food preferences, their ages, etc.?

2. How tall or short is the cook or cooks? The countertop should be right between your hip or waistline so that your elbows bend at a 90-degree angle when you're using the counter. Can you reach the lower shelves of the upper cabinets easily?

3. Do you entertain or cook from scratch a lot, have a garden, do canning, eat formally or informally?

4. Is the cook left-handed or right-handed?

5. How often do you go to the grocery store? How much food do you like or need to have on hand? What kind is it—canned, frozen, or fresh?

6. What daily routines do the cook and the other users of the kitchen follow? What's the traffic pattern to and from the other rooms in the house?

7. Cost and budget are of course always factors. You can do anything if you have enough money.

8. What accessories and appliances do you consider essential: bread bin, pantry, microwave, garbage disposal, cutting board, cookbook holder, spice rack, sink sprayer, trash compactor?

9. Personal preferences in decor must be considered.

A Ten-Minute Course in Kitchen Design

Every kitchen has a few basic ingredients:

Refrigerator

Stove

Sink

Counter space

Food storage

Dish storage

Your job as a kitchen designer is to combine these elements into an easy-to-maintain place to prepare and eat food. Because eating and preparing are things we do often, the *easy-to-clean* aspect is absolutely essential.

A basic design that serves *your* lifestyle is very important to a low-maintenance kitchen. Here is where the questions above come into play. If you entertain a lot, you'll want a large service area and a closed-off kitchen. If there is more than one cook in the kitchen, you must provide a place for the second cook that doesn't collide with the main cook's work area. If you garden, you need good access to the outside and a clean-up area that will keep you from bringing the mud into your main work area. If you are 5'1" you need a lower counter than if you are 5'11". Your kitchen has to fit *you*.

To design this perfect kitchen, let's first look at the traffic pattern between the three main components in the kitchen—the refrigerator, the stove, and the sink. Since those three appliances are the key work points in the kitchen, a layout that places them in a triangular pattern is almost always the most efficient. This is the work triangle.

One of the three main work stations should be at each point of the triangle. There are all kinds of theories (and counter theories) about kitchen work triangles but all you need to know for our pur-

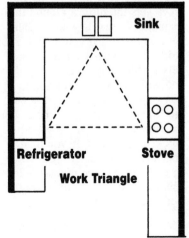

Sink

Refrigerator   Stove

Work Triangle

poses is that you will travel the path between the sink and the stove the most, so that's where you should put your main work area—the area where you prepare the food. You then locate each of your other centers (the eating area, if you have one, and food and dish storage) in a spot convenient to this work triangle.

The more you design the kitchen around this concept, the more efficient it will be. **A low-maintenance kitchen minimizes the steps you must take to prepare food and clean up after eating. The easier things are to reach and put away, the less tiring your work will be and the cleaner the kitchen will stay.**

To help achieve this, the main work area, the space between the range and the sink, should be both long and wide enough. The ideal length is five to six feet for a family of five. Your bowls, pots, flour, sugar, spices, spoons, etc., should all be in this area so you don't have to dash all over the kitchen to perform a single cooking operation. **Be sure to concentrate your most heavily used items into the work triangle and put your secondary items out beyond the edge of the triangle.**

In many ways a compact kitchen is better than one that is more spread out. The farther apart the points of your work triangle, the more dashing around you'll have to do. And your kitchen floor always gets the dirtiest around the main work area. If your kitchen isn't compact and you have lots of work areas, your kitchen floor gets a little dirty in a lot of places and will always need cleaning. If you concentrate your work area, the floor will get dirtier there, but that smaller area can be wiped up quickly and easily. If you plan your kitchen properly, you won't be cutting down on much-needed counter space—just concentrating it in one location.

Using the Triangle Theory

There are many kitchen styles that use the work triangle—including the L-shaped, U-shaped, and double-corridor. There are also modifications of these styles incorporating features such as islands, china hutches, service carts, etc. Of these, the U-shaped and double-corridor kitchens are the most convenient.

The U-shaped kitchen and the double-corridor each have a 10x3½-foot work area that can be cleaned with a couple swipes of a broom or dust mop. Two cooks can work together more easily in a double-corridor kitchen. The U-shape is more suitable for the individual homemaker.

The L-shaped kitchen has the same twenty feet of counter space as the U-shaped and double-corridor kitchens, but the walking distance is greater. The single-corridor kitchen is one of the least efficient.

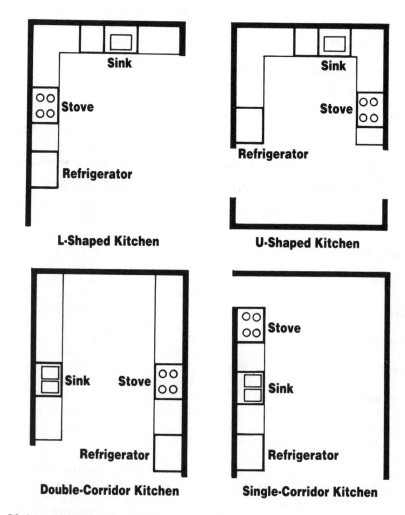

L-Shaped Kitchen

U-Shaped Kitchen

Double-Corridor Kitchen

Single-Corridor Kitchen

Of the most common kitchen arrangements, the U-shaped and double-corridor are best.

Ceilings

No matter what floor plan you choose, you should also give some thought to the ceiling plan. Almost everyone tries to choose easy-to-clean materials for the kitchen floors and cabinets, but many people forget that the ceiling gets a good share of the smoke, splatters, and splashes, too.

Don't let anyone talk you into putting an acoustical tile ceiling in the kitchen. These ceilings absorb grease and moisture and in no time they look like the filter inside your range hood.

The most maintenance-free ceiling I've seen in a kitchen is one of solid Plexiglas with fluorescent lights behind the Plexiglas panels. If the entire ceiling is Plexiglas, you'll never have to paint it. Cleaning it will be as easy as cleaning a picture window. You'll have direct light everywhere in the kitchen, so you can eliminate spot lighting. This treatment is especially nice when continued into the dining room. Instead of an ornate chandelier hanging over the table dropping dust and bugs off into the salad, you'll have a solid ceiling of light. You may want to install a dimmer switch for different atmospheres, but when you need to, you *will* be able to see. A glass ceiling looks sharp and is easy to clean.

Even if you can't construct a ceiling of light, you should strive for built-in lighting. Recessed lights along the tops of walls and boxed fluorescents are by far the most maintenance-free.

If your ceiling is painted, use a smooth enamel (no heavy textures). Don't use dark colors—a light color will give the kitchen a spacious, airy, "clean" feeling. If you have wood beams up there, seal them well.

Walls

As with every other part of the kitchen, the rule for walls is to spend as little time on them as possible. The easiest way to do that is to get rid of them altogether. We're eliminating the kitchen walls in our maintenance-free house. One corridor is an island and the other is against a glass wall, looking into the backyard. **Unless you love to cook in private, an open kitchen is more inviting and it can be more fun, too.** You can chat with dinner guests while tossing the salad or, if you're a show-off chef, entertain them by tossing the pizza dough or flipping the pancakes (if so, pay close attention to the section on easy-to-clean ceilings!).

If you can't eliminate walls, try painting with a good semigloss enamel. Or use a good, durable washable vinyl wallcovering. I'd even suggest you take a soapy cloth and try the paper out before you buy it. The most genteel kitchen will get an occasional spot of food on the wall and if the paper absorbs it, that spot will be there until you replace the wallcovering. A good heavy vinyl wallcovering will cost a bit more but it's well worth it in a kitchen. And the slicker the wallcovering the better. When mustard or spaghetti splatters, it just dries up and flakes off.

When it comes to the color or design of a kitchen wallcovering, choose something that won't show smudges, flying food, and little spots. A printed pattern is your best bet. Plain solid color wallcoverings will show the dirt *fast* and have to be cleaned more often.

You can do anything you want with your wallcovering pattern. If you're being conservative with your cabinet surface and hardware selections, as we suggest later, live it up with the pattern in your vinyl. Knickknacks printed on the paper don't take a second longer to clean than a solid-colored paper. In fact, they're preferable because grime doesn't show. Just make sure the wallcovering is scrubbable. Then you'll have a maintenance-free wall. You won't need trinkets or pictures or doo-dads on the wall because you already have your decoration.

Wood with a smooth, hard finish is a natural in the kitchen. It's warm and appealing and dirt-and-damage disguising and goes with anything. Choose a midtone wood stain. Too dark a stain shows nicks and spots, too light shows wear and grime. Solid wood is more durable than wood veneer, so look for solid wood when buying paneling.

Floors

If you pay attention to television commercials, you'd think kitchen floors were the bane of most people's housekeeping existence. With the right choice of material, they don't have to be. Sheet vinyl flooring is the best—it's easily cleaned, inexpensive, and cushions the fall for anything you might drop, more so than terrazzo or earth tile.

In the kitchen, as well as the rest of the house, you can cut down on maintenance if you "cove" your floor coverings. All that means is to bring the floor covering up the wall about three inches. (See page 142.) That way you have just one surface to clean, eliminating a baseboard that has to be dusted often and maybe even repainted. You also eliminate cracks and sharp corners that collect dirt and are hard to clean. Make sure the installer puts a coving strip down behind the floor covering before installation.

Your kitchen floors should be a little darker than you might imagine. Floors that are white, light tan, etc., have to be mopped more often, and they look bad between moppings. Don't choose a floor covering with indentations or texturing. There's plenty of flooring that gives the effect of being textured when in fact the surface is completely smooth. Choose those. Your dust mop or broom will pick the dirt up easily and you'll still have the look you desire. Floors with smooth surfaces also can be easily cleaned with a floor squeegee.

Why would anyone carpet the kitchen? I've seen carpeted gymnasiums—different, but okay. I've seen pickup trucks with carpeted beds. I've seen carpeted barns, garages, briefcases, and horse's hoofs. I can understand carpeting ball fields, even basements or beauty parlors—but *kitchens*—how could you do it? Are you a gambler? There isn't a 90, 95, or even 99 percent chance that spills, stains, and odors will occur; it's a 100 percent sure thing that you'll get all of these on the kitchen floor! **Carpet in a kitchen or anywhere food or drink abounds will eventually be recognized as a mistake—plush and kitchen don't go together because as we know, if an open-face jam sandwich falls to the floor, it falls face first.** If the floor is carpeted, that's ten minutes of your life gone—only ten seconds if it's a hard floor. Every stain and spill is an emotional strain and they all add up to a very good reason to avoid kitchen carpet!

The Cabinets

If I were allowed to make only one recommendation about cabinets, it would be to build your kitchen cabinets all the way to the ceiling. You won't believe the extra storage space you'll have. Instead of building a soffit or leaving this space open to get caked with settling grease and grime, ask for 42-inch upper cabinets—the kitchen designer will know what you're talking about.

An empty space above the cabinets also becomes a tempting space to stick pretty little plates and such. Whatever decoration you put up there will get twice

Cabinets that go all the way to the ceiling not only provide an extra shelf of storage space, but also eliminate the space above the cabinets that collects dust and grease.

as dirty as it would in any other spot in the house.

Cabinets to the ceiling will give you one extra shelf in every cabinet. Even though you can't reach these top shelves readily, they're the perfect place to store all those seldom-used but sometimes-needed things such as serving platters, cake dishes, picnic baskets, etc. And if you're worried that you won't be able to reach the top shelf easily, think how frustrating it will be to climb up there to dust those decorative knickknacks every week!

The trouble with having a lot of things to store is they get stored away and you forget that you have them to use. With this upper shelf you see them every time you open your cupboard. You're reminded of what you have, but it isn't in the way or taking valuable low storage space.

Your other shelves will also be less crowded, thus more maintenance-free. The fuller a cabinet gets, the more of a maintenance problem it becomes. Things get knocked over, you have to hunt for them, and you can't get at them easily.

An extra row of cabinets around the top of the kitchen:

1. Uses otherwise wasted space to provide extra storage

2. Enables you to concentrate your kitchen storage in the kitchen and not all over the house

3. Eliminates the space between the ceiling and the top of the cabinets that usually collects dirt and clutter, thus saving you an additional surface to clean

4. Gives the illusion of a higher ceiling

5. Costs no more than building a soffit and storage somewhere else

Ideally, kitchen cabinets should have a perfectly smooth surface. Aesthetically, this may not appeal to everyone, but it's still a good idea to stay with flat surfaces and straight lines in your door decoration. It's much easier to run a cloth or sponge over a smooth surface than to take your pinky and weave up

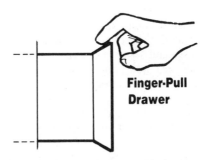

Finger-Pull Drawer

Drawers or cabinets with beveled edges eliminate the need for handles.

and down, over and under to clean the crevices and grooves in a fancy door.

Porcelain-coated steel is the most carefree material for kitchen cupboards, but many people find these stark and institutional. The best compromise is medium-colored hardwood with a factory-applied finish.

The handles you choose for your cabinets can also cost you five or ten minutes a week (that's more than 400 hours in a lifetime). If you can't live without fancy handles, put them in the den or living room to enjoy. You *won't* enjoy cleaning crud out of them in the kitchen.

Use recessed or hidden hinges (sometimes called invisible hinges) and eliminate exposed hardware entirely wherever you can. Most cabinets are available with finger pulls or beveled edges for easy

Wire Shelving in the Kitchen

Wire shelving is a great idea in most cabinets. Wire shelves scarcely ever have to be cleaned or dusted, they allow more air circulation, and it's easier to see what's stored on a wire shelf. Use wire shelving as top shelves to store things like smaller pans or mixing bowls. Towels, canned goods, and oversized objects can also be stored there. But don't use wire shelves for heavy items such as cookbooks and small appliances, or small items like utensils.

Wire storage racks on the inside of the doors of your kitchen cabinets are great because the less you have to dig and hunt for the things you use most, the better off you are. I'd also put light wire storage shelves on the pantry door.

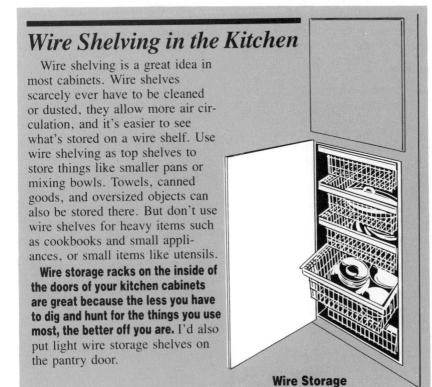

Wire Storage

opening without a handle. **If you've already got fancy hardware on your cabinets and you'd have big holes if you took it off—replace it with smooth, simple, rounded hardware. It's safer and easier to clean.**

Keep Down the Deposits in Your Dust Fund

Seldom-used things such as cake decorators, cookie cutters, or muffin tins collect dust between uses and sometimes even wire shelves aren't enough to keep the dust under control.

One solution is a covered or multi-tiered lazy Susan. This minimizes the dust and grime settling on your rare spices and other little-used items. The dust still settles, but most of it only reaches the top tier.

As far as possible, store all your seldom-used items together in one area—if they are seldom used, that cupboard or cabinet will be seldom opened to the dust and grime.

If dust is a big problem where you live, you can also seal your cabinets. That isn't as hard as it sounds. You know those little felt tabs some people put on the corners of cabinet doors to soften the "bang" when the door closes? Well, you can buy the stick-on felt in strips instead of tiny little circles. Put the strips around the entire edge of the door so that when the door is closed the felt takes up any gap between the door and the front edges of the cupboards. Then when the cupboard is closed, it's sealed and much less dust gets in. This can be done to any door, china cabinet, hutch, gun cabinet,

etc., where unused items sit year after year. (Of course, you should also get rid of a lot of these little-used items that demand your care.)

Sealing your cabinets will also save the semiannual, ceremonial washing of glass goblets and display dishes that haven't been used since the *last* time you washed them. I wouldn't hesitate to put those strips on every cupboard that presents a dusting problem, especially in the kitchen where glassware is stored. There are also dust-free cabinets available from a number of manufacturers. Some have routed strips of protruding wood that automatically seal the cabinet. These are nice but expensive.

Counter Intelligence

Your countertops get harder use and even more mess on them than the floor, so they should be models of cleanability. What are your choices in countertops?

1. *Plastic laminate:* It's the most common countertop material. It isn't as durable as some surfaces, but it isn't as expensive either—for the difference in price, you can replace it when it wears out.

2. *Marble:* Has a luxurious look but it's porous as well as hard to install. Its cool, smooth surface is great for working with candy or pastry. It is quite resistant to abuse, but can be damaged by acids such as vinegar and harsh cleaning compounds.

3. *Ceramic tile:* Since a tile surface has joints, it isn't completely smooth but it is one of the most durable countertops available. Many people love a tile countertop and food doesn't stick to one. The grout in tile surfaces does make them a little harder to clean than smooth plastic laminate. No matter what color your tiles are, make sure *the grout is medium to dark.* You'll never have to scrub stained grout and your counter will always look nice. Also, don't edge the countertop with tile—it's too prone to chipping on exposed edges and corners. Use a beveled hardwood edging that matches your cabinets.

4. *Wood:* Has to be treated to be used in a countertop and even then it isn't very long-lasting. It is nice to have butcher block in a few areas for cutting, to serve as a hot plate, etc., but not overall.

5. *Corian:* This synthetic sheet material developed by Du Pont is considered the Cadillac of synthetic countertops by most cabinetmakers. It is smooth, seamless, resilient, and very resistant to damage. But it also costs about three times as much as plastic laminate.

6. *Stainless steel:* Used widely in restaurant kitchens, it is almost indestructible and is easy to maintain. Better grades of aluminum—especially those with a brushed finish—can look good for years. But cheap grades soon develop a scratched, "used" appearance that isn't very elegant looking.

7. *Granite:* Extremely long-wearing and almost impervious to abuse, granite is prohibitive in price and its installation requires skilled craftsmen.

8. *Onyx:* It's okay in a bathroom but a little too soft for the hard use a kitchen counter gets.

The choice is yours—just remember the principles of maintenance-freedom here and then fit them to your pocketbook.

A countertop surface must be:

1. Smooth—you don't want any type of texture

2. Able to stand up to hard use

3. A neutral color (not too light or too dark) to help disguise dirt

4. Simple—don't give yourself a lot of different surfaces or seams and crevices to clean

5. Safe—no sharp corners or edges (see page 57 for information on how to avoid these)

6. A good trade-off between cost and the time and trouble it saves

7. Appealing to you!

A Matter of Splatters

The backsplash is the extension of the countertop up the back wall to protect the wall from splatters. **Don't let anyone tell you that six inches is high enough for a backsplash, because it isn't.** Food and grease don't know that they're only supposed to splash six inches and then stop. There is usually an 18-inch gap between the upper cabinets and the countertop. Often we think a good enamel paint or vinyl wallcovering will be sufficient here, and for the first couple of years it is. But paint or wallcovering isn't as durable as the countertop and eventually, after you've scrubbed flying grease or cake batter off time and again it will look dull and spotty. With a 6-inch backsplash, you've also given yourself an extra ledge and two separate surfaces to clean. Run the backsplash all the way up the wall to the upper cabinets. One big smooth surface of plastic laminate or whatever your counter material may be will save a minute or two of cleaning time every day.

Height

It's important to consider the height of the counter in relation to the height of the user. The standard counter height is 36 inches. If that's too low, you can adjust ready-made cabinets for a tailor-made fit. Put a few sheets of particleboard or plywood beneath the standard 36-inch cabinet. Upper cabinets can be hung lower or higher than standard, depending on your needs. It's tougher to make the bottom cabinets lower, though, so you may have to turn to a custom builder if you're shorter than average.

Many people overlook one of the places where a backsplash is most needed—behind the stove.

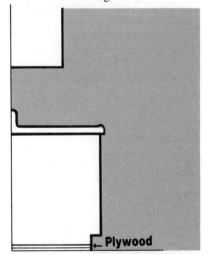

Insert a few sheets of plywood beneath bottom cabinets to make them higher.

Plywood

Decorate with Color

Here is a decorator's tip for making a kitchen seem cleaner. **If you are using plastic laminate on the countertops, trim the counter edge with laminate in a complementary bright or dark color.** It will carry your eye around the kitchen faster and the kitchen will seem crisper and sharper. Your eye is immediately drawn to the dark sharp edge and the whole kitchen will appear cleaner.

You can also get a decorator effect by using a laminate in a pattern. The accent won't create any work, since it's made of the same material as the countertop, but it will give the kitchen some added interest.

Faucets and Fixtures

For years, both on the job and at home, I accepted the faucet that happened to be available or on sale. It wasn't until I began to repair and replace faucets that I realized that some fixtures were twice as easy to install, fix, and clean. **Changing faucet hardware and fixtures is a project that's well within the range of the average do-it-yourselfer.** So choose a faucet fixture that's not only easy to maintain but also easy to install.

Once again the simplest hardware—the single-handle faucet with a knob at the end—is the best. There are thousands of fixtures on the market and you could look forever and still get a lemon. Even the big-name companies have some bad models. So we'll make an exception here and name a couple of specific brands. For good overall fixtures that will last, Delta and Moen are both good—if you spend the money to get one of these, you will be happy. Remember to keep things compatible and put the same brand

of faucets throughout the house and the same model, at that, in all the sinks. The single-handle, washerless faucet is smooth and easy to clean, with no crevices or corners to trap gunk. The internal workings are relatively durable and trouble-free, are easily repaired, and the parts are widely available.

Sinks

Double sinks are handiest in the kitchen, and in the kitchen or the bathroom, the deeper the sink, the better. If water cascades into a deep sink, less will splash out onto walls, counters, cabinet fronts, the floor, etc. When you drain potatoes or pasta in the sink, you're less apt to get scalded. When you're mixing juice or scrubbing a greasy skillet, it keeps any splatters in.

Stainless steel sinks take little upkeep, last a long time, show dirt very little, and are hard to damage. Stainless steel *will* stain, though—it comes in several grades, and the lower grades will streak and get blotchy-looking.

Porcelain over cast iron is also very good. If you absolutely love the look of porcelain, use it, but avoid dark colors such as red, black, and brown, as well as pure white. Dark colors are sure to show scratches, water spots, and detergent residue. Choose sand, beige, or ivory instead. Neutral colors like these clean up fast and don't show the dirt as much. Solid cast-iron sinks with porcelain coatings probably retain their good looks longest, and are quiet when the disposal is running.

When installing a sink, be sure to leave at least an inch between the base of the faucet and the back wall or backsplash so you can get a sponge or cleaning cloth through easily.

The Fountain of Youth

A drinking fountain can be a maintenance-free appliance if you have the traffic to justify one. How often do people get drinks of water? Kids, at least five times a day. Visitors, at least once—and if they eat or snack (which they usually do)—three times. How many glasses is that to take out, wash, and put back in the cupboard, and worry about breaking? And of course when the kids do it themselves, they drag a chair across the floor and ding the cabinets. When they're finished, they never put the chair back.

Water fountains are a luxury, but the trade-off may be worth the cost. They offer instant hassle-free cool water. **I'll bet a drinking fountain pays for itself in the first three years by cutting the cost of broken glasses, electricity to cool an often-opened fridge, damage to the sink and floor, etc.**

A drinking fountain does require a water supply, a drain, and an electrical source. And they do burn energy, probably about $40 a year. If your crew is always heading for the water, I'd put one in. Your local plumbing store (or architect) can give you names of a source. Be sure to buy the wall-mounted type to prevent overspray and *recess* it when you install it. A refrigerator with a cold-water dispenser could be an alternative if your water demands don't warrant a fountain—it has all the benefits of a fountain except that you still use a lot of glasses. There are also faucets that double as water fountains—the head swivels around to direct water wherever you want. The disadvantage of these is that the water isn't as cold as it would be from a bona fide fountain.

Appliances

Every year, every appliance company comes out with something new; some of these are good and some are bad. Instead of recommending brand names, we're going to give you some principles of appliance buying and let you take it from there. There are some features *you* like and need that *I* don't like and need. If this weren't so—if there were one overall best model—it would be the only one on the market.

You know which of your present appliances are *not* maintenance-free because you rarely use them—it's too much of a hassle. Think about why you don't use them and what you don't like about them when you're looking over those shiny new appliances in the store.

Whenever possible, choose appliances with a fingerprintless front. This is a slightly textured finish and almost all manufacturers have realized how good an idea it is. It hides the little fingerprints that you usually have to polish or wipe away.

When it comes to color, choose a medium tone—dark colors are hard to clean and so is pure white. Avoid black-fronted appliances—they show every drop and fingerprint. They *have* to be shined and will get dirty fast. Almond is one of the nicest dirt-minimizing colors there is. Look for plain simple handles and knobs and as few of those as possible. The new electronic touch controls are immensely easier to clean than the old exasperating ridged and decorated knobs and dials.

If you can manage it, a built-in appliance is the best, no question about it. Whenever you seal the top, sides, and underneath, you eliminate all those places to collect grease and dust and flying food that has to be cleaned off.

There are two drawbacks to built-ins, though. A built-in appliance is there to stay, so it better be installed in its permanent location. If you don't plan to stay in your present home permanently, this can be a problem. Also, built-in appliances are slightly more expensive than standard ones, and you may not plan to replace your major appliances now, anyway. But if you're doing major remodeling or building new, built-in is best.

The Stove

This is your biggest mess-maker. There are more and more ranges with sealed-in heat elements on the market. These have coils just like the stove you're using now—only the top is completely sealed so nothing can get down under it. At least three manufacturers currently make them and I'm sure every other manufacturer will follow suit, so shop around for the one that suits you. We prefer these to the glass-top models that require a special kind of pan to cook on them, but glass-tops are great for clean-up and have been improved considerably over the last few years.

The new cooktops on the market also have a downdraft venting system that is wonderful. It's said

The Trials of Too Many Knobs

45

to be 80 percent more efficient in getting the grease and grime out of the air before it gets to the rest of the house. It works like this: Grease and smoke that come from cooking settle down toward the floor, so a vent that is below the cooking surface traps the grease and smoke more efficiently than an overhead vent that pulls fumes up to dispose of them. That flying smoke and grease are what cause the layer of grime you find on the top of your fridge—that stuff is landing all over your house; you just don't see it because you clean your counters daily and you rub it into your carpets and floor.

There are now several major brands of appliances offering this system and every six months something new comes out so you will soon see this system available in a wide variety of stovetop models. **If you are building in, put your venting fan down near the cooktop and vent it *to the outside.*** Filtered, circulating hoods don't do a good job no matter what the salesperson says—you want to get the smoke out of the house, not recirculated back into it.

What about those cooktops that are steak barbecues, rotisseries, and deep fryers all in one? They are harder to clean. If you actually do barbecue a lot, you'll love them, but make sure the use will justify the extra cleaning. Attaching and deattaching all the parts is questionable otherwise.

If you're not ready to buy a new stove, you can still cut back your stove upkeep time. There are burner pans available now that have a Teflon surface. Ask at your appliance store—if they don't have them, you may be able to order them.

Ovens

By all means get a self-cleaning oven. Laura says she didn't believe they could work as well as

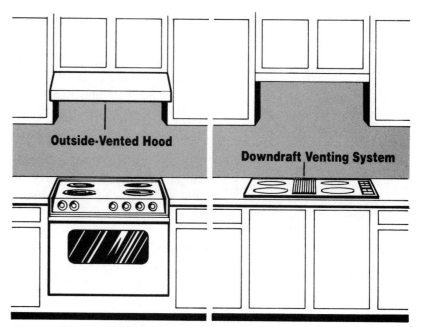

Two good types of built-in cooktops.

they do until she rented out her house one year and the new oven was left a mess. She put off and put off cleaning it even though it was "self-cleaning" because she just knew she was in for a job. One day her husband just turned all the knobs and turned it on. "That oven was spotless—and I mean every little drop of burned-on mess was gone and I didn't even touch it," she says. Think

what that would save in cleaning time over the years—kitchen mess, floor mess, sink mess—not to mention the cost of oven cleaner. **Self-cleaning ovens are a definite must for your low-maintenance house—don't be without them.**

Built-in ovens also save work—they sit higher off the floor so they don't catch as much dirt as the lower ones do.

The Self-Cleaning Oven

Microwaves

Microwave ovens are timesavers for many household jobs. Not only do they boil water almost instantly and cook food in much less time, there's less cleaning, too, because food doesn't splatter all over the microwave when it cooks.

Build them in if you can. If you already have a microwave and don't want to buy a new one, you can buy a kit to convert your countertop microwave into a built-in—ask your cabinet dealer or at the DIY store.

A word of caution about your microwave's location: If your microwave is set too high, the danger of tipping something out on top of yourself is great. Don't put a microwave higher than mid-chest. Any higher and you greatly increase the chance of burns, and burns from spattered microwaved food can be severe. Food from a microwave comes out HOT—often hotter than food from a conventional oven.

You should also consider everyone else who will be using it, including kids. Built in at the 3 to 3½-foot level is just about right for most people, but here again is a place where you should tailor proportions to fit *your* family.

Refrigerators

For a fridge, anything but frost-free leaves me cold. **Defrosting a freezer is a major, messy job that isn't necessary in this post-Ice Age era.**

An automatic ice-maker is also handy. If you have a large family, the job of keeping the ice trays full can be titanic.

Take a hard look at the design inside, too—all those little shelves, drawers, and compartments. This interior architecture can get very tricky to clean—so run your mental washcloth over it

and check it out. The various devices and major drawers should not only store things conveniently and efficiently but must be easy to remove for cleaning.

While buying built-in appliances is always a good idea, built-in refrigerators are particularly handy. They're wider and shallower than regular refrigerators—and are easier to maintain because you have less "back of the fridge mess." Also, things don't get pushed to the back and then forgotten or knocked over and spilled.

Because built-ins are more expensive, you may opt for second best. Build a cabinet over the top of a regular refrigerator and put a panel of wood that matches your cabinets down both sides. Instead of the usual arrangement, in which the fridge top is exposed to collect grease and grime, extend the cabinet out over the top of the fridge. The side panels are attached to the countertop. This means you don't get that dirt dropping off the counter down between the fridge

and the cabinet. The top cabinet also makes an accessible storage place—some people like to put slots in it for lids, cookie sheets, mail, etc. This arrangement eliminates two sides and the top to be cleaned.

Other Appliance Musts

Any kitchen that aspires to be maintenance-free should not be without two timesaving treasures: the dishwasher and the garbage disposal. In addition to the obvious benefit of freeing you from dishpan hands, a dishwasher helps hide clutter between washings, stores clean dishes, and encourages you to deal with the dishes right away rather than letting them pile up in the sink—where the job just gets harder the longer you wait. A garbage disposal eliminates food seepage from garbage bags, aids in speedy cleanup, and makes for less frequent trips to the garbage can since you have less perishable waste.

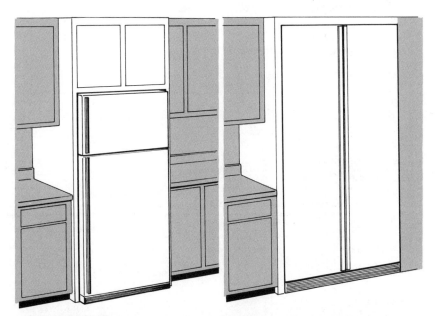

Built-in refrigerators are best—but if you don't have a refrigerator that's made to be built in, you can construct your cabinets so that your standard model works like a built-in.

Suspended Appliances

Count how many things you have on the counter—canisters, can openers, coffee makers, toaster ovens, microwaves, knife blocks, utensil holders—they all add up. Every time you wipe up the counter, what do you do with these things? You have to pick them up and put them down again. What do they look like when you pick them up? Invariably, they have a glob of jam or a bit of spilled tomato paste on them so you have to quickly wipe them down, too. You do this at least weekly and more likely two or three times a week. That's a lot of extra work. And with many new homes being smaller and more compact, the need for efficient use of counter space is greater than ever. **Many appliances and containers can be mounted underneath the upper cabinets or on the backsplash to eliminate that constant handling and free up counter space.** Since manufacturers have grasped the convenience of having fewer things sitting on the counters, you can now get almost any appliance suspended or built in. Some are less common, so you have to pay more for them, but some of the things you use every day, like can openers and mixers, are available for about the same price as the countertop models.

Eating Area

If you're lucky enough to have an eat-in kitchen, you face a decision about the best styles and materials for kitchen furniture. A table with suspended chairs is the way to go in almost any kitchen, but particularly in those that serve large families. It makes mopping easier and saves the floor from the scourge of scuff marks. (See page 120 for a full discussion of tables with suspended chairs.)

A solid hardwood table is elegant for light use, but most woods have to be treated with special cleaners or oils. A tabletop with a plastic laminate holds up much better for a more rambunctious household and tolerates (if not thrives) on soap and water. Glass is easy to clean and very durable, although it does show fingerprints and water marks. **Make sure the backs of your chairs are open so they let crumbs fall easily to the floor.** Don't get chairs with elaborate upholstery, either. Buttons, puckers, and tucks collect every speck of dirt that comes their way.

Oh, That Kitchen Windowsill

Everything piles up here! You find one of your daughter's hair barrettes on the floor. You don't drop everything and run to her room—you set it on the kitchen windowsill. Somebody drops a dime on the floor—you park it on the kitchen windowsill. You find a crayon in the silverware drawer, you don't scoot to the playroom and put it in the box—there it goes on the kitchen windowsill. You take the rubber band off the morning paper—and drop it on the kitchen windowsill. Then, when there is danger of an avalanche, you finally have to face putting everything away. It may be smarter to consolidate the putting

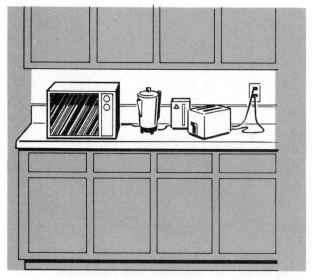

Before

After

away—your time is valuable—but how do you deal with that messy pile in the meantime?

You need a "control center" with room for all this. The reason you use the kitchen windowsill is because it's central and convenient. The control center can include a "mail center" with slots or bins for the bathroom, the bedroom, the kids' room, your office. Those slots will invite people to police their own things—even though they never touched the mess on the kitchen windowsill. The slots will also save you a solid hour of sorting—you sort as you go. The control center also organizes many other kinds of messes and messages. (See page 23 for an illustration of one example of a kitchen control center.)

If you want to go a step further, you can eliminate the windowsill altogether by setting the window in so that it is even with the wall. Then there's no place for things to accumulate.

But don't get rid of the kitchen window completely! In fact, consider putting a giant picture window in the kitchen. Nearly everyone puts a big window in the living room, but you don't really *live* in the living room like you do in the kitchen. You're usually there in the evening when it's dark and you can't see out anyway. The kitchen, however, is the headquarters of the house. Most of the talking on the phone, babysitting, family decision-making, etc., goes on there. So if there's any place light should come in, where people should see and feel the outside, the kitchen is the place.

Accessories

A lot of the work you do in the kitchen is generated by the dishes, napkins, tablecloths, and other accessories that go with the territory. So while lessening the labor caused by these items won't exactly make your house do the housework, they're probably worth a moment or two of thought.

Opt for modern dish styles that are truly serviceable—the plates aren't too ornate, the glasses aren't too small to clean easily, the cups are neither too heavy nor too fragile to handle. Choose a material that is smooth and cleanable.

One of the best ways to make sure you're wasting as little time as possible on the dishes is to make sure you have plenty of storage space for them. You need at least four feet of dish storage for an average family. Tablecloths and place mats need a lot of care. Except for very formal occasions when you want the elegance they can provide, omit them from your table setting. They have to be washed, ironed, and stored after each use. Place mats often cause more spills than they catch because they create an uneven surface that can tip over glasses and bowls.

Paper napkins are a lot less work than cloth, so decide if the luxury of "real" napkins is worth the washing, ironing, and folding they require.

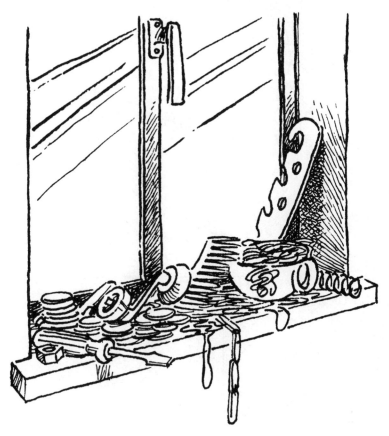

The Kitchen Windowsill

Chapter 7

Transforming the Toilet Zone

In a surprisingly short time, the bathroom has evolved from a simple outhouse to an overdone penthouse. For decades it was one of the most functional rooms in the house; now it's more like a trip through Disneyland. Floors have been carpeted, phones, bars, bookcases, exercisers have been installed. Shower handles and nozzles have been so complicated that many of us just skip it and use more deodorant.

Somewhere along the line someone put the word "boutique" after bath and it has hypnotized people ever since. Now there are even bathroom specialty stores,

which hawk everything from a full plumage of plumbing to velvet toilet seats and heated towel racks.

Then a water relaxation craze steamed across the country, lining bathrooms with hot tubs, whirlpools, Jacuzzis, and shower massage units. With them came lots more plumbing, valves, drains, steam moisture, mildew—and of course, increased expenses for cleaning and repair.

In her days as a kitchen and bath designer, Laura saw plenty of examples of the overdone, but perhaps the worst was a couple who ordered faucets plated with *real* gold for their master bath. The contractor had to guard the fixtures day and night until the house was ready to move into, and now the owners have to worry about and guard over a bunch of *bathroom fixtures.*

When it comes to the bathroom, forget the frills. Don't let the bathroom beauticians unload all those unneeded accessories on you.

Why seek glory in the bathroom? The quickest and easiest to use and clean would seem the ultimate honor.

For example, what value is art displayed in a bathroom? The bathroom is used with a sense of either urgency or relief—and neither is conducive to aesthetic appreciation.

As in the other rooms of the maintenance-free house, put your decorations in the pattern of the wallcoverings or curtains. If you are a lover of flowers, get a flowered print instead of a vase of silk flowers that sits on the counter and has to be cleaned around. (And horror of horrors the flowers themselves have to be cleaned. Does *anyone* know how to clean a bouquet of silk flowers?) Bear in mind though that if you choose a very large print or design for the wallcovering, you will "shrink" the size of the bathroom. Keep it

simple. **If you have too much going on (that's the decorator term for too many colors and textures in one place), your bathroom will appear smaller than it is and it will never look clean.**

Privy Information

Aside from the kitchen, the bathroom is the most expensive room in the house to remodel. Because of the plumbing problems and tear-out work that usually has to be done, more time and money *per square foot* is spent on the bathroom than on any other place under the roof.

When Laura worked as a designer, bids for remodeling a bath seldom ran under $6,000. More often, the bill ran to $10,000 or $11,000. (It seems that when the time arrives for a bit of remodeling, home owners want it to arrive in *style*.) It's not uncommon these days to have a hot tub or whirlpool and either would cost at least $1,500 and could go as high as $8,000.

Size Up the Situation

There is no law that says the bathroom has to be 5x8 feet. If you are building, insist on a little

larger bathroom. Give yourself room to move. These days we dress, groom, relax, and even exercise in the bathroom. The people of yesteryear did most of their personal grooming in their bedrooms and they also did less of it. We moderns wash our hair every other day and generally are accustomed to a higher level of luxury.

Before you decide how big your bathrooms should be, decide how many there'll be. As a general rule of thumb for comfort and convenience, figure two people per bathroom. Adults, that is— four children can share one bath. This rule isn't hard and fast, though. If that ratio sounds a bit luxurious for your budget, you can have fewer baths without sacrificing all the convenience. A "Hollywood bath," for example, is almost as good as two bathrooms. Or install a separate shower stall in the master bath and it can do almost double duty. On the other hand, don't use that rule of thumb to rule out extras, either. A bath, or half bath, off the garage may be worth the expense in the time it saves by keeping the dirt from the kids' outdoor games and your tinkering with the car outside the house.

You should also think about any special needs you might have. You will need extra room if you have children that you must bathe and dress in the bathroom or if

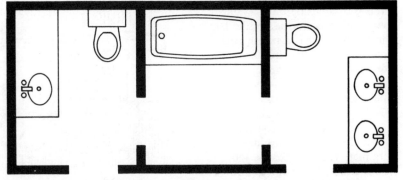

A Hollywood bathroom is almost as good as two separate baths.

you anticipate that it will be used by someone in a wheelchair. You should plan for these things. It doesn't take much longer to clean a large bath as long as it isn't full of junk and clutter.

It's very important to get the right size. Too big and you have a living-room-size cleaning job. I've seen homes where neither expense nor expanse was spared on the master bath—homes with a 15x25 foot bathroom complete with double pedestal vanities, crystal swan-head faucet handles, a chandelier, and a five-person Jacuzzi.

While you don't need a bathroom big enough to film a shampoo commercial, too small can be just as bad as too big. It will help to have things stored here that are going to be used here, including cleaning supplies, toiletries, cosmetics, towels, and to have enough room to take care of the kids when they're in the tub. We've found that a bathroom about 6x7 feet (or 10x12) is a nice family-sized bath.

The Big Three: Tub, Toilet, and Sink

Do you know this scene? There you are in the bathroom armed to the teeth with scrub brushes, cleanser, and disinfectant. But before you can unleash even the first sprinkle of amazing blue crystals, you recoil in horror before the Big Three. The tub has a bigger ring than Liz Taylor, the sink looks like a biology experiment gone haywire, and the toilet—well, the toilet's too terrible to mention.

It doesn't have to be that way. If you're remodeling, you can choose the right fixtures and the right materials to make the job easier. If not, you can add a few accessories that'll cut down on ev-erything from soap scum to floor flooding. Either way, you *can* control the Big Three.

The Tub

Buy and install a top-grade cast-iron porcelain tub, even if it *is* expensive. A tub gets a lot of hard use over time, so you'll never regret it. *Nothing* beats a cast-iron tub. You could slaughter a cow or run a still in one of these old tubs—they're solid as rock and hard as flint. Cast-iron tubs have a baked-on porcelain surface that stays glossy and is easy to clean.

Modern manufacturers have introduced cheaper porcelainized steel units to replace the cast-iron models. These damage and dull more readily than cast iron, but are more durable than the molded and fiberglass tubs that have also come into use in recent years. The fiberglass tubs have a relatively soft surface that scratches easily.

They look great when they're new, but depending on the quality, the surface wears off rather rapidly. Fiberglass also has a tendency to turn yellowish.

In an existing home, the design of the bathroom may limit you to a conventional 5-foot tub, unless you want to do extensive remodeling. But if you're building a new bathroom, you can consider exotic shapes and oversized tubs, if that's one of your dream house can't-do-withouts. For just taking a bath or shower, however, the conventional equipment is adequate.

When you buy a tub, stay away from dark colors and white. Midtones are more merciful on you. A deeper tub and a wider rim mean less splashes on the floor.

From a cleaning standpoint, those little non-skid tub appliques are an abomination. No matter how handsomely they're designed, their textured surface acts like a door mat, absorbing dirt. They

One of the biggest problems in the bathroom is keeping water where you want it.

look dirty and eventually *are* dirty and hard to clean. The best solution for non-skid safety is the good old-fashioned rubber mat you can remove and replace.

If lounging in a giant Jacuzzi is your idea of idyllic, be prepared to pay extra in purchase price and maintenance. Most of the large spas and whirlpools are made of molded plastic which, like fiberglass, is not as durable as porcelain-coated cast iron. Plastic and fiberglass require more care and maintenance if they are to retain their beauty over time. And that extra plumbing and water treatment equipment also mean extra upkeep.

Keeping Water Where You Want It

Conrad Hilton was once asked if he could solve one of the biggest problems in his hotels, what would it be? "Keeping the water in the tub and shower instead of the walls and floors," he said.

Water is the plague and ruin of many a bathroom.

How do you contain it?

Tub enclosures or tub and shower doors aren't the answer. I receive more complaints about these than about anything else in the house. Fiberglass shower doors get covered with hard-water deposits; their tracks crud up and won't slide; the corners mildew; the doors yellow, they crack, they stain, you name it. If they're the accordian type, they will never be clean. You're better off with a $7.98 discount-store curtain. You'll be spared all the headaches of shower doors, and if the water temperature goes wild, you can leap through the curtain instead of being trapped and scalded.

While an inexpensive shower curtain is better than a door, your best bet is to get a heavy plastic or plastic-coated curtain. A nice heavy curtain will resist mildew, holes, and wrinkling better than a cheap, thin one. It will keep the water in

the tub better, too. The heavier material will hang in place and allow water to run off. And keep it simple! Lacy curtains that are hung in layers have to be laundered and soon lose their crispness. One nice plastic curtain can serve both purposes—function and beauty.

Another easy way to keep the water where you want it is to place the shower head a little higher than normal. Splashing will be minimized because the water will fall straight down instead of ricocheting off the wall and bouncing onto the floor. There are also L-shaped brackets that curve the ends of your shower curtain to help contain the water, as well as plastic splash guards that can be glued to the corners of your tub.

The Shell Shower

For bathrooms where you don't need or want a tub, the new "shell" shower is by far the best choice. Its unique design eliminates the need for a curtain or shower door altogether and provides a place to store shampoo containers, etc., out of the water path and soap-scum zone. Its smooth, seamless interior is a cinch to care for. It's available from the Swan Corporation (see the Source List) as a pre-built kit, or your contractor could construct a similar one.

A smooth seamless "enclosure"—the technical term for a three-sided unit that covers the back and side walls of the tub or shower—is the next best thing. An enclosure doesn't provide the water containment of a shell shower, but offers many of the same maintenance pluses.

Fiberglass isn't the best material for an enclosure—it doesn't last and it yellows and stains. Corian, made by Du Pont, is a much better alternative in that it's almost indestructible and scratches can be

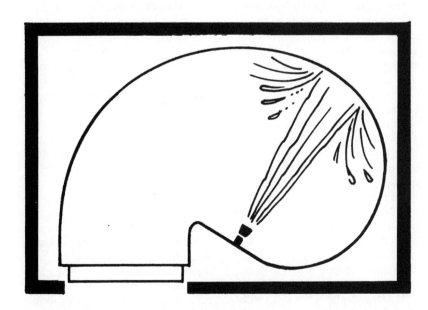

A shell shower doesn't need a door or shower curtain. It is designed so that water hits the back wall and runs to the drain with no chance of splashing out onto the floor.

sanded out. While Corian is the best sheet material to use, it can be expensive; cultured marble also works well. Avoid cheap plastic-coated masonite products with metal trim. Any sheet material with metal trim will mean lots of edges and crevices to get dirty—and they're hard to clean.

The Sink

Looking for a way to get rid of that sinking feeling? The best source of relief is a drop-in one-piece china sink with no metal rim. This is probably the most durable and maintenance-free sink. Porcelainized, one-piece cast iron is the second choice, and porcelainized cast-iron with a metal mounting rim is also good. Cheap steel sinks with a porcelain coating come in last.

Many sink tops are made of resin molded to simulate marble. This starts in a liquid form and so can be poured into any shape. The basin and the countertop surrounding it can be molded into one single piece—so there are no rims, cracks, or corners anywhere to get dirty and moldy.

The Perils of a Too-Small Sink

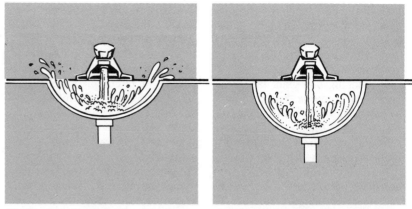

Much of the water mess in the bathroom is the result of a sink that's too shallow. A deeper sink keeps water off the counters and floor.

The backsplash is also molded in as part of the unit, which makes the countertop and sink one continuous piece that's very easy to clean. Because most of the corners and edges on a single-piece unit are molded in a rounded shape, you're less likely to get chipped or peeling laminate that needs to be repaired—and looks bad until it is repaired.

One-piece, molded countertop/sink combinations are easy to clean, but not as resistant to damage as the other materials. They are made of different materials such as synthetic onyx and marble, even fiberglass and Corian. Corian is the most long-lived, and onyx and marble are next best.

As for the size and shape of the sink: *The bigger and deeper the better.* Obviously, given all the splashing and soap, the more space there is in the sink to catch it and drain it away, the better off you are. The countertop around the sink will need less wiping and mopping up, and you won't be constantly bending down to wipe up the floor.

Stay far away from the sinks with little decorations like flowers or geometric designs. These are soap-catchers and will have to be cleaned with a toothbrush. Sinks shaped like seashells, etc, with little grooves and dips are also work causers—you have to clean in and out, over and under.

The best course to take when choosing a sink is to make sure that the bowl is a reasonable size, that the lines and corners are clean and smooth, and that the finish is smooth and glossy with no matte or rough areas (run your imaginary washcloth over it). Pick a neutral color such as beige, off white, soft pink, light gray—any color that is about the color of soap. This will camouflage some of the dirt so the sink will look better between cleanings. Dark colors will magnify the mess. The shape of your sink bowl doesn't make a big difference as long as the corners are rounded and the sink is deep enough to keep the splashes in.

Hardware

When you clean the bathroom sink, do you faithfully shine up the chrome—knowing full well that the first one who uses it will smudge it? Oh well, it does look nice for a couple of minutes. Wish there was a finish that looked good all the time? There is! It's an antique, brushed brass plating that

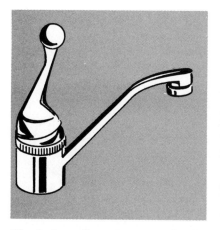

Single-lever faucets are easier to operate, maintain, and clean.

has a low-luster finish instead of a high gloss like chrome.

- Fingerprints don't show

- Just wipe off to clean—
  no polishing

- Water doesn't spot

- Wear and scratches don't show

I'd have this surface on every faucet from the kitchen to the utility room.

Another good material for the faucet handle is smooth hard plastic with no indentations or designs in the surface. These faucets have to be wiped off, but they don't have to be shined to a high gloss—so they won't show water spots and look bad the first time someone uses them after cleaning. White china faucets don't have to be shined either, but they show dirt more easily and aren't widely available.

One handprint is better than two. That's why a single-lever, pivoting handle faucet is less trouble than two handles. It's the most streamlined and easiest to operate. There are thousands to choose from, but the main things to guard against are little corners and crev-

ices that you can't get your fingertips in—they collect grime.

The common faucet with separate knobs for cold and hot water has three separate pieces—plus cracks, grooves, and crevices— that are virtually impossible to clean unless you use dental floss.

Be careful what kind of tub/ shower valve you build into the wall. Some are notorious for requiring constant repair, and once one of these is in the wall, you're in trouble! **Here again, Delta and Moen single-handle washerless valves are good ones. For something built into a wall and used every day like a tub/shower valve, the few extra dollars to go first class is money well spent.**

The Toilet

An article written by a bath designer, reviewing all the wares of the bathroom refiners, ended on this note:

"There are many new gadgets hitting the marketplace for the superbath of the '80s. But it still makes sense that the simple, less complicated bathroom equipment is the best."

When you buy a new toilet, think about this. Remember your old toilet and imagine yourself cleaning the new one (I know— this one will never get that dirty— but it *will*). Think about cleaning before you think about anything else.

At least half the bathroom maintenance woes come from the lower or base area of a toilet. In addition to those (*#!!) hard-to-clean-around little concealment caps that hide the anchor bolts, the base gets dribbles and messes from the top, combined with dirt from the floor. And if little children use the toilet you have another set of problems.

The way to eliminate cleaning the base is to eliminate the base. You've seen wall-mounted toilets in public buildings; we're putting them in our maintenance-free house. While it's usually not practical to go to wall mounting in most home replacement jobs, I'd install them whenever possible in new construction.

The next best bet is a single-form toilet where the tank and bowl are one piece, not two pieces connected with a bolt. This sits low, has a sleek modern look and streamlined design, and comes in a variety of colors.

| Standard | Streamlined | Suspended |

You can cut down your toilet troubles by installing the right kind. The sleek, streamlined models that are one single piece are easier to clean than the standard variety, and suspended toilets also eliminate cleaning the base.

In any case, pick out a toilet that's simple in design, with a minimum of ridges, knobs, and contours to clean around. What you want to avoid are little corners that cannot be reached or cleaned. They allow moisture to puddle, dirt to collect, and odors to develop.

A toilet seat is cleaned often and has to be simple and durable. It's a real lapse into tackiness here to have carved, padded, jewel-encrusted, scented, or flowered toilet seats. Buy the hardest-surfaced, strongest, least complicated toilet seat you can find.

Toilet seats come in a vast array of colors, finishes, and materials. The least expensive ones are made of cheap, brittle plastic or of wood, usually painted or plastic-coated. The cheap ones also have cheap hardware, and you often end up with broken or twisted hinges, rusted attachment bolts, etc. **The best seats are the solid commercial type made of a good, durable plastic that you buy at a plumbing shop, not an all-purpose discount store.** The finish doesn't wear off, they don't crack or peel, and the hardware is very durable. Padded vinyl seats are only good until the

first puncture, and fabric-covered ones are just about impossible to clean.

A lot of cheap toilet seats get broken or twisted because someone stands on them to change a light bulb or the like. The better ones will hold up to this kind of abuse, although climbing up on a toilet isn't the safest imaginable thing to do. (P.S. Always tighten the two fastening bolts on the seat extra tight. Once a toilet seat gets loose, it goes to pot fast!)

The Vanity

Since you'll be cleaning your vanity more often than anything else in the bathroom, it makes sense to make sure it's designed for fast and easy cleanup. Even when the rest of the room has the shabbies, if you can quickly clean the mirror and sink, the bathroom will usually look presentable. The trouble is the vanity usually makes that kind of jiffy spiffing up impossible. Toothpaste, hair, and crumpled tissues are everywhere, not to mention the brushes, combs, razors, bobby pins, blow dryers, curling irons, makeup, and

glasses left for you to clean around. It's a fifteen-minute job just getting the vanity ready to clean.

Solution: Make other, handier places for all these things. Nothing should be stored on the vanity top or you'll have to move all of it every time you clean. Drawers below the vanity or a cabinet beside is a nice solution. This keeps your vanity completely clear. Your blow dryer, towels, brushes, hot curlers, and shavers are all there on shelves (not on a little four-inch ledge beneath the mirror). The cabinet beside the vanity takes an extra eighteen to twenty-four inches of floor space, but it gives you all the storage you'll need for those items your vanity can't do without.

About the best bathroom vanity setup is one that is suspended about a foot off the floor. You won't lose any storage space because you just eliminate the kickboard, which takes up four inches, and then install the cabinet higher.

The suspension eliminates scuffs and kick marks that end up on the bottom of the cabinet front and keeps children from climbing on the cabinet doors.

56

What Material for the Countertop?

Now that you've got everything cleared off the countertop, you may want to give some thought to what it's made of. A smooth, hard surface such as cultured marble, granite, or Corian is the best. Plastic laminate is good and there's no limit to the variety of effects you can create with it. The price makes plastic laminate the number one choice for most homes.

A perfectly smooth surface is always best. Everything lands on a countertop and runs to the lowest points, and if the surface is textured, this means to the inden-tations, however slight. After the splashes and spills dry and settle in as dirt, they're not easy to get out. A cloth dampened with disinfectant-cleaner solution won't do it. A man we knew had a white, highly textured laminate countertop and it always looked dirty. One day I cleaned it for him; the lines and crevices had to be cleaned with a toothbrush, and in a week the crevices were dirty again. The low-gloss "suede fin-ish" laminates look rich without creating the problems of textured surfaces.

As for color, a neutral color with a faint speckled, geometric, or cowhide pattern is best. The ef-fect is essentially solid pastel and it hides the dirt and water spots.

If you do use plastic laminate, avoid sharp edges and corners. Keen, sharp edges do give a struc-ture a crisp, clean look, but they're also quick to make a struc-ture look shabby when they're even slightly damaged. To save "edge maintenance," make sure you slightly bevel the edges of plastic laminate to remove that sharp paper-thin point. For only a little more work and no extra ma-terial cost you will have elimina-ted a sharp corner to hit and a rough edge to split out and break off. And it looks ten times nicer.

High Lips Float Ships!

The outside edge or "lip" of any counter or sinktop should be raised a bit higher than the level of the counter itself. This keeps a big drip or splash from spreading little drips down the front of the cabinet to the floor. Better to have the water on the counter where you can wipe it up with a few quick swipes than on the floor.

Good builders do this. And many of the prefabricated counter-tops you'll find at DIY stores are made with a "drip-stop" lip.

Bathroom Mirror

Everyone wants to know how to handle the flying toothpaste and shaving splatters that begrime the bathroom mirror. The first thing you should know is what kind of mirror *not* to get. Don't get one of those single-piece mirror-with-vanity units that have the little box at the bottom with sliding doors (which may also be mirrors) for storing goodies. You buy them pre-assembled and slap them up on the wall above the sink. They are readily available and oh so tempting because they are fast and cheap. If you keep everything else, you have to get rid of these! They're ill-proportioned, have a

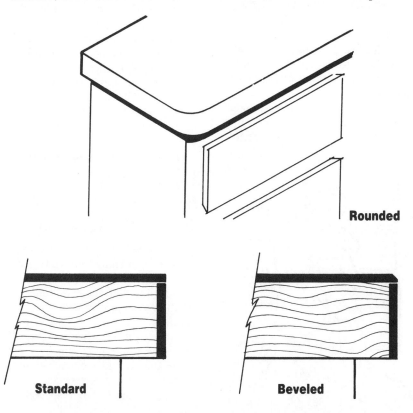

Rounded

Standard

Beveled

Sharp corners and edges are easily damaged. Rounded corners and beveled edges will save wear and tear on the counters, and will rid you of some danger points for young children. They're a good idea in both the bathroom and kitchen.

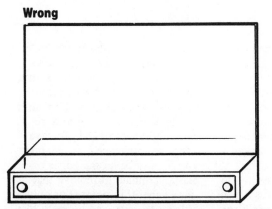

Wrong

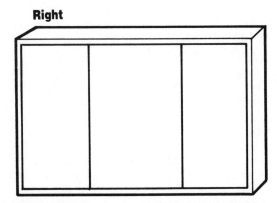

Right

Single-piece mirror-with-vanity units are hard to clean. A medicine chest with mirrored doors helps eliminate dust collection and has more storage.

lot of unnecessary surfaces located right in the line of fire—you don't stand a chance. The top of the storage unit provides a lovely place to collect things, and things will indeed collect. Then there are those gummy crevices called the sliding door tracks—you see how the problem snowballs. You've got all those extra places to catch dirt and toothpaste. And that doesn't count cleaning around the knobs, where there are always fingerprints. To top it all off, they often have a scrawny light fixture that does nothing but collect fried flies.

The Solution

Get a medicine chest with a mirrored door and no handles. You'll have more storage room, it'll look better, and you'll eliminate another place to collect dirt. If you want a frame get a light wood one and make sure it's simple and smooth.

Don't bring the mirror all the way down to the counter—water will splash on it and it will always look sloppy.

Bring the counter up and under the mirror to form a backsplash. You eliminate another crevice to

clean and water splashes won't show on a neutral-colored backsplash.

If you have room, you can put up a full-length mirror on the wall. This style is by far the easiest to clean. And remember the discipline of structure: Full-length mirrors can also be used to keep groomers and grooming mess (and drain-stopping hair) in a controlled area, away from the sink.

Ideally, the mirror should have no frame so it can be cleaned quickly with a squeegee without leaving lines on the side or top.

Lights in a Bathroom . . . the More the Messier

Ever notice that even the smallest bathroom tends to have two or more separate light units—one overall light and one task light, usually over the sink and mirror? Yet most of us only remember to turn one light out when we exit! One large fluorescent unit over the mirror that provides enough light for both uses is a better idea. (You may want to buy a special "natural color" tube for this room, so that your skin will look more natural.)

A full-length mirror can entice groomers and their drain-clogging messes away from the sink.

58

Wet dust—that persistent film that settles on lights in the bathroom—is the toughest in the world to deal with, so you don't want to have fourteen little lights all aching to be coated. And moisture billowing out of the steaming tub and shower area eventually rusts any metal it touches. Chrome and stainless steel withstand moisture well, but even so all the set screws get stiff and make changing a bulb a hard job!

Build in all the fixtures that you can, so that the bulbs are sealed behind a translucent panel of Plexiglas (see Chapter 14). And don't skimp on wattage. Good bright light will retard mildew.

A Makeup Mirror

A lighted makeup mirror is a good idea. A makeup mirror is just a mirror with built-in lights and you've got to have lights anyway. Why not recess a "natural color" fluorescent light on each side of the mirror or even at an angle and then encase the lights with Plexiglas just like the little makeup portable mirrors you buy?

Built-in and out of the way, they'll serve the dual purpose of providing light in general and light that's bright enough to shave or put on makeup by. They'll be easy to clean because they're flush with the wall and mirror and convenient because you won't have to store a makeup mirror and drag it out to use every day.

Walls and Ceilings

Your first thoughts about bathroom improvement naturally center on big items like the tub and toilet, but don't forget the walls and ceiling. Minimizing the maintenance is just as important here as anywhere else.

If your walls and ceiling are painted, use semigloss latex enamel paint. It's scrubbable, durable and resists moisture and peeling.

If you prefer wallcoverings, be sure to choose a fabric-backed vinyl. Fabric-backed vinyls have little or no paper to get soggy after years of sopping up bathroom moisture. You can tell a fabric-backed vinyl from a paper one be-

cause a sample won't tear easily.

Ceramic tile is (and has always been) a fairly common bathroom wall material, but there is one well-justified complaint about tile. To echo a TV commercial, "the grout"! Every square of smooth, tough, easy-to-maintain tile has trouble lurking around it.

A common 4x4-inch tile looks like a piece of true maintenance-minimizing material. But measure the amount of grout around it—sixteen inches of nuisance. Minimize the grout and minimize the grout problems. Use large tiles with narrow grout joints for shower walls. Just remember that nothing beats the cleaning ease of a single-sheet plastic laminate or acrylic surface, and be prepared to sacrifice some cleanability in return for the traditional look of tile.

As you choose your tile colors, keep in mind that midtones show dirt less. Beige, tan, pink, light green, and light blue are good. White is pretty good, too, because it reflects light, which helps hide water marks. Brown and black are horrible and highlight every speck of scum or drop of water.

Large tile means less time spent scrubbing grout.

Never Carpet Bathroom Floors!

There is always moisture in the bathroom. There is always the chance that the toilet will someday run over, and where does all the fallout from all that splashing, dripping, and hair spray go? *Into the carpet.* Floors of ceramic tile or sheet vinyl with no seams are classier and easier to clean, and much, much more sanitary. **Glazed ceramic floor tile is probably the best material in a bathroom, but be sure to color the grout a medium tone to disguise stains and discolorations.** Also, *seal* the grout to minimize staining. A little bit of texture to prevent slipping is okay, but don't use a heavy texture.

Sheet vinyl with seams isn't a very good choice for a bathroom floor. The again inevitable water splashes, leaks, and flooding will loosen and curl the seams and edges. Avoid marble and other flooring materials that are susceptible to damage from acid bowl and shower cleaners.

When it comes to bathmats, you want a mat made of natural fibers such as cotton so that the water will be readily absorbed. And for safety, make sure it's rubber-backed.

Never carpet the bathroom!

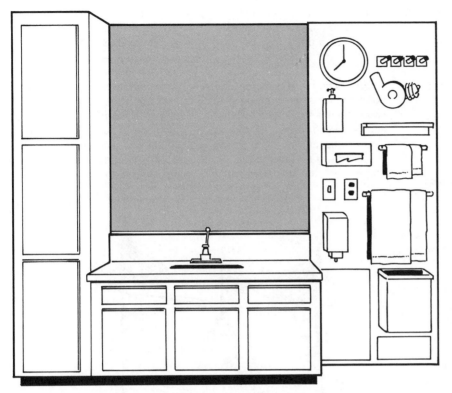

A bathroom control center can help confine the mess to one area. Put all the essentials in one place—tissues, soap and lotion dispensers, towel racks, trash can, hair dryer, etc.—and you won't have to clean the rest of the room nearly as often.

Take Control

Somewhere in the vicinity of the sink is a good place to put the control center of the bathroom—a storage space for essentials that need to be in easy reach: a box of tissues, hamper, wastebasket, etc., should all be built in right there.

Bear in mind that the bathroom is second only to the kitchen as a source of trash. More things are opened and unpackaged here than anywhere. When you replace the bathroom trash can, make it a little bigger—and *suspend it*. (For more on suspended waste cans, see page 87).

Curtains

As in the kitchen, it's important that bathroom curtains be washable. Given the moist atmosphere of the bathroom, you will need to wash and freshen them more often. We recommend a poly/cotton blend that will dry wrinkle-free. You want to be able to take the curtains out of the dryer and hang them right back up on the rod. Look at the tag and ask the clerk when you buy them—the cheaper they are, the more likely you'll have to iron. You can venture into darker colors for your curtains as it won't make a lot of difference in the care.

Use a simple cafe-type curtain rod and avoid metal hooks—they are likely to rust. In Hawaii this problem is especially bad; we have to evaluate everything in the house from a rust standpoint and so even our rods have to be made of something other than metal.

Because bathroom air is full of powder and spray, louvered shades are something you absolutely want to avoid in a bathroom.

Storage

A full-sized linen closet in the bath is such a good idea that it's hard to believe how few homes have one. It lets you store towels, toilet paper, extra shampoo and soap, and all the other grooming supplies right where they're needed—down the hall just isn't close enough when you've just stepped out of the shower and realized there are no clean towels. (See Chapter 12 for more ideas on bathroom storage.)

Towel Racks

Towels left on the floor are a big bathroom timetaker. When it comes to towel-hanging devices, remember that plain is sane and handy is dandy. Put an extra towel rod in if you possibly can to provide one more spot to "hang it up." The handier it is, the more likely it'll get used. How many times have you cleaned and polished your towel racks? Glass and chrome rods are the worst. The extremely ornate styles with lion paws and gargoyle heads are obvious no-nos. The best types are antiqued or buffed metal well coated with varnish or polyurethane.

Caulk, the Time Cutter

Few of us have figured out how to use that missile-looking tube of caulk. The caulk line meanders all over the place, the caulk sticks to our fingers a hundred times better than to any house surface, and even a seemingly perfect "seam" will in time gap, chip, and curl in an agony of surrender—yet other people seem to use it successfully.

Caulk can be a maintenance-freeing tool if used as it was intended to be. It seals tiny gaps and cracks to prevent moisture, air flow, and insect passage to and from your house. But it is a *sealer,* not a filler—too big a crack, gap, or hole won't benefit much from caulk. Caulk doesn't seem like a friend when you're trying to apply it, but once on, it immediately reduces the potential of damage from nature. Just remember these three rules:

1. *Buy the right stuff*—There is a whole arsenal of caulk on display at the store, at all prices, from cheap oil-base caulk (which cracks and chips with age) to latex (not bad) to silicone (which is *the best*)!

2. *Use it in the right place*—Remember, it has no structural strength, only sealing properties. Canyons left by bad construction should be filled with wood, shims, and glue, not caulk. You could almost think of caulk as a thick rope of paint.

3. *Apply it right*—The secret of good caulk is one thing only—*commitment*—you start rolling and you keep rolling, if you stop or quaver when you make a boo-boo, it's a disaster. If you don't keep steady trigger pressure and keep moving, you get scrawny thin spots or overweight humps. The more you try to fix it—take the gun off and try to amend the error with the snout—the more of a mess you get. *Commit* to it—and if after the run is over a slight adjustment is needed, wet your finger and push to smooth. If it's *really* bad, let it dry a week and then redo.

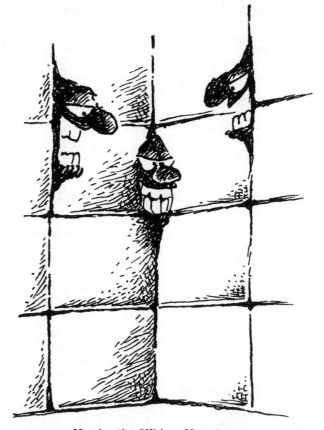

Murder the Mildew Monsters

Murdering Mildew

Another common bathroom complaint I get as I travel across the country is *mildew*. Three things that will help are:

1. Plenty of light

2. Air circulation

3. Use of disinfectant cleaner

A sure sign of poor circulation is the ceiling paint sweating moisture droplets and then peeling. Bathroom exhaust fans are a cheap, easy cure. All types of vents—even those combined with lights—can be fitted to most bathrooms.

The stick-on dispenser mounts on the wall or mirror and keeps the countertop free of soap scum and clutter. A dispenser in the tub or shower will eliminate one more sloppy mess.

The next best thing is to buy liquid soap in a pump bottle or, if you simply can't give up your bar soap, store it on a small cellulose sponge or one of your more presentable washcloths folded into a neat square. The sponge or cloth can be rinsed and wrung out easily, and it keeps the soap from getting so squishy.

The Horrors of Soap Scum

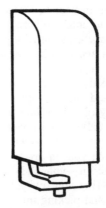

A soap dispenser mounted on the mirror or wall can keep your sink free from slimy soap mess.

Banish the Bar

If you put bar soap in the little "swimming pools for soap" molded into many sinks, or if it's been sitting in a wet dish or on a drippy counter for a while, it gets pretty goopy. The best solution is to build in a commercial liquid soap dispenser. You can get almost any quality or variety of hand soap in liquid form and eliminate all the hard-to-clean mess of bar soap.

Chapter 8

How to Keep a Nick, Bump, and Scuff Ahead of the Kids

What room in your house do you most fear to enter? Where dust bunnies have established a permanent hutch and crumbs live undisturbed for years; where closets resemble a Salvation Army collection box and smells laugh at straight Lysol; where bed covers should be called floor covers and the carpet hasn't been seen since the last time your in-laws visited? You guessed it—your kids' room!

Do you find yourself yelling at your kids and picking up after them twenty-four hours a day? Could it be that your house is furnished and designed so that it aggravates (or ignores) the problems caused by those amazingly active—running, jumping, poking, rolling, squabbling—creatures called kids?

The kids' rooms do present a special challenge because kids *use* a house more and harder than the rest of us. And besides extra durability, safety, education, and entertainment are also qualities we want to build into their spaces. If you have children, at some point in life they will be your number one time-taker, concern, and expense. If this is where you are now, read this chapter closely; it could do a lot to simplify your life.

A Pioneering Approach to a Boys' Bedroom

In the Fall of '65, my wife Barbara and I were in the middle of building our first home for our six children. One evening we were standing in the future "boys' bedroom" deciding where to put the beds, the dresser, the lamps, and all the other goodie trim stuff we'd seen in magazines and books. "The trouble is," Barbara said, "the boys don't really care what the bedroom looks like."

I agreed with that! She continued, "As for the dresser, the boys clutter like mad and even though most of the stuff ends up on the floor, the dresser top will be covered for at least ten years, so no one will ever see it." That too was an accurate appraisal. "As for the beds, they are going to jump, roll, wrestle, and do hobby projects on them. And kids don't care whether or not there's a framed print on the wall—they love hanging coyote hides, baseball gloves, football posters, scout awards,

rubber spiders, and school trophies. We ought to build the bedroom for just what it will be used for: sleep, play, hobbies, study, storage, a few fights, dreaming, and lots of display." I agreed. And that left us standing in the bare room without any good ideas.

We mused about how great it would be if the boys could enjoy the room but we wouldn't have to clean it. We joked about our ideal boys' bedroom: a large trampoline, a built-in vacuum, a center floor drain, two jungle hammocks, and a duffle bag.

The next evening as we were standing in the vacant, freshly Sheetrocked room Barbara said, "Let's build in the beds and put drawers under them." That seemed like a good idea, plus it would eliminate a place to hide dirty socks, clothes, shorts, food, and dead mice. "Let's put one bed in each corner against the wall," she said, pointing. I measured and said, "That leaves five feet in the middle—I ought to build a stagecoach there to play cowboy!" Barbara took me seriously. "That's a great idea. We

can put a clothes closet inside the doors of the stage, and the rear luggage box could be the dirty clothes hamper. And we could carpet the top for wrestling and jumping down on the beds." We decided the driver's seat could be a smooth stair riser, and "the gold box" could be used for storing ball mitts, bats, etc. By ten that night we had an actual plan for a combined storage and sleep center. With some ³/₄-inch plywood and a sabre saw we made the shapes we needed for the stagecoach and put on some fake wheels. It was downright simple to build.

Barbara then ordered some custom-sized foam mattresses and the boys were in paradise for the next ten years. That bedroom was built for use and required little cleaning and it looked smart, too. There wasn't one leg, cabinet, or underside to clean around. When the boys got older we tore out the little built-in coach and put in regular beds. But as long as we had it, the stagecoach room provided a center of growth, comfort, education, and enjoyment. And it cost practically nothing.

Was it a good idea?

The answer is that it was a good idea for *us*. You have your own individual considerations—the number and ages of your kids, their interests, and the size and shape of the bedroom. We could also have considered a race car with storage under the hood and in the trunk, set up in the same arrangement as the stagecoach. For a decorator touch the bedspreads or comforters could be grey or black with yellow or white "road stripes" down the center. Or we could have erected a skyscraper with storage drawers up the front that looked like windows and side openings for toys.

It's amazing what a simple structure like the stagecoach can do to reduce headaches in kid territory. Not only did the coach provide a great place for the kids to play while growing up, it housed their clean and dirty clothes, toys, provided a sleeping area, and kept the room from ever getting dirty enough to require a major cleaning operation.

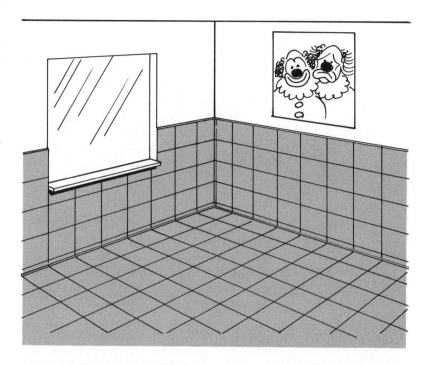

If you're putting cushioned vinyl on the floor of the children's room, go right on up the wall with it. You'll have a virtually indestructible wall at the level where the kids play.

Climbing the Walls

You want to make sure *every* surface you put in here is tough and scrubbable, but the walls above all. A child's room stays beautiful from about three feet up, where the kids can't reach. Everything within their reach is a high-maintenance item. Start your planning by remembering what it was like to be a kid. If you had jam on your hands, washing them wasn't exactly the first thing on your mind; in fact, it was probably the last.

If you paint the walls, use a good latex semigloss enamel. Medium-tone paints such as tan, gray, or beige will hide smudges best.

You can also cover walls with tough oak paneling or sturdy vinyl wallcovering (all kinds of bright, appealing designs are available). The figures in the paper will make the wall even more maintenance-free than paint because little imperfections will blend right in.

You can also carpet the wall. Carpeted walls are safe, durable, and maintenance-free. (For more on how to carpet the walls, see pages 148-149.)

Or you can also use the walls to entertain the kids at their level. If there's a chalkboard within reach, chances are about 50 percent less that they'll write on the wall.

One whole wall of the kids' room could just be a chalkboard or cork-board or some clever combination of both. The kids will have fun, and you'll never have to wipe off another handprint.

What's Underfoot?

The best floor for the kids' room is a hard-surface floor—sheet vinyl or vinyl tile. A carpet may never recover from all that painting, glueing, cutting, and other child-craft casualties. A hard surface is a little less hospitable to kid karate, but toys all work better on a hard surface than on carpet.

Vinyl floor covering is durable and scrubbable—and you can sweep the toys up to a pile when you're cleaning. There are thick "cushioned" vinyl floor coverings that are softer than regular vinyl. They're not so good in kitchens or any area where sharp or heavy objects (like appliances) can damage them, but they're a good compromise for a child's bedroom. They're soft and safe and more comfortable than regular vinyl, yet have a surface that resists spills and stains. **In a child's room go ahead and take the floor covering halfway up the wall. It's a softer surface if someone runs into the wall, and it won't crack, chip, or dent. It will even help absorb sound.**

For ages one to eight I'd use vinyl with a strong pattern to camouflage "project" scars—toy truck "wheelies," finger paint, paste, cherry Kool-aid, gerbil tracks, and fallout from a hundred other wild and woolly activities in a child's life. It'll be easier to clean and allow freer fun.

Low-pile tight-weave carpet can accomplish almost the same thing and is a softer surface to wrestle on, but carpet is more susceptible to damage. Stay with vinyl while your children are young, and move to carpet when they're older. From ages eight and up, go for carpet with a medium to long nap and not a solid dark color. Make it nylon and be sure to treat it with soil retardant.

Furniture, Kid Style

Anyone who puts fine adult-style furniture in a child's room is asking for trouble. Kids won't appreciate or respect its quality or cost. On the other hand, if children's furniture is bright, attractive, and scaled to their size, they might like it and actually use it.

For safety, I'd put soft modular fold-out furniture in the kids' rooms. It may not be everyone's idea of beautiful, but the kids absolutely cannot get hurt on it, it's just their size, and if they get bored they can rearrange the pieces. Laura put a modular couch in her son's room—it's great—he drives his trucks on it, jumps on it, moves it around, and runs into it. It's low enough that he can't get hurt and soft enough to take the blows. Plus it sits on the floor, so nothing gets under it. Soft modular furniture such as fold-up chairs and couches have many uses and are safe.

To lower the odds of the drawers getting hit, build them under the bed. The advantages are:

- It eliminates a place ("under the bed") for kids to shove junk—so you won't have to dig it out.

- It saves the cost of box springs and frame (all you'll need is a good mattress).

- It saves carpeting (and vacuuming!) the under-bed area

- Because the dresser has been eliminated the room will have more play area.

- The less furniture, the easier and faster it is to vacuum.

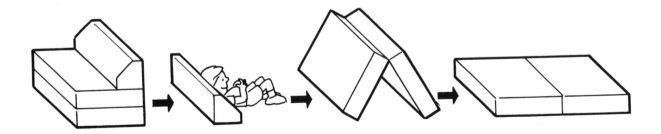

Fold-out modular furniture is perfect for children. It can be transformed into almost any kind of toy without hurting it or the kids.

Easy-to-Get-at Corners—No Furniture to Move

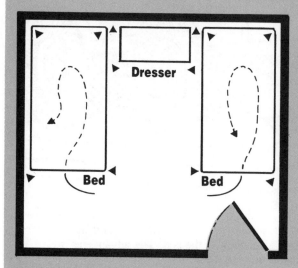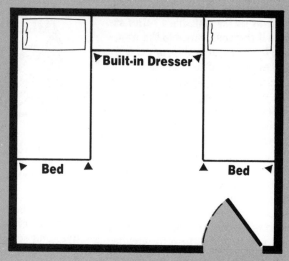

Most children's rooms provide dozens of places for dust, toys, and dirty socks to accumulate—under both beds, behind the dresser, in the corners between the beds and the dresser. A room with built-in furniture eliminates those hideaways.

A built-in child's bedroom vs. a regular bedroom:

• In the regular room you have *12* corners to collect junk and bump into and be cleaned.

• In the low-maintenance built-in room there are only 6 exposed corners to be cleaned.

Time Saved: Half the time to clean a built-in room than a regular room.

You can also build in: seating, shelving, trash can, work desk, reading lamps, and hooks, hooks, hooks (kids will hang things on hooks before they will hangers).

Less Kid Mess

What's the major obstacle to keeping kids' rooms presentable? It's the "obstacle course" all over the floor! Toys, games, Play Doh, coats, coloring books, crayons, paper, squirt guns, broken pieces of things, etc. Not many children think to put away their projects when they get tired of them, and with a child's attention span of about thirty minutes, that's a lot of project mess. Let's eliminate as much of the clutter problem as we possibly can.

Make Your Toy Box a Toy Bin

When you clean out the bottom of your child's toy box, can you believe all the little things a kid can collect (broken crayons, doll heads, puzzle pieces, Tinker Toy parts, rocks)?

When Laura moved into her last college apartment, her little boy was two years old. "My sister happened to be selling those stacking plastic bins, and she talked me into buying some. I decided to use them as his toy boxes, since I wouldn't be living in the apart-

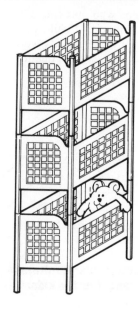

ment long enough to justify building a permanent toy storage system. They worked great and were bright colored and attractive, too. The little bits of junk fell right through to the floor where I could pick them up easily.

"I still have them today and I've never had to clean them out—not even once. They're unbreakable and lightweight, can be rearranged and moved around easily, they don't have to be painted, and they store the kids' toys, at their level, in whatever order the kids see fit.

"If you have children, make this one of your maintenance-freeing projects."

Put plastic stacking bins for toys storage in kids' rooms—dirt and little junk falls right out of them.

Make their storage a game or a place to learn. If it's fun, or seems like a game, the kids are more likely to do some picking up and putting away. Put bright, appealing pictures on their furniture (you don't want to put valuable furniture in their rooms anyway) that help them identify where each of their belongings goes. Children like to get involved and *need* to learn; sometimes we adults don't allow them the opportunity. Make their room for *them*—it'll make them happier and save cleaning time.

When we talk to mothers, a common complaint is that there's no storage really designed for children to use. It's all too high for them.

Countless nicks, spills, and injuries are caused by a child trying to get up to an adult-sized drawer, sink, or shelf. They drag chairs, climb on toys, or just dig their little shoes into the ledges and handles trying to get up.

If children can easily reach the closet rod or the drawers in the dresser, they'll put things away and form a habit for life—maybe even grow into teenagers who clean up after themselves.

Children's storage should be low enough that they can reach it easily and attractive enough that they'll want to put their own things away.

Kid-Sized Closets

Make the rod adjustable to the children's height. One way is to set the rod into a notched board at each end of the closet so it can be adjusted as they grow.

Two 1x6 inch pieces of wood (one for each end of the closet) with notches cut out to hold a closet rod can make a closet that is instantly adjustable to all ages and allows smaller children to care for their own clothes.

Put a tilted wire shelf at the bottom of the closet for shoes—the dirt will fall off to the floor where it can be vacuumed up easily—and the shoes will stay in order.

Sporty Decor

If you have active youngsters, your closets, hallways, and stairways are probably overflowing with sports equipment. Why not decorate your children's room with their sports equipment instead of piling it in the corner of the garage or losing it in the backyard? Mount their balls and bats and gloves right on the wall. When not in use, they'll provide decoration your kids will love and that you won't have to dust or worry about. And this way, the kids always know where the equipment belongs and might even put it back. It unclutters the closets and lends personal pride to a kid's living space.

You could also try decorating the room with their toys.

Eliminating Stress Points in the Rest of the House

Many houses are in effect jungles of sharp points. All of these points and edges are right at kid level and if a kid runs into them, he's a goner—he'll have a cut forehead or eye.

Every house should be kid-proofed to some extent, but if you have young children or a large family, you'd better kid-proof your house for sure.

How to Choose Child-Safe Furnishings

Avoiding injuries and stress is as much a maintenance issue as avoiding housework. (After a time or two of rushing your kid to the emergency room, you're sure to think housework is easier). Take a minute to check over the furniture you buy.

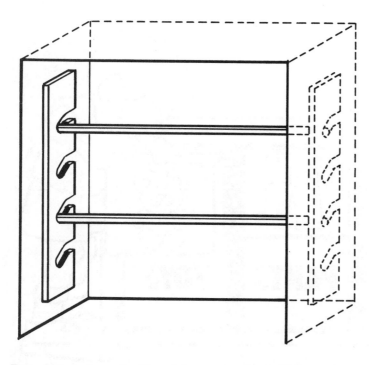

Two pieces of wood with notches cut out to hold the clothes rod make a closet instantly adjustable for children of all ages.

Children's Art Gallery

An art gallery for children is a must! It's a special place to display paintings, drawings, and school papers (and helps prevent tape, glue, and tacks from destroying the finish on walls throughout the house). You can hang a bulletin board in the kitchen or recreation room, or cover a door with corkboard to create a giant space for family masterpieces and mementos.

This kills two birds with one stone: you have one less door surface to maintain and a neat place to show off the things your child is proud of.

No Tablecloths with Freestanding Lamps, Vases, Figurines

Children are naturally curious: you were once, too.

No Sharp-Edged Furniture

Or furniture with a lot of exposed wood or metal. Also, watch out for things that tempt children to climb. If there is a way to climb to it, children will try.

No Sharp Corners

The first two years of a child's life are spent learning to walk—falling, bumping, and grabbing at everything in his or her path. Tumbles are part of the game. Besides checking for sharp edges, be sure that furniture isn't loose or unstable—that it can't be pulled over.

Eliminate Throw Rugs

Throw rugs are aptly named; they're a menace for kids *and* grownups.

Keep House Plants High

Or you'll have a mess—and maybe a hurt or poisoned child.

For Kids Only

During an autograph session in a popular bookstore, I kept noticing kids running past me and disappearing into the wall. I hadn't noticed a door, because there wasn't a normal door—there was a miniature one, just right for kids. A trip on hands and knees through the door revealed all! The bookstore owner had made a 6x6 room for kids. A cartoon video was going, and the room was decorated with colorful chairs, pictures, etc.—just for the kids! Where did kids love to drag their parents to shop? Into that bookstore, of course. The parents and store owner could relax and browse without worrying about grubby little hands pulling over displays or brow-beating books.

Why not alter a room in your house for Kids Only? You don't necessarily have to make any structural alterations. Just assemble some attractive toys, games, and maybe a TV and WOW! Your home will be a favorite spot for your children and their friends.

Like the bookstore did, we made a bright little kid-sized doorway leading into a delightful playroom for the grandkids. What kid can resist an open door? It worked! They file in that room like little troopers and play for hours. They have fun, and don't mess up, break, or get into things in the rest of the house.

Use your imagination! You were a kid once. Your brainstorms will pay off handsomely, because taking care of children is ultimately more time-consuming than housework.

Without Structurally Changing a Room, Make It for Kids Only!

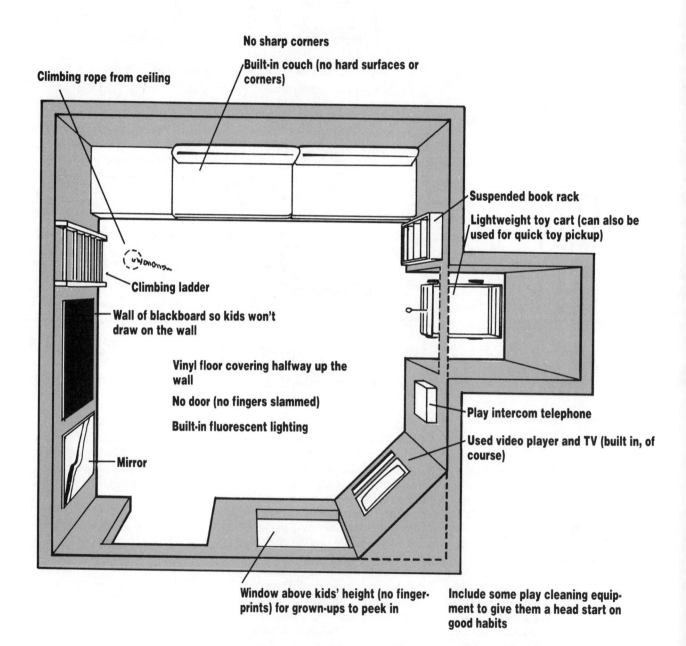

No sharp corners

Built-in couch (no hard surfaces or corners)

Climbing rope from ceiling

Suspended book rack

Lightweight toy cart (can also be used for quick toy pickup)

Climbing ladder

Wall of blackboard so kids won't draw on the wall

Vinyl floor covering halfway up the wall

No door (no fingers slammed)

Built-in fluorescent lighting

Mirror

Play intercom telephone

Used video player and TV (built in, of course)

Window above kids' height (no finger-prints) for grown-ups to peek in

Include some play cleaning equipment to give them a head start on good habits

You can make a kids only room using simple materials and without structural alterations.

Confine the Fun

Small children aren't the only causers of mess and damage—older kids, teenagers, and adults also generate clutter in the process of entertaining themselves. But if you design, build, and organize for vigorous or messy activities, giving them their own place, the cleaning and maintenance of the house as a whole will benefit immensely.

The following are some ideas for confining messy activities to places that can take it, so they can be enjoyed without adding unmercifully to the burden of housework.

Create a Recreation and Fun Room

"Rough house" needn't be a negative concept, especially if a designated rough-housing area exists. If there are pillows to play with in the recreation room, there'll be fewer pillow fights in the bedroom. A trampoline in the yard will provide an outlet for a child's innate desire to jump on the furniture. A handy chalkboard or markerboard may just save a wall from the creative outpourings of a budding Rembrandt. If there are dart boards and blackboards in the recreation room, there'll be lots less wall damage in the other rooms.

Pick out a place in the house and make it a true recreation room. You don't know where you'd find the space for such a thing?

That pretty spare bedroom used once every four to eight months is a waste. Give it a more active purpose.

Basements are a common re-course for recreation. A family fun room is far more useful and life-enriching than a basement of old junk, and if nothing else is available, you might even consider converting the garage. (For specific garage ideas, see pages 82-83.)

If you're really pressed for space, an unused wall could have weights, exercise equipment, etc., attached to make sort of a mini rec area out of an existing room. Set up games, art tables, wrestling mats, building blocks, punching bags, mobile toys, and dollhouses. Make sure things are arranged so children can't get hurt or break something important while playing. Modular furniture is nice here as well as in the kids' rooms.

There are thick vinyl wallcoverings available today that are almost like padding. Soft, safe, and pliable, they cover any blemishes in the wall. When hit, they don't crack, chip, mar, or dent. They even absorb sound.

For the floor, consider cushioned vinyl or low-pile, tight-weave carpet. If you opt for vinyl, you may want to take it halfway up the wall to make a softer surface for reckless rough-housing—as well as to absorb sound. If you choose carpeting, be sure it's well padded, and you might still want a section of vinyl flooring for messy activities, such as finger painting.

Buy a couple of sturdy six- or eight-foot folding banquet tables (an office furniture store or a discount store is sure to have them) and some folding chairs. Get the kind with adjustable legs for small children, and get junior-sized chairs. You'll use these for all manner of projects and activities and they're also handy for kids' birthday parties and large patio dinners.

We always have a table tennis tournament going in our rec room. It's easy to set two light Ping-Pong table halves on your folding table.

Invite Them Outside

The whole idea of having is using. Don't keep a yard only for display; the more people stay outside, the less clutter and abuse the inside will get.

If you had your choice of sitting and reading on a bench in the fresh air, would you choose a stuffy living room? If there are ropes on the trees and swing sets outside, the kids are less likely to be swinging on the drapes inside. By making the outside of your house inviting, a lot of playing, eating, visiting, and projects will be done out there—and you won't have to vacuum afterward!

Yard Furniture

When you consider how often you have to replace them, flimsy, collapsible units aren't as "inexpensive" as they seem. Furniture that needs regular repainting to prevent rust is one more chore you'd happily chuck if you could. And who feels like running outside at the first sign of rain to tack a plastic or canvas cover over everything? You want *permanent* furniture—tables, chairs, benches, garbage cans, etc. Wooden picnic tables and benches are okay if you move a lot, but if you have roots down, why not build things to stay? The initial cost is only slightly higher but the furniture will last forever. For ideas, look at what public parks and rest areas use—furniture of concrete and heavy galvanized steel.

Built-In Recreation

We're not suggesting that you convert your home into a public recreation facility, but if you can't flex your physical, emotional, and mental muscles at home, where can you? By building in recreation, we don't mean that you have to install heated swimming pools, tennis courts, or horse trails—the simple things are usually the most used and enjoyed. Some of the most fun things call for the simplest equipment.

You know the things your family really enjoys—pick two or three of their favorites and build in for those things. Don't overdo it, or you'll end up having too much to take care of. You want to avoid building in equipment for short-lived enthusiasms, but pastimes that have stood the test of time are pretty safe.

Here are some simple things you can set up to make your yard a place to use and remember.

A few simple graphics and some inexpensive equipment can convert part of your yard or driveway into an activity center for volleyball, basketball, badminton, horseshoes, shuffleboard, soccer, or whatever.

Your local sporting goods store should have instructions for the official layout for all ball courts; if not, have the kids get it from their coaches. Lines are easy to apply (buy striping paint for asphalt or concrete), especially if you put tape down to guide you.

Basketball Hoop

These are not unattractive and will occupy a sporty child (or adult) for hours. Once they're up, they're up!

Avoid the bargain-basement particle board and spindly steel hoop assemblies—get a good sound unit that will last a long time. Galvanized steel and heavy-duty plastic hold up well outside.

Ball and Frisbee Area

All you need for this is a wide open expanse of lawn or blacktop—with no obstructions to trip over and neighbors' windows safely out of range.

74

A Sandbox

A sandbox is cheap and easy to build, and I doubt if there's a kid (or adult, for that matter) in the world who doesn't like to build sand castles. Build the box a good distance from the house, provide a cover to protect from rain and cats, and make sure there's a hose nearby to wash off sandy hands and feet. You'll have almost no maintenance with a sandbox, especially a concrete one.

Make a Playhouse

For twenty years, as our kids gradually grew up and left, we were always going to make a playhouse outside. The most we managed was a shaky treehouse (the kids did most of the work themselves), but never the playhouse we had in mind. This year we finally did it, and believe me, it's worth almost as much as a full-size house. Our grandkids and

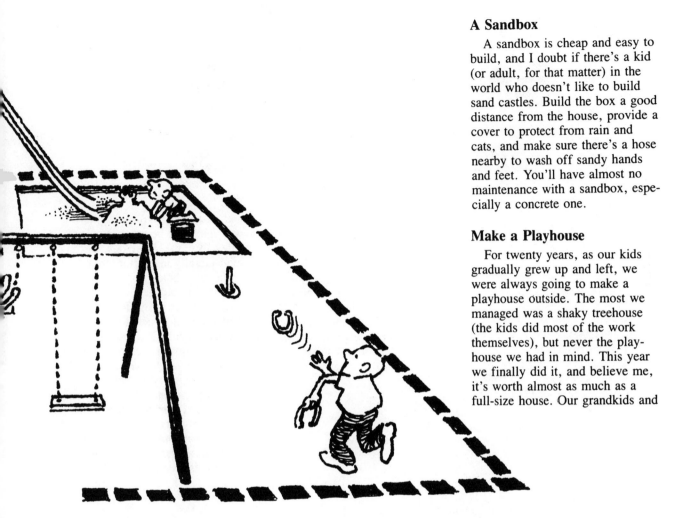

Swings and Climbing Towers

Playground equipment made of heavy galvanized steel, stainless steel, and treated lumber is available from commercial supplies. One set will last a lifetime.

Horseshoe Courts

These are zero maintenance areas and can be installed for under $25. (A character-builder as well as enjoyable!)

the neighbors' kids play out there—they can make a mess and be as noisy as they want. **In ten years, a $60 playhouse can save you $600 worth of repairing and cleaning time inside the *real* house.**

Our playhouse is 10x8; you could build yours any size you want. You can also make it, like ours, on a skid so that if you move you can take it with you. Inside we built little benches, a table, beds, and a loft, added some plastic dishes, a blanket, and doormat—the kids have it made!

Chapter 9

Stopping Dirt in Its Tracks

The innocent entranceway into your house is the single greatest source of control you have over what cleaning is done inside.

The American Carpet Institute estimates that 80 percent of the dirt and debris in homes rides in on our feet. Just because it's wet outside doesn't mean it's clean; rain and snow often contain dirt and dust which will work their way into your house from a wet sidewalk. On a rainy day, dirt and mud literally march into your home on people's shoes.

Once the dirt gets into your house it takes ten different types of equipment to get it out. This means sweeping, mopping, vacuuming, dusting, carpet cleaning. It can also accelerate the overall depreciation of your house.

The logical approach, *prevention*—keeping dirt from getting in, in the first place—not only saves wear and tear on your home, but cuts cleaning-supply costs and reduces your cleaning time dramatically.

Mats: A Must

To eliminate most of this tracked-in dirt, you don't have to build anything—just install the right kind of mats at your doors. It's as simple as that: dirt will be caught by the mats instead of being tracked in.

We're not talking about what most people think of as "mats"— flimsy rubber mats with your name or "Home Sweet Home" printed on them, shedding hemp mats, or rubber "link" mats made of old truck tires. We're talking about professional entranceway matting—sturdy olefin or nylon fiber walk-off mats with vinyl or rubber backing. The nylon creates a static charge that actually helps pull particles from your shoes and clothes. They will absorb mud and water from foot traffic and hold it in the roots of the mat. They won't show dirt easily and can be vacuumed like any other carpet.

You've seen these mats used in schools, churches, offices, supermarkets, and other commercial buildings. They can be purchased in various sizes and an array of colors at your local janitorial supply store; they cost less than $40

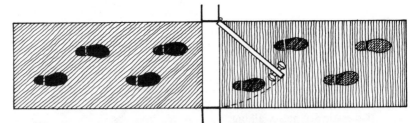

Mats are great work savers. Use commercial, nylon-tuft ones inside and synthetic grass or rough textured ones outside. Make sure the mats are long enough to cover four steps on either side of the door.

and should last for five to ten years. Place these inside the entrances to your home and use polypropylene (AstroTurf) matting on the outside.

A large mat will lower the maintenance of your house—the bigger, the better. If you set up your mats to cover at least four steps of any person who enters your house, you'll be amazed how much dirt you *won't* have to clean out of carpets and clothes, off furniture, etc.

Proper matting alone can save the average household approximately 200 hours of work per year, slow down structure depreciation, and save over $100 in cleaning supply costs. The cost of matting all the entranceways of the average home is about $80-$120. But that 200 hours of work they'll save means thirty minutes a day cut from your chore time.

your home through the door. In designing or redesigning a house, controlling access should be a major priority. Use only one or two entrances instead of four or five, and at the entrances you do have, provide the facilities to "quarantine" all those clutterers and messmakers. (More on how to do this later in the chapter.)

We had eight outside entrances to our farm home—*never again!* It was worse than a sports stadium, with people—and litter—streaming in from all directions. When someone knocked it was a two-mile marathon to find and answer which door they'd chosen! There were more doors to look after and more doors to be abused.

Ships at the docks have the right idea, one plank in and one plank out. Start with that idea when working on your maintenance-free home.

Control Access

Step in a creek with a pair of hip boots that have a hole in them, and in minutes you'll notice your foot getting damp. Put five holes in the boot and step in the water and in a minute you'll have as much water inside your boot as outside it. This is exactly the same principle as the doors (holes) into your house.

Most things that cause maintenance in your house (dirt, dust, insects, moisture, people with dirty or muddy feet, etc.) enter

A Hard Path to Beat

Sidewalks can do more to keep dirt from getting into the house than anything except their allies, good mats at the entranceways. Wide sidewalks around the approach to a home will knock dirt and grit off footwear so rain and wind can send it back to its natural setting, instead of into your house. Here's how to make the sidewalk work even harder at keeping dirt out of the house.

Rough Up the Surface

When someone has mud on his feet, it's usually up in the cracks and designs of the sole of the shoe. If the surface he's walking on is smooth, the dirt will just stay there. If the surface is rough, it will hit up against the dirt and knock some of it off.

Rough up the surface of your concrete sidewalks when they are being laid, or have your contractor do it. A roughed-up sidewalk will serve as a dirt knocker. If the sidewalk is smooth, you'll be cleaning a lot more dirt out of your house. If you rough up your sidewalk by running a stiff broom across the almost-set cement, the rough edges will actually be rounded a little on the tops and it won't be too hard on kids—we did that when we roughed our sidewalk and haven't had a skinned knee yet.

A textured sidewalk is also much safer when wet, because you're much more likely to slip on a smooth, wet surface. This is the traditional reason for broom-finished concrete.

Sidewalks aren't the only things that can be "roughed up." Textured concrete patios and driveways will also help sidetrack dirt before it has a chance to get tracked in.

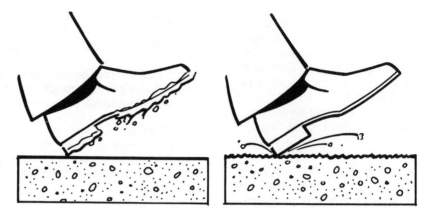

A smooth sidewalk will let the dirt walk right in, but a rough surface will knock dirt off your feet before it gets in.

Don't Let Runoff Run On... Your Sidewalk

As we said, rain and snow have dirt particles in them so when your entry gets snow and rain on it, it also gets dust and dirt. Water running off your roof also carries dirt that has settled up there.

When installing a sidewalk or driveway, make sure it's slightly "crowned" in the center to provide good water runoff without puddling.

Effective drainage away from the concrete is also essential to avoid soil washing away from under the walk, patio, or driveway.

If the gutter's runoff spout is right by the sidewalk, mud and water will splash up on the sidewalk and be fair game to get tracked into your house. A downspout too close by a sidewalk can also cause the sidewalk to crack. (More on gutters in Chapter 19.)

Safety on the Walk

Anytime you have drops, rises, or level changes in a pathway where people walk, you're asking for trouble. Little stone pathways are cute, but what happens when you try to maneuver over them? You have to slow down and carefully plant every step or you might trip. And what about the kids? They don't slow down, as a rule, and a fall on a rock can chip or knock out a tooth, or inflict a cut that calls for stitches. Different levels in walks also trap dirt and create hard-to-clean corners that leaves and debris blow into, adding to your maintenance woes.

If you live in a northern area, you might consider building a heater into your walkways and stoops. Ice and snow removal means maintenance time, and ice isn't just a nuisance to keep salted and removed, it accounts for a great number of injuring falls. The salt is also another thing to track into your house. A sidewalk heat unit is a simple mat with heating wires similar to those in an electric blanket; you just lay it in the concrete and pour over it. Your builder or local utility company can give you details.

Cover the Entryways

Though you'll want to be sure you have sidewalks and good matting at the door to catch the dirt, it also helps to minimize the dirt that collects here in the first place. Put a roof over as much of the entrance as you can. Ten to twenty feet is ideal. Covered entrances help prevent dirt from settling on the sidewalk closest to the house where it will surely be tracked in.

A long overhang on your roof, a canopy over the door, or a recessed entryway give visitors to your home time to stomp dirt and moisture off their feet. **Extend the roof eaves farther than normal—even as far as three feet—to keep the rain from splashing dirt onto the windows and sidewalks, and to keep the sun from bleaching the drapes.**

Easy-to-clean materials are essential in an entryway, especially on the floor. For outside covered entries, concrete is best. For a totally enclosed entry, use a sturdy flooring material such as terrazzo, quarry tile, natural stone, or vinyl. You don't want any finish that has grooves or indentations where dirt and grit can lodge and stay. A hard surface is better even if you do have mats down, because the heavy traffic in this area will cause a carpet to be dirtied quickly. The floor should be durable, more so here than in any room of the house, as this is one place gravel is going to be ground in.

The walls of an enclosed entry should have a smooth surface such as paneling, vinyl wallcovering, or semigloss enamel paint. This is not a place for texture; textures give flying dirt a place to settle.

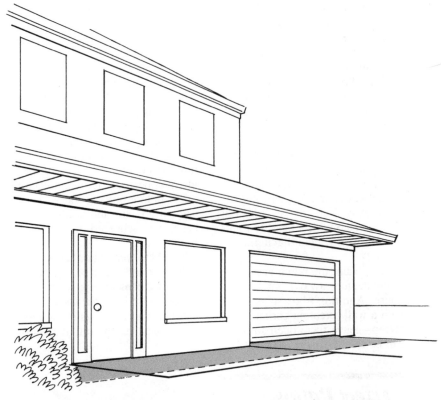

A long overhang helps keep rain off sidewalks and windows, in addition to giving guests shelter when they arrive in bad weather.

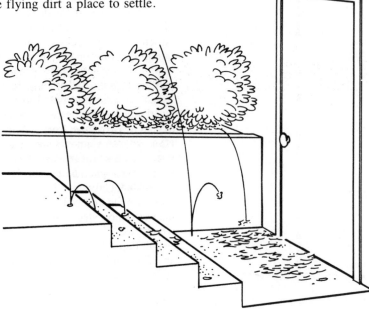

Avoid Sunken Entries and Patios

When there's a hole in a flat surface, what usually happens? It ends up collecting everything loose. That's exactly what a sunken entryway or patio does. Wind-blown leaves, papers, and wrappers sail through the air, hit the wall, and where are they trapped? Rocks and pebbles roll out of your garden, acorns and catkins fall off the tree, and they all end up in the sunken area. You can guarantee that all of this will stay there until *you* pick it up or sweep it up. You can't hose it off unless you have a drain—which will probably clog.

You can eliminate threshold troubles by avoiding sunken entranceways that collect leaves and debris.

79

You have to get out your dustpan. An above-grade entryway could just be swept off—not to mention that Mother Nature will help with wind and rain. Make sure your outside surfaces are all one level or elevated. It'll save your back a half hour or so every week—add that up!

If you can arrange or design your steps so that you step up to your entry, you'll be able to sweep *off* instead of *up*—and a lot of the leaves and dirt will just blow away. You can also clean off a raised step with a hose and not have to worry about having a drain.

Also, slant the porch and steps a few degrees away from the house. And don't box steps in with a wall, creating corners to sweep—leave them open so dirt can be swept off the edge.

ground floor sits above grade, you may also want to drop the patio level about a foot down from the door so any dirt that's on the patio won't blow into the house when the door is opened. However, for a covered patio, with less of a leaf and dirt problem, a patio floor on the same level as the house is safer and easier to maintain.

The easiest care surface for patios is concrete, with quarry tile the next best and redwood decking third. Indoor/outdoor carpet is bad—it absorbs and holds dirt and has to be vacuumed or swept hard.

One of the worst surfaces for patios is brick with loose sand joints. It presents a constant opportunity for tracking sand into your house.

When you're designing a patio, try to visualize the traffic pattern

and plan accordingly. Build benches and furniture *in* wherever possible, for both safety and worksaving (much of your cleanup time will be spent rearranging the furniture otherwise), and you don't need another "room" to clean. And don't forget a trash can—a nice big one in a handy location.

Whether or not the patio should be covered depends on the area in which you happen to live. In the East and South where the foliage is thick and fruit and pod-bearing trees are abundant, it may be worth the effort. A cover is another thing to maintain and you must decide if it will save more work than it causes.

To cover a deck or patio, use conventional roof construction—just carry it out over the patio. Walls can be screened, especially if mosquitoes are a problem, or open, depending on your preference.

Perfect Patios

For patios, the ideal height is about six inches off the ground; it's hard to kick dirt that high and so the patio will stay pretty clean. Depending upon how high your

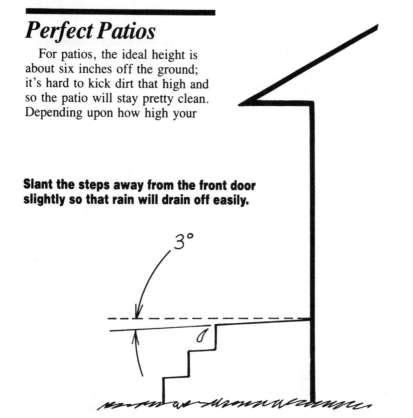

Slant the steps away from the front door slightly so that rain will drain off easily.

3°

Stack the Deck in Your Favor

Redwood is probably the most widely used wood for deck material. But unless properly constructed, wood decks require frequent attention or they'll quickly deteriorate. **Wooden planks in direct contact with the soil or close to it should be pressure-treated with a wood preservative before they are installed to keep them from rotting. All other wooden elements should be coated with a preservative deck stain, best applied *before* the deck is assembled.** Galvanized steel or aluminum nails and bolts are better than common steel nails and bolts, which rust.

Paint should never be used on any flat portion of a wooden deck, as it will quickly peel and blister.

The Garage

The garage is another great place to stop dirt in its tracks, because in our wheeled society the garage is often the first line of defense. It can control and confine a lot of the mess that otherwise would molest the house. But before you can ask your garage to help out with the housework, you have to declutter it.

Dejunk It

A mere thirty or forty years ago most homes were built without garages, but once this added-on edifice entered our lives, we more than made up for the years of absence. We've filled it with so much stuff that our automobiles aren't sure they belong in there, and we only dare open the garage door under cover of darkness.

As you read this, a guilty smile crosses your face because you know you not only hauled all that junk in there but you've shuffled it around, dug through and crawled over it, and inventoried it several times for your "someday" garage sale. If you don't have the gravel in your gizzard to tackle the job yourself, pick up a copy of my book, *Clutter's Last Stand,* and read it. That's all you'll need to help you dejunk your garage so it can eliminate some nasty housework for you—what a deal!

Finish It

The garage is usually left unfinished because it's just "the garage." But I'd finish my garage before the family room in the basement! So will you, when you think about it. If you have extra room in your garage it can be used for *living* space; a large, sturdy, dry space, convenient to the outside and able to tolerate the abuse of tools and toys is a great place for family projects and play. A garage is made for heavy action, fixing, fiddling around; a lot of the mess can be confined here if we make sure it's somewhat snug and welcoming.

You can do this simply by:

1 *Covering the Walls*—If you use plywood rather than Sheetrock, then you can easily mount shelves and hang even heavy things.

2 *Painting It*——Don't use just one coat of leftover paint, but two or three coats of a good heavy-duty off-white enamel.

3 *Lighting It*—Do-it-yourself stores have nice fluorescent light units all ready to plug in. Get a 4-foot unit (8-foot tube lights are too hard to store and replace). You can install it in thirty minutes with a few feet of Romex (plastic-shielded electrical cable).

If you need outlets in a few more areas, run Romex from an existing receptacle. It only costs about $5 for each unit you install, and you'll save yourself a lot of dragging and stringing of extension cords all over. Be sure to use Romex cable with a ground wire and make sure the ground is hooked up.

4 *Adding a Workbench*—If you don't have one. A couple of 8-foot 2x12's and some 2x4's will do it. A workbench keeps the clutter of projects up off the floor.

By the way, put your electrical outlets on the front of the bench—not on the back where your cords will tangle.

5 *Installing a Sink if Possible*—It's much more convenient than running back and forth to the house for water. It also keeps the house mess-free—no drips, spills, banging against sinks, or gymnastics with faucets you can't get a bucket under, not to mention keeping unwanted things like poisonous cleaning solutions, lawnmower parts, and fish guts out of the kitchen sink. Most houses have washer and dryer hookups or bathrooms near the garage wall—in a few hours, with some pipe and a prefab sink unit, you can have water in your garage.

Here are a few more housework helpers for your garage.

A good smoke alarm and fire extinguisher—Chances are if your house ever has a fire, it will be in or around the garage—prepare for it. Besides the obvious safety benefits of this equipment, cleaning up is far easier (and less costly) after a small fire than after a widespread one.

Compactor—An attached garage is the *best* place for a trash compactor—odors and all. Lots of nice new garage models are available, and some even come with a hand truck for transporting gar-

6 *Wall-hanging As Much As You Can*—Try to get everything off the floor. Common sixteen-penny nails driven in a plywood wall will hang most things, or use the hooks, dowels, and hangers of every race, creed, and color that are available at the hardware store. Wall-hung storage is a lot better than stuff flung all over the floor. It saves space, time (you'd otherwise spend searching for things), and looks neater too.

Put a 4x8-foot sheet of plywood up on the wall behind your workbench to organize your tools. Outline the tools with a permanent felt marker while they're hanging. Those graphic silhouettes are a great visual reminder to put things back where they belong, and you know instantly if something is missing.

7 *Sealing the Floor*—Too many of us suffer from the illusion that if we paint our garage floor no one will know it's concrete. But a garage floor is going to get abuse, and after the assault of scrapes, nicks, scratches, leaks, and abandoned dog bones rattling around on it, a painted floor looks tacky. It's much better to do what commercial cleaners do to stadium, factory, and other floors that get a lot of abuse—clear-seal them.

To do this, mop with a solution of degreaser, followed by etching acid diluted in water. (Your janitorial supply house or paint store has these—with specific directions on the label.) Flush the solution off and rinse with a hose. Allow the floor to dry for at least five hours, then apply transparent concrete seal or an all-purpose seal, either of which can be obtained at a paint or janitorial supply store. Use any applicator that will distribute the seal in a nice thin even coat, and let it dry. A second coat is a good idea to ensure that all the rough surfaces are filled. Presto, your garage floor is now glossy and smooth—a snap to clean as well as good looking!

8 *Slanting the Floor*—If you're building a garage, slant the floor toward the door so that car drippings and spillage will run out the front and down the driveway to the street drain. A slanted floor will do the job much better than a floor drain. Also, raise the garage floor one inch above the driveway level just inside the garage door. This will keep rainwater from splashing inside.

9 *Matting the Doorways*—At the doorway into the garage and into the house from the garage, place walk-off mats of at least three by five feet. Plenty of sawdust, oil stains, project residue, and outside dirt gets tracked into the house from the garage. Concrete dust and garage-type soils and dirt are especially abrasive and damaging to carpet and waxed floors.

bage to and from the compactor. (For more information on trash compactors, see page 89.)
Built-in vacuum—If your garage is attached to the house, this is where the vac unit for your

built-in system is usually located. Be sure to include outlets to make it easy to reach your vehicle and workbench area. (For more information on central vacuums, see page 105.)

Old files—Four-drawer metal file cabinets (full suspension roller types) can provide sturdy storage for all kinds of tools and supplies. You can find these through newspaper ads and at liquidation stores for $25-$50.

Laundry Room/Mud Room/Utility Room

These are technically three different concepts—but in many houses all three or at least two are combined. Whatever combination of the three you have, you want to make sure it's designed and finished to serve the utterly utilitarian purposes of stopping dirt in its tracks.

All three of these rooms, the laundry room, the mud room, and the utility room, combined or separate, should have some basic maintenance-freeing features.

- Central location near the rooms they serve, and ideally not located at either end of the house.

- Walls and counters of durable, water-resistent materials.

- Simple, hard-surface flooring— never carpet!

- Light-colored paint for cheerfulness and ease of cleaning.

- Enclosed fluorescent lighting.

- Enclosed cabinets or open shelves—make sure you have plenty of them. Remember, wire shelves and hampers keep clothes ventilated and don't accumulate lint, dust, or dirt.

- Built-in and suspended design wherever possible.

- Lots of hooks for coats, towels, extension cords, brooms, etc.

- A large utility table for projects, clothes-folding, etc.

- An open closet to hang up things that are in transit or being repaired.

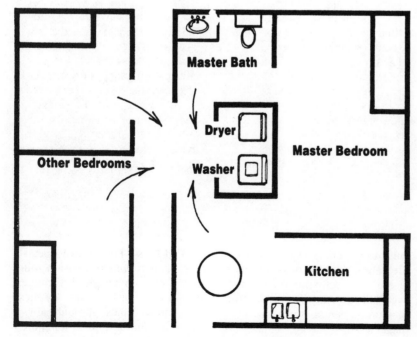

Master Bath

Dryer

Washer

Master Bedroom

Other Bedrooms

Kitchen

If you have room, put the washer and dryer close to the kitchen, bedrooms, and bathroom, the three greatest laundry-generating areas.

The Laundry Room

This is where the washer, dryer, and laundering supplies are kept, ideally along with room for folding and storing clothes in various stages of laundering and redistributing. Some people use this room to store sewing supplies as well.

A laundry room on the main floor saves a lot of steps. If you have a two-story house, put in a laundry chute from the second floor.

If you're building new, locate the washer and dryer as close as possible to bathrooms, bedrooms, linen closet—in other words, where most of your laundry is generated.

If the bedrooms and bath are upstairs and the laundry is down, a laundry chute will save lots of steps.

The laundry room needs a large work space for folding clothes and lots of shelves to hold the folded laundry until you're ready to distribute it. Or better yet, label those shelves with family members' names and when they need them badly enough, they'll come and get them. **Rolling wire clothes baskets for distant bedrooms will save bedroom and laundry room mess and make it easier to transport clean and dirty clothes to and from the laundry.**

Wire baskets are a must here for ventilation of often-damp laundry, as well as to prevent dust and debris from accumulating in the hamper. Make sure there's a rod in the laundry room for hanging clothes on hangers, and think

about installing a built-in ironing board, *where you iron!* This is basically a small (5 feet tall, 5 inches deep, 18 inches wide) closet, which when opened produces a fold-out, suspended ironing board. The iron and sprinkling bottle can be stored in there when not in use.

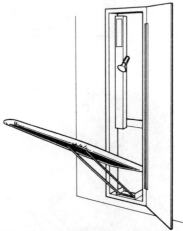

A built-in ironing board is easy to use and put away.

The Mud Room

This a buffer between the outdoors and the indoors, a place to clean up or unload stuff before entering the house proper. It usually has a sink, toilet, and mirror, and would ideally be designed to store shoes, boots, outerwear, etc.

It should have immediate access to the outside or the garage and be located near the kitchen and other main work centers of the house.

The Utility Room

This is an all-purpose workroom, cleaning-supply center, and storeroom which often houses the hot water heater, water softener, freezer, etc. A utility room should ideally be combined with a mud room and, like a mud room, it should have direct access to the outside and be near or in the main work area of the house.

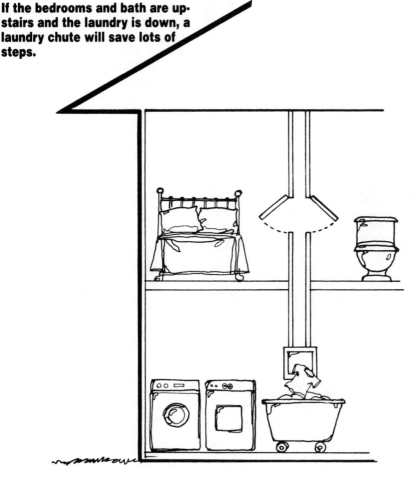

Chapter 10

Managing the Unmentionables

What are your home's best-kept secrets? Every home has them— no matter how decorator-perfect it looks to the casual visitor. It's the thing you most hate to deal with. The dark, dank corner of the basement that's been taken over by mud since last spring's flood. The brigade of ants who are steadily colonizing your kitchen pantry. The dented, rusty trash cans hidden out back where no one can see the piles of fast-food wrappers, half-eaten apples, and empty milk cartons.

You can manage even the worst unmentionables. In this chapter, we'll clean those maintenance skeletons out of your closet so they'll never come back to haunt you.

Garbage In . . .

The computer people came up with a nice excuse for errors and problems relating to their magnificent machines: "Garbage in, garbage out." Unfortunately, homemakers have to say, "Garbage in, garbage in and around the whole place." Homes would require a lot less maintenance without garbage. The average American generates two tons of trash a year! Multiply that times how many of you are in your home, and you have a mountain of refuse.

Garbage

- It's messy

- It's unsightly

- It stinks

- It's in the way

- It has to be taken out

- It dirties the walls and floor around it

- Kids tip it over

Convenience is the biggest secret here!

Trash receptacles should be conveniently located and easy to use—some trash cans have lids that Houdini couldn't open. And if your trash can is hiding behind a door or in some cubbyhole where nobody ever goes, chances are that the trash will stay right where it is, relaxing in the kids' room or on exhibit throughout the rest of the house.

Having your trash receptacles visible encourages people to use them, especially children. Recessed, hidden, or covered receptacles look nice, but sometimes don't get used because they're inaccessible or forgotten; guests can't find them. All of us would-be basketball players love a chance to practice our hook shot—would you take that away from us?

Stick with plastic containers—flexible plastic cans are light, unbreakable, and easy to clean. Metal cans will rust, leak, and beat up your walls; baskets, wicker, and lightweight wood are impossible to clean; hard plastic cracks easily. And while a 32-pound, stainless-steel-lined oak unit might look classy, would you really want to wrestle it down the hall?

In the kitchen, you'll probably need a large container—or maybe even *two*—a lot of waste is generated here. It's a good idea to use trash can "liners" (plastic bags) in the kitchen and the bathrooms because of the wet trash in these rooms. The polyethylene liners used by professional janitors can be purchased by the case in various sizes from janitorial supply houses for considerably less than they'd cost at the supermarket.

Hang It

An attractive, open-top polyethylene waste can mounted on the wall is a good choice because it won't tip over and you can sweep under it easily. It can be small enough to be unobtrusive, and can be found in a color that will blend well with your decor.

You need one in each room where trash is generated.

A backboard of hardwood, plywood, or Formica-covered plywood protects walls from scuffs as the receptacle is removed for emptying and replaced. Stain, don't paint, an unfinished wood backboard. With any abuse, the paint would chip.

Suspended Trash Can

The lip of the container just slips down over the mounting strip and hangs there very nicely. It goes on and off for dumping very quickly and easily, and if stooping is a problem for you, it can be mounted a little higher.

Having the waste containers up off the floor makes floor sweeping and vacuuming easier, and it also discourages the clutter that tends to accumulate around a can on the floor. Those "missed shots" look so disgraceful lying there all alone under a wall-mounted can that most of us will go in for the rebound and try again. The backboard is great for "bank shots," too! Your kids will love it.

Kitchen Garbage Mess

Food is one of the prime mess-makers, and the kitchen is Food Central. No wonder we spend so much time cleaning here. You have several choices, according to your working style and the floor plan of your kitchen. Your objectives are to:

1. Save steps

2. Eliminate smell

3. Prevent floor mess, both around the garbage container and in the can itself

4. Cut garbage take-out time

A freestanding can in a traffic area is probably the most maintenance-multiplying way to go—besides being unsightly, a freestanding can is always in the way and periodically gets kicked over. And since it's not usually located in your high-need area, you're forever stringing the garbage across the kitchen floor to the can, making a mess all over. Shorten the distance from your working area to the garbage container and you'll cut down the mess caused by garbage.

Remember the basic principles for making something low-maintenance? Whenever possible—*build it in!* If you can't do that, *suspend it!*

One of the big problems with the kitchen garbage is the mess around the garbage container. If

the can sits at the end of the cabinet or up against the wall, food and juices and coffee grounds get splashed on the wall and the cabinet—not to mention the floor—what a mess!

One of the nicest solutions is a pull-out suspended garbage can. I'd locate it right in your work center, the place you use the most. This will do a lot to minimize preparation mess—which is most of the mess in a kitchen. If you are building new or remodeling, ask your cabinet dealer for a "built-in suspended garbage container" and see what he has to offer. There are many different styles, so you'll need to decide on the one that will best serve you. The way to do this is to pretend you are actually using it *before* you buy it. Often things look neat and usable

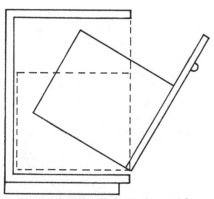

A trash can built into the cabinets can make trash disposal neater and handier.

but when you actually go to use them they don't function smoothly and cost you more time than they were supposed to save. Check it out!

Go right now and look under

the trash can in any room there's a mess, isn't there?

There are options in built-in garbage receptacles to fit any home.

Garbage Disposals

One of the best ways to minimize mess is to catch it at the source. Garbage disposals are great because they allow you to dispose of perishable and wet garbage right at the point of origin (food preparation), and reserve the trash can for dry waste. This way, cleaning the can isn't a major chore, the garbage doesn't rot and stink, and animals don't invade it when you put it out for collection. It saves cleanup time because it's located right where you're preparing those foods—in the sink. You

never even have to handle the mess except to push it down the drain.

If your kitchen isn't already equipped with a garbage disposal, by all means, purchase one! They are relatively inexpensive (less than $100), and can be installed in almost any sink. But it's important to buy a good one, because cheap ones will let you down time and time again. Good ones aren't finicky—they'll eat just about anything, they're quieter, they don't often break down, and they last a long time. A good disposal has a resettable overload circuit breaker on it, and many have a wrench that can be used to turn the shaft from underneath the sink to clear jammed items.

Trash Compactors

Cut down the amount of trash you have to handle—a compactor can squeeze an entire week's worth of garbage into an 18x24-inch bag! A compactor not only reduces the volume of garbage you have to tote to the can, to the dumpster or dump, but reduces odor and pest problems with garbage. You can put anything in it from milk cartons to glass bottles to tin cans, and it smashes them flat. Wet garbage can be put in too, but because you'll only be emptying the compactor once or twice a week, it will begin to smell. It's better to use a garbage disposal for wet garbage.

The main question is where to put the compactor—in the kitchen or the garage? I say the garage, but suit yourself. Mounting a compactor under the sink right next to the food preparation area is a convenient option, but odor may be a problem even *without* wet garbage. **Some trash compactors have bins with wheeled dollies that make disposal a snap. I'd get one of these, and keep the compactor in the garage.**

Trash Cans Outside

Your outside trash cans should also be convenient. The farther trash has to be transported to its final resting place, the more likely the garbage will be ignored as long as possible, left to become a festering monster. Trash mess multiplies when your "trash can runneth over." You find yourself picking up greasy eggshells and tin can lids after they've tumbled off the overloaded pile and come to a messy rest on the floor (usually just as company walks in the door).

If you put your garbage out for collection in cans, you should look into the heavy-duty molded cans such as Rubbermaid "Brutes" or Continental "Huskees." They have nice weatherproof lids and even casters. They can be ob-tained at a janitorial supply house in 30- or 44-gallon sizes, they are virtually indestructible, and will outlast a metal can many times over. They're also a lot more durable than the plastic garbage cans you're likely to find at the department or discount store.

Putting the Lid on Yard Litter

In this day of disposables, trash is a big problem outdoors too. Public places make sure there's a handy and highly visible trash receptacle; in our yards and patios we often fail to do the same. Convenient outdoor litter containers make it much less likely that you'll have to pick or rake it up yourself.

For outside, you can buy a commercial swing-lid dome cap to fit a 30-gallon metal drum, a barrel, and even some of the large garbage cans. Rain and animals can't get in, and the spring-loaded flap hides the mess. A top like this only costs about $10 at a janitorial supply house.

Compact garbage is much easier to handle—you don't leave a trail of broken eggshells and fish bones every time you take the trash out.

Airborne Dust and Dirt

A research article reports that your house gains or collects forty pounds of dust in the course of a year! We might question the exact poundage, but not this fact: Dust, airborne dirt and oils are not only responsible for a great percentage of daily housework, but also cause soiling, discoloration, and stains that eventually demand repair or replacement.

If you don't believe in airborne dust, dirt, and grease, go wipe the top of your refrigerator, bookcase, light fixtures, or doorjamb. What you find there is all over your house and everything in it. You don't see it on the floors because you've hoofed it into the pattern.

What is dust caused by? Dirty furnace filters, leakage from worn vacuum bags, dirt tracked in by people and animals, open windows and doors, lint escaping from the clothes dryer—you name it. Dust is everywhere, and here to stay.

The cure is in using your head and a few secret weapons.

Good insulation—It not only saves energy, it saves cleaning. Drafty, poorly insulated homes have a lot of air migration, which soils walls and ceilings faster.

Seal it up—Good weatherstripping and caulking will cut down the amount of dirt and dust that gets in through cracks and leaking doors and windows.

Furnace filters—Almost all forced-air heating systems have filters. The magic word is *replace*—do it *often* to cut down on dust in the home and increase the efficiency of the furnace. Furnace filters are inexpensive and can be installed in minutes.

Airlocks—If you have a mud room, utility room, or small entry-

way from the garage, consider a door between this room and the rest of the house that would remain closed most of the time. This creates an "airlock" or double entry effect like many commercial buildings use to control blown-in dirt and loss of heated/cooled air each time you open the door. Without it an open door or window somewhere else in the house can turn your entry into a wind tunnel.

Vents—These are required by most building codes for attics, stoves, and bathrooms. Keep them clean and in operating condition.

Vacuums—Use vacuums with good bags, or better still, install built-in central vacuums. Vacuuming consistently will help prevent most of the damage to carpets and furnishings caused by airborne dust and soils. Just remember to *change the bags* regularly, too!

Dust mop—Most brooms just strain and stir up the dirt. A good dust mop sprayed with *professional* dust mop treatment is the fastest and most effective way to clean all hard-surface floors.

Treated professional dustcloths—Wool dust wands pick up and hold the dust instead of just moving it around as feather dusters do.

Professional walk-off mats at your entranceways—Mats catch tracked-in dirt at its source (see pages 101-102 for more information on mats and other equipment).

Remember—if it doesn't get in, it won't have to be taken out!

Heating and Cooling

If you're building or doing extensive remodeling, you might want to consider heat types in terms of not only availability, installation, and fuel costs, but also the contribution they make to cleanup chores.

The *cleanest* heat is radiant heat (hot water is best, followed by electric). To have air conditioning, though, a forced-air system is required, which moves air around, creates dust, dirties the drapes and walls by the vents, etc. The cleanest forced-air systems are electric—but they also have the highest fuel cost. Gas-fired is next best, then oil. Coal is the dirtiest. Again, changing furnace filters often is the key to controlling dirt.

The outlook on fireplaces is dark, from a maintenance standpoint. Soot from fireplaces damages walls, ceilings, drapes, and furnishings. Fire and flame are almost alive, they have to be fed and their leftovers disposed of. Fireplaces are a fire hazard in general as well as a burn risk for children, and they introduce toxic hydrocarbons into the living quarters (many people are allergic to these without knowing it). If you have a wood-burning fireplace, the chimney sustains a slow creosote buildup: if it should ignite, the chimney becomes a blowtorch.

On top of all that, fireplaces are a tremendously fuel-inefficient heat source, plus they draw cold air into the house from windows and cracks. Their only real advantage is "charm."

Anytime you go in the direction of chimneys you are moving away from maintenance-freedom. But if you enjoy the cozy glow of a fire on cold winter nights, be sure to have your chimney swept every three years.

Smoke Gets in Your Eyes

Outdoors, we can usually count on smoke being whisked away by the breeze. But that's not the way it works inside. It sticks to everything—wall and ceiling surfaces, windows, drapes, upholstery, and appliances. The smoke that doesn't stick undergoes chemical changes and becomes airborne fallout. That's because smoke is composed of tiny particles of oil and tar, as well as water vapor and other substances.

But what kinds of smoke are we talking about?

Cooking smoke

Fireplace smoke

Woodburning stove smoke

Cigarette smoke

Smoke from scented candles, incense, hobbies that involve soldering, hot glue, wood burning, melted wax, etc.

Smoke can dirty everything in a room, and the smell lingers on indefinitely.

Smoke is one of the most insidious mess-makers because it's almost "invisible," so we tend not to worry or even think about it. But smoke travels so freely it can sully our furnishings and surfaces at will—and do a lot of hard-to-clean-up damage in a very short time. What can you do about it? Make sure there's a place for smoke to go.

Up the chimney is one logical place, but David Stol, the nation's leading chimney sweep authority, says the majority of chimneys are not efficient due to creosote build-up or because of their design. So smoke that is supposed to be going up your chimney is probably settling comfortably on your (once clean) possessions.

Exhaust fans can be installed in any room. I'd definitely put one near all fireplaces. They're also good for bathrooms, kitchens, basements, or any place where moisture or odors develop.

Cooking grill vents are better than ceiling exhaust fans or hood vents in the kitchen because they suck smoke and gases in right at the level where they occur. They put gravity on your side. The downdraft type of vent is said to be 80 percent more efficient at getting the grease and smoke out before it can rise and settle around the house.

If a vented hood is already in place, keep it clean (the fan, ductwork, and filters) and working at top efficiency. If a circulating-air hood is in place, change the filter *often*. (This type is not nearly as effective as a vented hood.)

Room air filters. Cigarette smoke inside a building is especially devastating in that the tars and oils in the smoke yellow everything imaginable. Many non-smokers don't allow smoking in their houses, thus eliminating the problem. You can also use room air filters, or limit smoking to certain areas.

Water, Water Everywhere

Water is usually associated with cleaning but can be one of the worst mess-makers and work-causers of all. It has the power to stain, rot, rust, mold, and mildew things, and to create hard water deposits and leave rings.

Anyplace there is water close by, it will get in. You can depend on it. Uncontained or uncontrolled moisture can even split a slab of granite.

Water is all around us, so be sure to take it into account. One coat of latex paint on a shower ceiling, for example, won't do it. Water condensation will soon disintegrate it into a flaky, sloppy mess.

Leaky hoses or connections are simple problems, but can end up causing lots of maintenance and repair chores. Water from these leaks lifts tile, rots the flooring underneath, and stains the wall base. Check periodically under sinks, behind the washer, around the toilet base, tub, and shower for slow leaks.

Roof leaks can be a problem with flat roofs. Keep your roof in good repair and fix it at first sign of leaking. A little water can do a lot of damage over time.

Window casing disintegration is caused by condensation of water on glass during cold weather. Double-glazed glass helps, as do sills of plastic laminate, cultured marble, tile, etc.

Drainage is very important. If water can't get away, it gets in! (See page 178.)

The maintenance-freeing secret is to *keep water-susceptible surfaces sealed* with a coating that won't let water in:

Wood—paint or varnish

Concrete—clear concrete seal

Vinyl floor tile—acrylic floor finish (wax)

Earth tiles—acrylic tile sealer

Grout—silicone water seal

Cracks & crevices—silicone caulk

Carpeting—soil retardant

Fabrics—soil retardant

Will De-humidifiers Help?

High humidity encourages the growth of mold and mildew and accelerates rust and deterioration of many materials. Humidity control for a whole house usually costs more than it's worth from a strictly maintenance standpoint, but it may well be worthwhile if you have allergies or respiratory problems. Vented fans for bathrooms are a big help and air conditioning also tends to dry the air.

Or Water Softeners?

In areas of very hard (high mineral content) water, a water conditioner is almost a must. Without one, you're always fighting lime buildup and water spots on plumbing fixtures, shower walls and doors, etc. Where the buildup really hurts, though, is in the water pipes and in the hot water heater. It's not unusual for the lower element in water heaters to burn out from hard-water buildup in only one year's time. (That $100 plumbing bill would almost pay for a water conditioner for the year—the conditioner would make your laundry detergent more effective, too.)

Pet-Proofing

There's no getting around it—house pets are high-maintenance. Dealing with hair, odor, litter, pet food, scratches costs time and money. Animals create trash, damage, and residue just like humans, but unlike us, they can't pick up after themselves.

Pets Ranked from Best to Worst for Maintenance Ease

1. Fish

2. Small dogs

3. Cats

4. Large dogs

5. Birds

A Pet's Best Friend

Pets *do* add maintenance—and though you can minimize some of the mess—there is no such thing as maintenance-free pet ownership. If they are kept outside your house will stay a lot cleaner.

But if you do keep your pet inside, here are a few ways to keep house-pet ownership tolerable:

1. Seal and protect. If you apply the general maintenance-freeing strategies we suggest for your walls, floors, and furniture, you'll be taking the first step toward protecting them from your animals. Animals rub against and shed on your furnishings and the house must be able to repel it.

A pet rake will lift the hair off furniture and out of carpet like nothing else. And have a good vacuum with an energetic beater bar.

2. Provide a place. Establish a place for the animal—a comfortable bed or pad, preferably covered, so he feels secure there. If he likes his home, he'll spend a lot of his sleeping, rolling, and shedding time there instead of on your furniture and carpet. Cleaning hair and mess out of a little cat bed is easier than cleaning it up all over the house.

If your animal has a favorite chair (and you let him stay there), it may be worth putting a slipcover of terrycloth on the cushion that can be removed and washed regularly.

3. Provide a bathroom. Make sure his litter box is kept clean and usable. If it gets too full, the odor-killers in the litter won't work and your house will stink. To make matters worse animals won't use it if it's too full—they'll find *another* place in the house to go—most likely the carpet.

4. Suspend, secure, and mat food dishes. If you secure the animal dish, the water and food won't get tipped over—by you or the animal. Put an absorbent mat or towel under the dish to catch the inevitable slopping food as the pet eats and drinks.

5. Trim and clean your pet! Keep your cat's or dog's claws trimmed to minimize scratching damage. If you don't know how to do this, ask your vet. Bathe the animal when it's dirty to keep dirt from being spread throughout the house.

6. Use disinfectant cleaner. When you're cleaning in pet areas—around his dish, or the walls around his bed and litter box—use a disinfectant to keep germs to a minimum.

Pests

Even the most tender-hearted of us have to admit that "critters" can be a real maintenance headache. These little buggers gnaw, nest, burrow, litter, contaminate food, spread disease, and have been known to scare some people silly.

Are new homes and suburbs, maybe, more pest-free? Not necessarily. Garden compost heaps, outdoor firewood piles, storage bins, sewers, and spacious attics and garages in suburbia provide fertile new ground for rat and mouse infiltration.

Mice, roaches, flies, termites, silverfish, ants, hornets, spiders, and birds can all cause a lot of cleanup and damage, and sooner or later you have to either pay someone else to eradicate them or do it yourself. Logic plays an important part in stopping them.

No Place, No Face

Rats and mice can always get in. Insects, too. How, we don't always know, but they do. The trick is to have no place for them to go if they do get in—in other words, no living and hiding places.

Getting rid of pests' living environment is the best way to get rid of them. Seal up cracks and holes in walls and foundations, and you seal out pests. Get rid of gaps, crevices, tiny corners or openings— every little empty unusable space.

Caulk every crack and hole near the foundation with silicone caulk.

Several companies make canister "foam" generators. You've all seen this styrofoam-looking stuff—it comes in do-it-yourself insulating kits. One tank is filled with liquid, the other with oxygen under pressure. When you activate the unit, these materials are mixed into a bubbly foam that expands and fills the space, then dries into a solid bread-like material. Drill a small access hole into the spaces underneath your cupboards or other hideouts and fill them with the foam; you can also fill the openings around the pipes and conduits. An ant couldn't even live there after that, and you can be sure that nothing else will.

In some areas of the country, the battle of the bugs is pretty intense, and you may have to resort to full-scale professional exterminating. But these steps will help cut down the amount of chemical warfare needed.

Bugs, rodents, and all their relatives can cause a lot of stress as well as maintenance. *Eliminate easy-to-find food and hiding places!* Then they'll disappear.

No wood—no termites.

No rat's nest—no rats.

Build a birdhouse, and they won't use yours.

Bird Roosting

Some of my professional jobs include "operation pigeon potty" (removal of bird droppings). A high pressure garden hose will wash the little heaps of droppings away. We use rubber snakes to

scare birds away, and if the problem is really serious there is an appliance like a dog whistle (a high-frequency sound generator) that can be mounted near the roof to keep it maintenance-free.

Again, the structure itself through features such as closed-in eaves can help—by eliminating the roosting place you'll eliminate the problem.

The "Ups and Downs"

Do you have the basement blues or attic attacks? These two places can make you sick once in a while, because most basements and attics look pretty sick most of the time. Let's start from the top and work down.

Attic Attack

Attics are notorious as caches for seldom-used or worthless junk—they're usually dimly lit

and covered with dust. Your once-in-a-while visits to that lofty hideaway are just enough to keep you vaguely aware of what's there and to add a few new pieces of junk and fire hazards. On the way back you spread dirt and dust down through the house. **If your attic has the potential and the room for storage, spend a few dollars on it and make it truly serviceable.** Lay down a nice subfloor of ¾-inch plywood, wall in the storage area so it's protected from dust, give the

walls and ceilings a couple of good coats of paint, and seal the floor. Be sure to carpet all stairs going up and coming down, too.

Next, make sure there's good lighting up there—not the usual single wobbling 60-watt incandescent bulb with a dangling string. One or two good 4-foot fluorescent tube lights will last ten to fifteen years before you need to change them. Then use the attic to store valuables that you seldom use.

Before

After

Attics should have vents at the very least (exhaust fans are better) to dissipate excess heat and moisture. Moisture causes insulation to lose its "fluffiness" and effectiveness.

Many people convert attics to small extra rooms for guests, a den, or a bedroom for older college kids who come home only on weekends or college breaks. If you do this, a good sanding and a couple of coats of paint will make it fast and easy to clean. In an extra room especially a lot of built-in furniture and storage—in fact a totally built-in room—is a maintenance saver.

Make sure your investment balances with what it will save—spending $1,000 to make the attic low-maintenance would be a waste unless you actually *use* the attic. Spending $6,000 to make the kitchen low-maintenance can be well worth it because you use it daily.

Beating the Basement Blues

Basements can do a lot to help the rest of the house be maintenance-free. The first hurdle to get over is the negative attitude that a basement is a damp dingy catchall for leftovers. It isn't—it has a real value to your house, it's absolutely the best place in the world for certain kinds of storage—it keeps fruit and vegetables and other foods cool and out of the upstairs traffic flow. It's also the only place in a modern house you can make and store wine and grow mushrooms. The basement can house all kinds of hobby and craft projects. If you just put as much money in it as you do into a couple of weekend dinners at a fancy restaurant, you could really perk it up. The structures—walls, ceilings, and floor—are already there and guaranteed sturdy; you simply need a covering of paint, a light fixture or two and some *closed-in* storage and often it's like doubling the

size of your house. Don't leave the basement in its primitive state! Cleaning it up, lighting it, and organizing it discourage its use as a hotel by every homeless bug and rodent in the neighborhood.

A functioning floor drain is a great asset in any basement, but absolutely essential if you have a hot water heater or washer and dryer located there. And good ventilation is important to keep the space from becoming damp in hot, humid weather. A damp basement will rust and damage moisture-susceptible things stored there, and can create a mildew problem in other areas of the house.

If your house is built on a grade, the ideal arrangement is a basement designed so that one wall has sliding glass doors that open directly onto ground level. This not only provides good ventilation and light but makes the basement an attractive living area. An alternative is to install several windows in each of the four walls of the basement. These should be a type that will open easily to allow fresh air in.

The Basement Blues

A basement can provide a lot of extra living space, if it lends itself to finishing. To be a candidate for finishing, the basement needs to be *dry*—no flooding from subsurface water or dampness seeping through the walls. If your location has constantly encroaching subsurface water and you need a sump pump, or your basement walls "weep" because of inadequate moisture-sealing, you're better off to give up on finishing the space and just use it for storage. Fixing the moisture problems, if possible, would probably cost more than you'd gain.

Stairs

I've attempted to design stairs out of every house I've owned or built, but I couldn't. If a house has more than one level, inclined ramps, lifts, and elevators are usually either impractical or prohibitively expensive except for people with special needs. Stairs are going to be a fact of life for a while yet, until we learn to levitate.

I've cleaned every type of stair there is, and no matter what genius of design or efficiency you apply to stairs, you won't manage to make them truly easy to clean or fully safe unless you eliminate the stairs. You can at least improve your odds—safer stairs that are easier to clean.

Safety First

Hard (uncarpeted) stairs aren't bad in heavy use and abuse (commercial and industrial), but carpeted stairs are far superior in a home for appearance, safety, and dirt-catching ability. A slip or fall on stairs (which is bound to happen sooner or later) can really be compounded by a hard, sharp-edged stair. The harder the material, the more injury. Solid concrete

One Way to Avoid Stairs

or steel stairs with sharp edges are the worst, wood stairs covered with carpet are the best. Stairs with rubber treads, etc., fall somewhere in between. Carpet is a slip-resistant covering that assures solid footing.

I'd definitely carpet any and all stairs, and not purely from a safety standpoint—they'll also be quieter and give you a more cushioned step. Contrary to what you may think, carpeted stairs are *not* hard to clean.

The wear—and dirtying—of stairs is almost wholly on the center of the tread, so a carpeted stairway can be vacuumed in minutes. The dust that collects in the corners can be wiped up in seconds with a damp cloth.

Wear It Well

All stairs have accelerated damage and wear points at the top of the risers and the lip of the tread, but carpet hides and minimizes

that wear. Low, dense-pile carpet with a pattern wears best. Always carpet the whole stairs—don't give yourself two surfaces to clean.

As a second choice on stairs, try a cushioned vinyl. It is still a soft surface and even the corners can be swept or wiped out easily. Never *paint* stairs—they'll require frequent repainting, and can be very slippery when wet. Grooved rubber treads decrease slippage, but are hard to clean because they require a broom *and* a vacuum (you have created two surfaces to clean). Not only that, dirt and pieces of things get under the tread and then you've really got a cleaning problem; you've got to reach under them with your fingers and get it out. Your broom or vacuum can't reach them. Forget about using rubber treads; they aren't worth the trouble.

Stairway walls should be painted a darker color as more

99

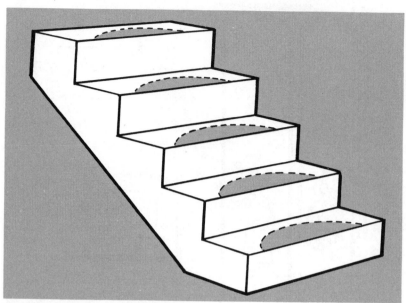

The wear pattern on stairs is mostly in the center of the step, so carpeted stairs can be vacuumed easily.

handprints concentrate here. Never use *white* paint, unless you really need to lighten up a *very* dark stairway. Use semigloss paint, or better yet paneling or vinyl wallcover—you need to hide prints here more so than on other walls.

Open Up!

Each stair on a conventional home staircase has four separate areas to collect dirt and damage. **So why not have an open staircase? Since there are no risers, there's nothing to scuff and no corners to collect dust.**

Little bits of things don't collect on them because of the open de-

sign. Everything tends to get kicked through to the floor below, where it's more easily dealt with. And open stairs can be designed with wider treads than traditional stairs, so there's more room for you to step, and consequently *less* danger of falling.

However, often the stairs are over some very good and needed storage space. You can enclose your storage space and leave the stairs open, providing the dirt has a place to go when it falls through the stairs.

Designing Safe Stairs

Most of us have fallen down the stairs at least once. Some of us were only shaken, others were injured, but there are people who have actually died as a result! The following list will help you reduce the chances of accidents on stairs in your home.

1 If you're designing a new house or building an addition that will have stairs, make sure they have a landing and a turn. It'll make the stairway look less formidable and break the fall midway if someone does slip.

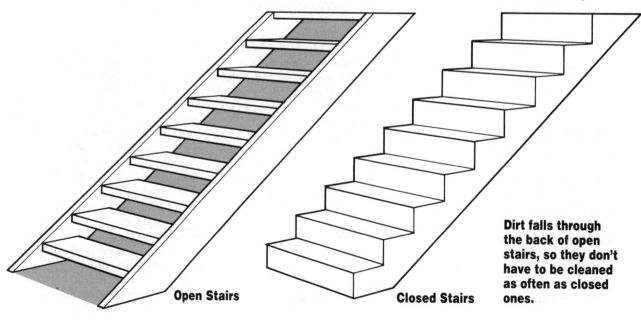

Open Stairs

Closed Stairs

Dirt falls through the back of open stairs, so they don't have to be cleaned as often as closed ones.

2 Make stairs wide and long enough, at as gradual an incline as possible. Because stairs are a necessary evil to get up or down in a house, the first mistake we make is in putting our stairs in whatever place is left after all the "living" room is planned. This cramps stairs' width and often steepens their pitch. Wide stairs—an extra foot (4 feet wide instead of 3 feet)—not only feel more open and spacious, but save a lot of wall dirt and damage. This also allows easier access for moving furniture—or even just carrying armloads of things up and down the stairs.

3 Make sure the steps are spaced correctly for safe, comfortable use. Some stairs are just plain uncomfortable to use because they're too steep, the tread is too narrow, or the risers are too high. The angle of the rise, depth of the tread, and height of the riser make a lot of difference in the "feel" of a stair, and if they throw you out of synch as you go up and down, they are dangerous.

4 As noted earlier, carpeted stairs are much safer than hard-surface stairs because there's less chance of slipping on them.

5 Try to avoid having a door directly at the top of a flight of stairs, even one that opens away from the stairs. Opening the door and stepping out without looking could mean a real bad trip (down the stairs!) for a visitor to your home. And a door that opens toward a staircase is a double safety hazard.

6 Install *two* handrails on each side—one for juniors and one for seniors.

7 Always put a light on the stairway with a switch at the top and the bottom of the stairs.

Chapter 11

The Right Equipment and Supplies Will Help

Using the proper cleaning tools and chemicals is basic to our low-maintenance approach. The right equipment and supplies will not only dramatically reduce the amount of time required to do a job, they'll also accomplish the task safely and protect your home's surfaces from unnecessary depreciation. More damage in a house comes from maintenance than from usage. How can you damage a bathroom by using it? It's the maintenance of it—the scouring, scrubbing, and scratching—that ruins things. The same goes for light fixtures, stove tops, and furniture; moving things, putting them up, taking them down, and cleaning them makes them wear out.

Many popular cleaners are overly aggressive, and will hasten deterioration of your expensive furnishings and fixtures. The right tools and supplies are almost always easier to use, and can be stored in much less space than the hodgepodge of cleaners most homemakers use. **Knowing the right tools and cleaning agents for each task is an important key to effective low-maintenance home care.**

The following are a few of the professional tools available at janitorial supply stores (just look in the Yellow Pages under Janitorial Supplies) or by mail order.* You can find a more complete list and descriptions in *Is There Life After Housework?*

Cleaning Cloth*

A far superior replacement for the "rag" in any job that calls for a drying and polishing cloth; especially effective in wall and ceiling cleaning. Made from a 9x18-inch piece of cotton terrycloth. You can fold it and turn it inside out for sixteen different cleaning surfaces. (See Chapter 14 of *Is There Life After Housework?* for details on how to make and use a cleaning cloth.)

Plastic Trigger-Spray Bottle*

Sturdy quart size or smaller with tough industrial spray head for dispensing your cleaning solutions.

Concentrated Professional Cleaners*

Can be purchased in plastic pre-measured portion packs or gallon jugs and diluted with water. Three basic types—heavy-duty neutral cleaner, disinfectant cleaner, and alcohol-based glass cleaner—will do most every cleaning job in a house and replace $100 worth of bulky closet-cluttering cans, jars, tins, and bottles.

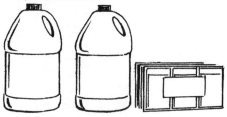

Lambswool Duster*

Does high dusting with ease. Actually *attracts* dust like a magnet and will not streak or scratch. Washable.

*For your convenience, items marked with an asterisk are available by mail. For more information and a free catalog write to: HOUSEWORK INC., P.O. Box 39, Pocatello, ID 83204.

Masslinn Dustcloth*

A professional treated-paper dustcloth that picks up and holds the dust. Inexpensive and disposable.

Scrubbing Sponge or Pad*

A white nylon pad or a white pad bonded to a sponge for scrubbing hard-to-remove soil safely. The white pad contains no abrasives and is safe to use on almost any surface. The colored nylon pads bonded to sponges contain abrasives, and should only be used on nondamageable surfaces. They can damage paint, chrome, glass, plastic, and porcelain.

Dry Sponge*

For cleaning surfaces that can't get wet, such as acoustical tile, lampshades, and wallpaper. They also work great on flat paint and oil paintings.

Vegetable Oil Soap*

Soaps such as Lin-Sol, Murphy's Oil Soap, or Wood Wash are designed to clean wood surfaces and leave them shining, not sticky. Mild and safe, great on wood paneling and kitchen cabinets.

Upright Commercial Vacuum Cleaner*

Eureka makes a good model with a heavy-duty 6.5 amp motor, 50-foot cord, wide furniture guard, and extra-strong beater bar/brush.

Dust Mop*

9- or 14-inch commercial mop with a swivel head is best for home use. Fast, maneuverable, effective (much better than a broom for cleaning hard-surface floors). Wash and treat occasionally with professional dust-mop treatment for best results.

Heavy-Duty Floor Squeegee*

Does a super-smooth job that beats mops and snow shovels on wet surfaces. Cuts water removal time on floors and walks dramatically.

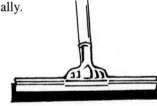

Mats (Indoor and Outdoor)*

Get the dirt before it gets in. For outside your entranceways, use a heavy-duty polypropylene simulated grass fiber surface with non-slip backing, made to stand outdoor use and foul weather. For inside, use nylon or olefin fiber on a vinyl or rubber backing.

Commercial Floor Finish ("Wax")*

A liquid polymer coating that dries to form a tough protective film on your floor and gives it a brilliant shine. For tile, linoleum, sheet vinyl, and "no-wax" floors.

Stripper*

A strong emulsifier that softens and lifts old floor finish, making it easy to remove.

Make It Easier for Others to Clean Up Their Own Messes

In one of my maintenance-consulting assignments, the architect had eliminated the janitorial storage closet on each floor of an 18-story office building. There was one large room for cleaning supply storage in the basement instead—the effect of this approach was a 20 percent increase in cleaning costs and triple the damage to the elevators, walls, and floors from hauling equipment

up and down through the building. Not to mention the extra labor required.

If they can't easily find cleaning tools and supplies, it's much less likely that they'll clean up after themselves. (This goes for kids and teens as well as guests and reluctant spouses.)

Have cleaning equipment handy anyplace in the house that requires constant cleaning, such as the bath and kitchen. Make cleaners, cloths, etc., easy and convenient to get to. If you have a built-in vacuum, provide lots of vacuum hoses. If there's a spot where you always get a buildup of dirt—such as an entryway—have a small hanging broom and dustpan available for a quick daily cleanup. Put a spray bottle of disinfectant cleaner in

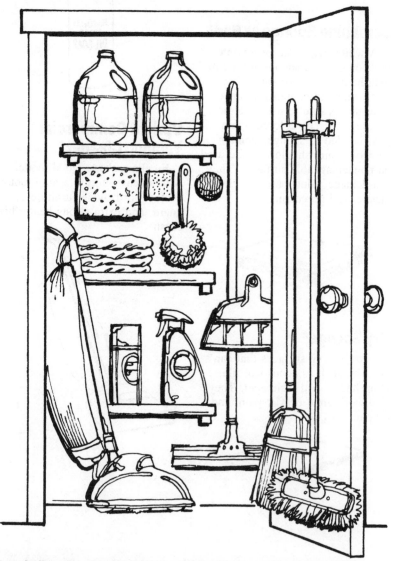

Store bulky cleaning supplies together in a location that's convenient to most of the work areas—the utility room is often a good choice. Often, smaller supplies can be stored right where they're used, in the kitchen or bathroom, for instance.

each bathroom along with a cleaning cloth.

Store Often-Used Products Where They're Used

If you quickly wipe up your bathroom with disinfectant cleaner every other day it will stay clean and require less "hard cleaning." Having the equipment right there on hand will make it a two-minute job that's likely to be done.

The kitchen with its inevitable spills and sticky messes requires quick cleanups daily—have the cleaners handy. A scrubbing sponge, some disinfectant cleaner, a cleaning cloth, and some window cleaner are essential.

If you have a two-story house that has a lot of carpeted area on the second floor (and you don't have a central vacuum), you might consider a second vacuum. It could save a lot of lugging up and down—not to mention nicks and dings on the staircase walls.

The rest of the supplies should be stored in a location convenient to the main work areas of the house—perhaps in the utility or "mud" room. This is where brooms, dust mops, bulk cleaning supplies, the vacuum, dustpans, dusting tools, etc., are stored.

A hanging clean-up board that will hold all your housecleaning supplies (Housework, Inc., is one source for these) can be mounted in the closet or on a door.

Central Vacuums

Alias "built-ins," "wall vacs," and "built-in centrals," these are timesavers and house-savers, well worth putting in even an existing home. The principle is simple— the motor that creates the suction is mounted in the basement, garage, or other handy utility area, then plastic tubing is run to key locations all over the house, where

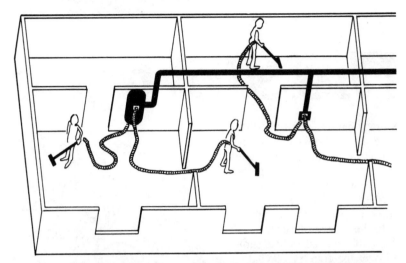

The power unit of a central vacuum can be located in the garage or utility room, and outlets can be installed wherever they're needed. Long, flexible hose lets you move easily without lugging around a heavy vacuum.

outlets are installed. You walk into the room, insert a light hose into the outlet, and presto—you quickly and quietly vacuum the area, then move on.

A central vacuum saves the hassle of lugging the vacuum from room to room, up and down stairs, banging it into the walls when you turn the corner. You don't have to worry about the plug always pulling out when you're in the middle of vacuuming, or all that noise (central vacuums are quieter).

Central vacuum hoses are light and convenient and make it easy to vacuum hard-surface floors instead of sweeping them. Some experts feel that from a health standpoint central vacuums are the only way to go because they push all the dust outside. All upright and canister vacuums, except the "Rainbow" water system, redistribute a certain percentage of the dirt they pick up back into the room. Dust seeps through the pores of a vacuum bag, and gets into everything, especially your lungs. This is a serious consideration for people with allergies.

Nineteen out of twenty owners of built-ins love them, but there are some complaints about weak suction and worthless beater-bars on the hosing. Both of these problems can be avoided if you buy the most powerful unit—it only costs a few dollars more, and then you can be sure you'll have enough "air power" for the air-driven beater brushes. (You *will* have to have a place to store the rather long hose.)

Be sure to put outlets in the garage, on the porch, off the stairs, and near the fireplace, to mention several places in the house often neglected. The hose length and style you need will depend on how many outlets you have and how far apart they are. At least fifteen companies now make central vacuums; for more information, see the Source List.

You can easily install a central vacuum while building a house. It's more difficult in an existing house but it can be done. There are models in which the pipes run outside the house, so you don't have to do so much tearing out to install one in an existing home.

Chapter 12

The Storage Solution

Storage can make all the difference. Entire books have been written on the subject, so we won't give it exhaustive coverage here, but we will pass along some of the best ideas we've heard to get you thinking along the right lines.

In the course of our research for this book, we asked householders all over the country: "What single thing would make your housecleaning faster and easier *today?*"

The answer—*better storage!* The cry is the same everywhere:

"Storage!"

"We need more"

"More kitchen storage"

"More room for our clothes"

"A place for the kids' stuff"

"Storage our families will use"

"Better *organized* storage!"

"Storage for outdoor equipment"

"More laundry storage"

It's easy to understand why the interest in storage is so intense. Inadequate and poorly planned storage means there are a lot of things in the way of your cleaning efforts, a lot more stuff that has to be moved out and moved back, lugged or carried away in the course of cleaning. The things that slow down professional janitors are boxes and other junk *on the floor* and *in the way*—they'll slow you down, too.

When you clean your house today, take the time to notice how much of "cleaning" is actually "transporting"—getting things out of the way, putting things back where they belong, trying to find a place for things. **Poor storage even adds to repairs—many an object got its nick, dent, scrape, or wrinkle in the act of being stuffed or crammed into an already too-full closet or drawer.**

The Joy of Positive Parking

Storage is just that—the positive parking of useful things near where you need and use them. If you have mainly junk in your storage areas, shame on you (stop right now and re-read Chapter 5—or, if you're a serious junker, consult *Clutter's Last Stand*). Good storage takes the not-presently-being-used things out of the traffic flow.

You want to distinguish between "live" and "dead" storage and stash things accordingly. Make sure that live storage—where you keep frequently used things—is close by and easy to get to. Put dead storage—the stuff that's only needed seasonally, or on special occasions, or for special purposes—in the less accessible places like the top closet shelf or the attic (close to heaven, where dead things should go). But bear in mind that anything bad enough to be "atticized" probably ought to be ostracized instead.

Well-designed storage will save you hours of shuffling and dig-

ging and thrashing and fretting. Cramped storage space is one of the most frustrating drawbacks of homes today. Most houses have the usual bedroom closets, hall coat closet, linen closet, and cabinets for kitchen storage, but we've all learned that these don't really provide enough storage space.

There's hardly a room in the house that doesn't need some form of storage. There should be places in the living room for books, magazines, records, and fireplace wood; a place in the dining room for linen, silver, and dishes; a place in the family room or play-room to hide the clutter of toys and games; space in or near the garage for garden tools and bikes. You'd never store your pots and pans two rooms away from the kitchen, would you? So why run down to the basement every time you need a dust mop or rummage through the upstairs closet to get an umbrella?

Storage facilities can be added after you move into a house, but you seldom manage to catch up with your junk accumulation ability. It's best to provide for storage before you move in, even if it means a few extra dollars in original building cost.

Finding New Places to Put Things

If building or adding on is out of the question, but you still need more storage, remember that storage can:

Go *in*

Go *on*

Go *under*

Some of the most overlooked and unused storage spaces are right

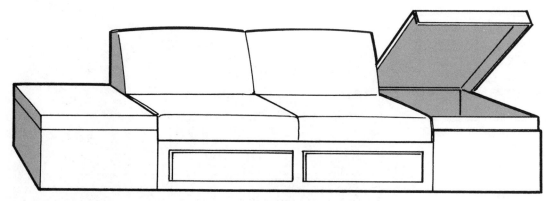

Storage doesn't have to be in closets. Built-in furniture provides plenty of storage possibilities, such as inside end tables or beneath the cushions.

under your nose. As we suggested in Chapter 8, you can build in drawers under beds. End tables don't have to be just for show—make sure they're designed to store things as well. Mount knife racks, towel racks, etc. under cabinets to save space.

Re-evaluate every surface in your home for its storage potential. Many pieces of furniture can double as storage, saving you both work and space. And the less crowded things are, the cleaner a room looks.

For example, the space under a built-in window seat can double as a chest for children's toys. Or replace partition walls with storage walls—special ceiling-high cabinets with shelves and drawers. They provide a great deal of extra storage space and also serve as the partition between two rooms. Storage walls are not in general use, however, so you will have to look around for them (try your DIY store) or have them made.

Likewise, you can make storage that serves as the partition between the kitchen and the dining room. If it has doors on both sides, you can load dishes in from the kitchen side after washing, unload them from the dining room side when you're ready to use them.

If you're in an apartment or temporary dwelling, you can buy or build freestanding storage shelves that will double as room dividers, and they can be moved when you go.

Beyond the Conventional

We know that you can come up with better storage arrangements than the conventional if you think about it, so here are a few thoughts to get you started.

- A clothes closet will save work if it contains all your dressing needs in one spot. And if it opens to both bedroom and bath, two people can dress at the same time.

- How about a dressing room adjacent to a laundry room, so there's no need for dressers or closets in the bedrooms? All clothing would be stored in the dressing room, which would have mirrors, hooks, and special shelves for clothes worn once but clean enough to wear again. Storing all clothes in the dressing room would save the wear and tear of carrying

clothes from the laundry to drawers and closets in other rooms. Also, when changing, you could easily deposit clothes in the nearby dirty laundry.

- If you've built a "mud room"where wet or muddy clothing and shoes can be removed and stored, you could set it up to store sweaters, jackets, and hats, too. That way you cut down on both dirt and mud being tracked in, and on loose pieces of clothing to keep track of.

- Convert a whole wall to storage. Instead of trying to figure out how to decorate a wall, why not turn it into extra storage? A large convenient storage area is far better than a blank, useless wall.

Wall storage can be as shallow as 12 inches or even less, depending on the room, and can be covered with nice factory-finished wood doors (you can get them at a cabinet shop). This will cost about the same as if you bought a chest or bookshelf to put in front of the wall—but your wall of storage will be built in and provide much more storage space.

- Use more hanging storage. Put hooks in the children's closets, utility room, bathroom, and entryway. Another way to make use of otherwise blank wall space, hooks also are less work than hangers or folding.

- If your home doesn't have storage space as needed throughout the house, you can still enjoy some of the benefits of stashing things where they're used if the storage you do have is in an area that's convenient to all the rooms. A floor plan like the one shown here can stretch your storage space.

Closets

Closets are our prime storage areas—the largest legitimate space we grant to storage in our main living area. Yet because closets have doors (fatal fact!) they're all too likely to become cluttered and crammed archives of junk rather than fully useful live storage.

If it's behind doors, nobody will ever see it, right? But *you* see it every single day—even if only in your mind's eye. You know what's up there and down there and back there. (You can remember at least some of it; some of

it's been there so long you've forgotten.) First, get the closets cleaned out. Then we'll go to work so you'll never have this mess again.

In general, each person should have a closet for clothes and personal effects that is at least 24 inches deep and 48 inches wide, or 8 square feet per person. A family of four needs a minimum of 40 square feet of personal closet space; 60 is even better. And that doesn't take into account family storage for items like linens, towels, etc.

Walk-in closets with no doors are best. They save you the hassle of opening and closing the door every time you want something out of the closet, and keep you from letting junk pile up simply because you can't see it.

Will you have dust in a doorless closet? No. Wire shelving in a closet, as elsewhere, lets the dust fall to the ground. Besides, things that lie on a shelf or sit on a hanger long enough to get dust-covered should be moved to your dead storage for items you seldom use. (See page 159 for a bedroom floor plan that does away with the closet door.)

If you've got to have doors, make sure they extend the full width and height of the closet, so that you don't have any dark corners to lose things in. You want to be able to see everything inside at a glance, so install an inside light and adjustable shelves.

Limit dresser storage. Most people prefer to hang clothes rather than fold them and put them away in a drawer. Hooks are even less work than hangers, and are especially good for the kids. Also, things stay in order better in hanging storage than they do in drawers; you can add or remove clothes from a closet without disturbing everything. When you add to a drawer or look for something in it, you inevitably disrupt the rest.

Instead of putting bits of storage all over the house, centralize it so that it's convenient to all areas. If it's handy, it's more likely to get used.

Checkpoints for Closets

1. Get rid of doors. All they do is take space and time and get in the way. How much of your life has been invested in handling the closet door? (Don't forget the time you spent on sticky or squeaky doors, or doors that went off the track.)

2. Enamel the interiors. Paint the inside of the closet with gloss enamel. Make sure all surfaces are sanded smooth before you paint.

3. Use wire shelving. Cleaning down inside little corners is a waste of good productive time (see page 115).

4. Have a strong closet rod. Use a commercial stainless steel pipe as a closet rod—not wood. Or you can even use a galvanized steel pipe from a plumbing store, but wipe the oil off with paint thinner first.

5. Use some self-stay hangers. These are the kind of hangers that hotels use, where a metal ring is permanently attached to the rod. They keep your hangers from getting dispersed all over the house, eliminating the problem of never having any in your closet when your kids' closets are always bulging.

If you stick with traditional hangers, one type that's useful is the open-ended pants hanger. It's plastic or rubber-coated, so pants don't slip off the hanger onto the floor. These hangers don't require clipping, either—just a quick draping of the pants over the open bar and they stay put. Any garments that can be draped without wrinkling—such as skirts or scarves—can be hung on these hangers.

Suspend the Shoes

Do you have to pick up thirty pair of shoes to clean the closet floor? You can't just skip around them because lint and dust build up in there if you do. Plastic-coated wire racks are ideal for the closet: You can put your shoes on them and then simply remove the rack, shoes and all, to vacuum underneath. Your shoes will be a little easier to reach every morning, too.

Another approach to organizing shoes is a built-in sloping wooden shoe rack with small cleats to hook the heels over. It keeps pairs together, visible, and easy to reach.

Closet Inserts

Are you seeing lots of ads lately that show overstuffed "before" closets turned into tidy, organized "after" closets through the clever use of a shelving system called a closet insert? The ads are telling the truth. **Well-designed closet inserts can double your closet space. This kind of organized storage makes good use of all the available space and gets things off the floor and out of piles.** The closet is light and airy and you can see what you have.

Change your closet from a cramped, disorganized mess to a versatile and convenient storage space. Good quality inserts are easy to assemble and install. These closet organizers come in hundreds of styles and in materials from all-wire shelves to all wood. No one style is best because it depends so much on what you have to store, but wire shelving is almost always better than wood in a clothes closet.

These units force you to maintain order instead of letting the closet get fuller and fuller and more and more disorderly—to the point that you must take everything out and "clean out the closet" (an all-day project). The slots and shelves provide a specific space for everything. Thus when

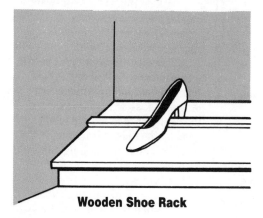

Wooden Shoe Rack

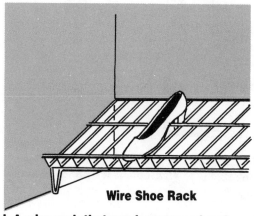

Wire Shoe Rack

A shoe rack keeps your shoes orderly and easy to find. A wire rack that can be removed makes cleaning the closet floor a cinch.

something is put in the closet, it stays where it belongs and doesn't get shoved, tipped over, buried, or crowded by other stuff. Put closet inserts into as many closets as possible. Your closets will stay cleaner and more organized and your time won't be spent re-organizing the same closet day after day.

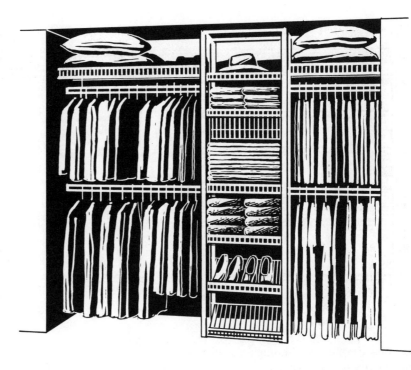

Closet inserts are great because they don't allow messes to build up inside the closet. They can be tailored to meet your needs and can give you more room— you can fit in double rows for items like shirts and skirts, for instance.

Bathroom Storage

Most bathrooms today have no big storage areas. The only place most bathrooms have to store things is a little shallow three-shelved unit behind the mirror.

A full-sized pantry or closet in your bathroom is one of the handiest storage spaces possible. It will let you store all your bathroom necessities— towels, soap, and paper goods as well as cleaning supplies—in one place. You also gain a good enclosed place to install hooks for clothes and wire shelves for all those bottles, cans, brushes, jars, and combs.

The area over the toilet, while not ideal, can be used for storage if space is tight. Make sure it's a suspended unit and be careful to place it so as to avoid bumped heads.

When it comes to shelves in the bathroom, vinyl-clad wire shelves are the best. All the stray little

An entire wall of shelves suspended off the floor provides
plenty of storage that's easy to
clean under. Because everything's visible, shallow shelves
keep items in better order than
deep ones.

bobby pins can fall right through them and you'll never have to clean or dust the shelves again.

Wire shelves keep towels and linens nicely ventilated. Likewise, wire baskets make ideal clothes hampers. Your clothes won't mildew and you'll never have to clean out the bottom of the hamper.

We don't, however, recommend the wire shelves you loop over the shower head to store things in the shower. Exposed to a constant stream of water, soap, and shampoo, they get coated with soap scum and hard-water deposits that are hard to get off. A place for shampoo storage should be built into the shower area.

Storage for All Reasons

Somewhere in your house you need some all-purpose storage for hobbies, filing, small tools, etc. The best idea is to put an entire wall of suspended storage in a utility area, and use it to organize all your ongoing projects.

If this storage is suspended off the floor, you can clean up around it with no problems. These shelves in your general storage area should be labeled with names such as: outdoor things, sewing, canning supplies, out-of-season clothes, hobby scraps, nails, wires, cleaners, painting supplies, kids' crayons/drawing tools, wrapping paper, and games.

You may want to organize the shelves according to who the item belongs to (for example, Dad's tools or Mom's pictures), what its function is, or any other method that makes sense to you. But *do* label the shelves. Otherwise, family members may not know what goes where and may find a *new* place to put it. Any system will work as long as everyone knows what the system is.

The key to this is to have everything *visible*. **Make the shelves no more than 12 to 15 inches deep, so that piles of junk don't accumulate and nothing gets stuffed behind something else.** If you have to look at it every day, you'll keep the shelves from getting too junky.

The Shadow Knows

The visual beckoning of a silhouette can't be beat! On the basement, garage, shop, or even utility room walls, inside your cupboards or out, simply trace the form of the tool in permanent marker to show where it goes. Hanging tools are a lot easier to find than ones that are crammed together, or leaning against a wall, or scattered all over. That kind of storage can damage tempers as well as tools.

For lightweight tools you can use magnetic strips (see your DIY store for information) that can be screwed to the wall. They will hold all your metal tools firmly in plain view; don't try to use these

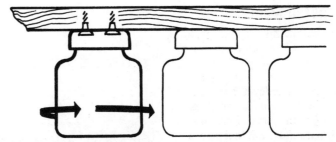

Baby food jars suspended overhead are perfect for storing small items such as nails and screws.

for heavy items like shovels, though.

The rolling steel toolboxes auto mechanics use are also a good idea. The multitude of sliding drawers and trays organizes tools well, and the whole unit can be rolled right to the job site.

For handy storage of screws, bolts, and small parts above your workbench, collect some junior-size baby food jars or something similar and mount them on a board suspended horizontally above the bench. Nail or screw the jar lids to the underside of the board (use two nails so the lid will be firmly anchored and won't turn); then screw the jars into the lids. Clear glass jars allow you to see what's inside and you can reach up with one hand to retrieve what you need.

Hanging tools and other items in the garage or shop keeps them neater.

Project Fold-Outs

Most worthwhile projects make a mess, but while you don't want to look at the mess, you don't want to discourage creativity either. **If the project (quilt, birdhouse, artwork) takes awhile to complete, then design your own built-in, fold-out storage unit—a unit that closes up neatly when not in use, but when opened exposes all your project tools and accessories.** You can buy them ready-made, have them made to order at a custom cabinet shop, or build one yourself. You'll be amazed at how inexpensive high-quality custom-made units are. Easy storage and maintenance of hobbies and projects encourages ambition. If you need ideas, DIY and women's magazines often have plans for fold-up storage units. Find one that suits you and your project.

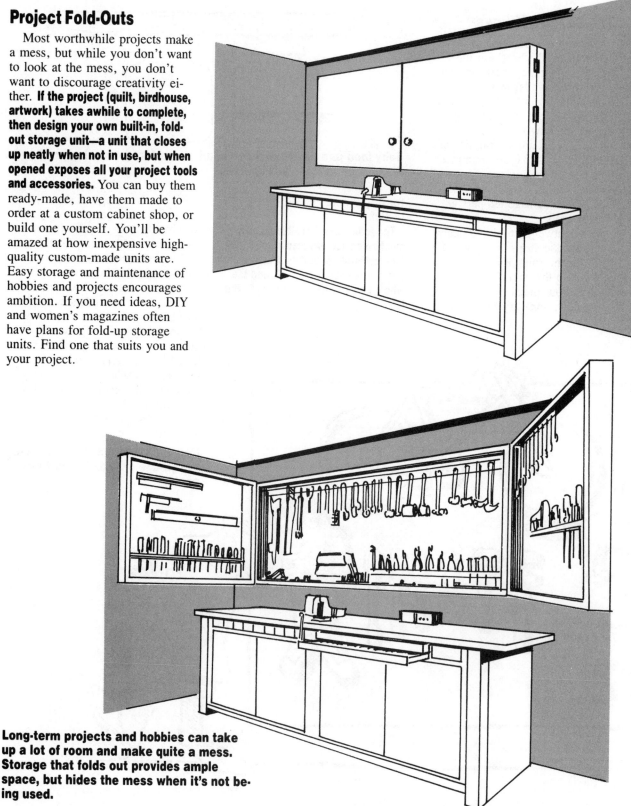

Long-term projects and hobbies can take up a lot of room and make quite a mess. Storage that folds out provides ample space, but hides the mess when it's not being used.

114

Dust-Busting Storage Ideas

You never have to dust or wash another storage shelf. If you use the right kind of shelves they can be almost self-cleaning.

Unless you happen to live on a ship or in an earthquake zone, you don't want lips on the front of your shelves. They only serve to complicate your cleaning. Instead of one easy swipe of the cloth, you have to wipe, then clean out the corners, and then you've got to manage to get all the little particles up and over the lip. A dowel rod installed slightly above the shelf is better because you don't have to get particles over a lip.

Flat wood, particleboard, or aluminum shelves are all right but you still have to wipe them off occasionally.

As in the kitchen and bathrooms, shelves anywhere else in the house will be nearly maintenance-free if you use wire shelving. Dirt and particles just fall right through to the floor where you can sweep them away with other floor dirt.

Wire shelves are great for ventilation, great for being able to see what's up on the shelf. They're light; they can be installed by anyone, anyplace, whether you own your dwelling or are renting; they can be put up and taken down with ease. Things stored for long periods of time on them are less likely to mildew because of the air circulation wire allows. And you can easily add wire shelves until you have an entire closet full.

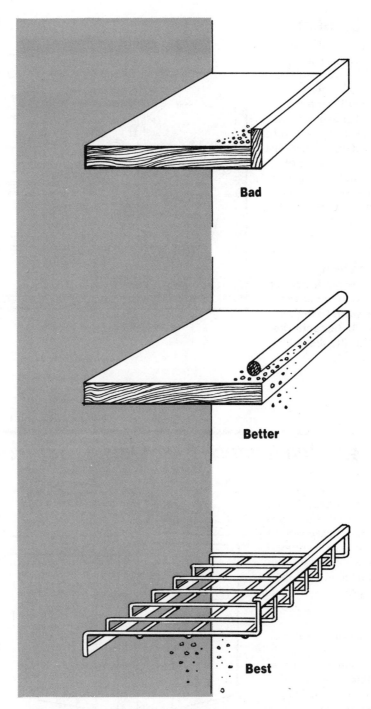

Bad

Better

Best

Wooden shelves with lips are the hardest to clean. A wood shelf with a dowel rod to hold small items on allows you to whisk dirt off with little trouble, but a wire shelf never has to be dusted at all.

Pleasant Under Glass

If you have scores of little knickknacks and displayables and you know you'll never part with them, make or buy a glass-enclosed case that'll protect your treasures from dust and breakage. It will show your things off to full decorative advantage without that weekly picking up, dusting off, and replacing. The case should have sturdy shelves and a built-in fluorescent light so that everyone can see and admire the things inside, but dust can't get in.

Glass-enclosed storage keeps items dust-free while letting you show them off to good advantage. You may want to install fluorescent lights beneath the shelves to make the display even more effective.

Build Some Maintenance-Free Outside Storage

I'm on record as saying that those little backyard storage sheds reduce your home's image and appearance 371 percent. But if you must resort to this, make sure that what you put up back there is maintenance-free—not just a duplication in miniature of all the exterior house problems of treating and painting and caulking and replacing.

Go to your masonry dealer or DIY store and get some plans for outside storage buildings. If you don't see anything you like, design your own. (Just remember that it's a good idea to have a big door and a ground-level entry for ease in storing lawn care equipment.)

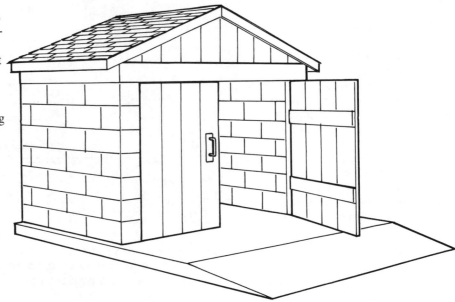

A masonry storage shed with a ground-level entry and extra wide doors is best for outside.

Beware the Junk Bunkers

A word of caution: You don't want to just fill up your home with "junk bunkers"—wicker, wire, plastic, or wood units that help you "organize" unneeded belongings. Junk—no matter how much room you can afford to give it—is the biggest enemy of maintenance-free living. If things really aren't being used, you don't just want to find a (perhaps expensive) way to stack them higher and pack them in tighter.

Junk bunkers come in many different models: desk organizers, shadow boxes, gun racks, pen-pencil holders, trophy cases, entertainment centers, and china cabinets are just a few. There are slick hangers you can buy (or make) to hang up coats you never use (coats that should be given or thrown away), racks for hats you never wear, see-through boxes for sweaters you've outgrown, drawer organizers that take up a good 10 percent of the drawer's total space, and tiny trinket shelves with which you can clutter your walls with utter abandon.

If your floors and furniture are crowded with clutter, there are devices for hanging clutter from the walls or ceiling. Some instant junk bunkers come in kits—just snap them together and presto—a clever rack for the back of the toilet, the top of the TV, or under the sink—you can stash three times the junk.

Junk bunkers are like a shot of morphine: they momentarily ease the pain, but they don't really take care of the problem.

There is no redeeming way to better organize and store clutter! Use these units only if they truly fill a need—only if they truly help you organize and store items more effectively.

Chapter 13

Furniture: Friend or Foe?

In thirty years of professional housecleaning, I've seen home furnishings that were at least as unusual as they were usable—everything from a swing set in the living room to Styrofoam assemble-it-yourself furniture.

In all the progress we've made since the times when furniture was just a fallen tree you sat on, all we've accomplished is that we have basically helped a log evolve into an overpriced torture device. Furniture's first name should be function. Instead, we often base our purchases on words like fine, fancy, facsimile, and first edition. Functional furniture can be beautiful and a joy to use, but little that is fancy is also functional. It sits there forever making you uncomfortable and taking up your care time. That doesn't mean a bean-bag and bear rug are the answers for all settings, but we could apply a little more horse sense when it comes to buying furniture.

Do you know where much of our present-day furniture designs come from? From the European Renaissance era. In those days only the very rich even had furniture and as a way of showing their friends how rich they really were, they had their furniture designed and carved—the fancier the better.

Don't let excess furniture turn your home into an obstacle course.

Of course, their homes were populated with forty maids and servants so it didn't matter if it was hard to clean—there was a footman for every chair. These styles set the standards and few have questioned them since. Some of them *are* very handsome and imposing, but many of them are cleaning nightmares.

Times have changed. Now *you* buy it and *you* clean it.

Get Rid of Excess

Remember how clean your house stayed when you first moved into it—how big and spacious it seemed? Wasn't it a pleasure to clean? What happened? You filled, added, saved, stuffed, and hung things in every room until each had four thousand things to move and manipulate every time you cleaned.

One of the first ways to turn furniture from foe to friend is to get rid of excess. Some of us have our places so jammed with stuff that *moving* through them (never mind cleaning them) is like running an obstacle course. Most Americans have 25 percent more furniture than they need.

One woman had enough extra furniture to furnish a whole housing development—not counting the three extra refrigerators in the basement. Almost anyone who has ever bought a new couch has had trouble throwing out the loyal old sofa it was supposed to replace. You save it, stuffed in a corner of the basement or the spare room, trying to get your money's worth out of it.

One way to cut down the excess is to buy foldable furniture to meet those occasional demands. If you have a small family, you don't need a 15-foot trestle table that could do lunchroom duty. Buy a 6-foot folding table with a laminated top—you see these in schools and churches all the time. You can use it when you have picnics, extra guests for dinner, hobby or sewing projects, etc. When you're through, just fold it up, snap it shut, store it in a closet, and forget it.

The next time you're tempted to rearrange the bedroom so that you can fit in both your mother's antique nightstand and the bedside table that your oldest child built in shop, remember that the average five-person home accumulates forty pounds of dust a year. Every extra piece of furniture is just one more place for it to settle.

Furniture Styles Rated for Maintenance Ease

	Worst	Better	Best
Couch			
Desk			
Table and Chairs			

The Magic of Wall-Hung and Built-In

Are you building, remodeling, buying new furniture? The key words are . . .

Suspend it

Build it in

These two approaches share one advantage—they get rid of all those table and chair legs that not only complicate cleaning, but also *cause* a lot of it. Suspended or wall-hung furniture is attached to the wall for support; built-in is built into your home's structure—perhaps the most common examples are built-in bookshelves. Both styles are great for preventing and streamlining housework.

Get a Leg Up on the Housework

Think of every chair and table as four on the floor—four obstacles to fast, efficient cleaning. Any time you eliminate legs you make cleaning easier. Look at most modern motel rooms. The desks and dressers are all suspended. Motels have realized that cleaning time is money—not to mention that when the furniture gets damaged (more from cleaning than from use), it has to be replaced.

The Shakers, in one era, had handy little stools they used as chairs by their tables. After use the stools were hung up like coats on a rack. We aren't going to ordain you to the ministry of maintenance-freedom by telling you to hang up your chair, couch, or coffee table after use, but we would like you to see the possibilities and rewards of getting things out of the way and off the floor.

While most of us today might not care to copy the sparseness of a Shaker home, we all have a great variety of items that can be built in, recessed, or wall-hung:

End tables

Lamps

Beds

Benches

Tables

Couches

Chairs

Display cabinets

China closets

Desks

Coat racks

Tissue boxes

Bathroom scales

Dispensers of all kinds

Ironing boards

Vanities

Ranges

Ovens

Magazine racks

Stereos

TVs

Suspended furniture can keep the floor from becoming a forest of legs.

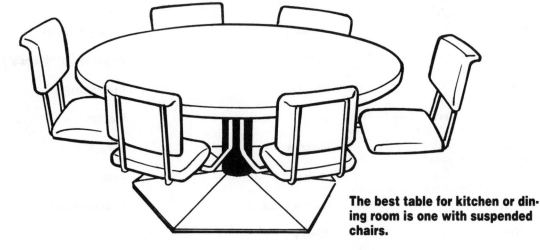

The best table for kitchen or dining room is one with suspended chairs.

Suspend Your Disbelief

There's one single furniture adjustment that will save you more time than any other—suspending your chairs and bar stools.

Suspending will eliminate a lot of surfaces to be cleaned (the legs themselves) and clear out that forest of things on the floor that catch falling dirt and have to be swept around. Suspended chairs can't tip over or fall and get nicked or broken. They can't be used for unsafe and potentially damaging purposes like serving as a stepladder or a doorstop. But best of all, *no one can move them from where they are supposed to be*. That means you don't have to straighten them, you won't trip over them, and they'll always be there when you do want to use them. You won't have to round up the chairs from all over the house at dinner time. The discipline of structure will keep your chairs orderly and looking good longer.

There is one thing to consider before you suspend your chairs, though—namely the problem they pose for handicapped, oversized, or pregnant people. You can solve this problem by leaving the ends of the table open. This leaves two places to seat anyone unable to use the suspended chairs. Or a bench can be put at each end to seat the children. This design gives it more versatility.

Surprisingly, it doesn't cost much more to suspend your chairs from the dining room or kitchen table or to specify suspended counter stools. If you are considering a nice new dining room set, find a kitchen remodeling or cabinet shop that carries suspended tables and chairs.

Seven Reasons to Build It In

1 Built-in furniture needs much less cleaning. A free-standing unit has to be cleaned around, under, and behind—a built-in has only a front to be concerned with.

2 Building in reduces damage to structures and appliances—since they aren't exposed, they aren't as vulnerable to abuse. So they don't require repair, refinishing, or replacement as often.

3 A built-in unit can't be scattered, lost, or disorganized—its orderliness is self-preserving.

4 It's safer—it eliminates tripping on trailing electrical cords, etc.

5 It saves space and makes the room seem less congested.

6 It looks better. The simple, streamlined look is pleasant and neater.

7 You won't need a case or a cabinet for items like the TV or stereo.

Go through your house (or the plans for your new house or dream home) and see how many things you can build in. Maybe first take a drive to a mobile home sales yard and look through their units for built-in brainstorms. Since it's important that everything in a mobile home be firmly attached, mobile-home makers have done a good job of coming up with ideas and designs for building in furniture.

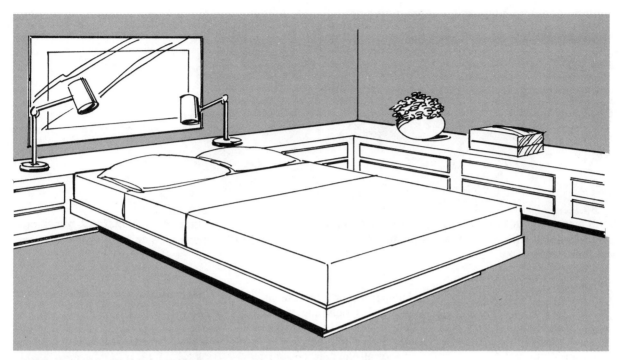

Built-in bedrooms, above, and dining areas, below, are less work than the traditional arrangements.

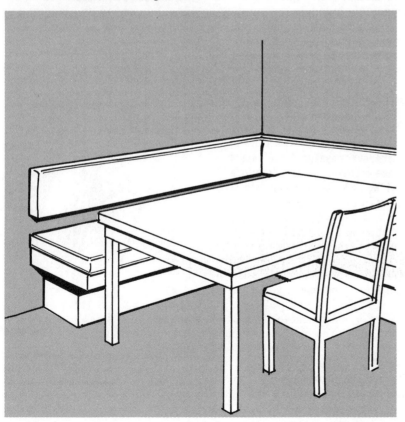

All the Angles on Arranging the Furniture

Of all household chores, vacuuming is probably the one you do most often, with the possible exception of dishwashing. Depending on the use a room gets, you may vacuum every day. But the way you arrange the furniture can make this task nearly impossible.

The first mistake is placing furniture at acute angles to the wall or another piece of furniture. Since most furniture is square, placing it at an angle creates a triangular space between, for example, the sides of the chair and the wall. How does a vacuum fit into a narrow triangle? You don't need the Pythagorean Theorem to tell you it doesn't.

If your furniture is placed at an angle, you have to:

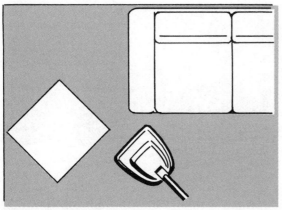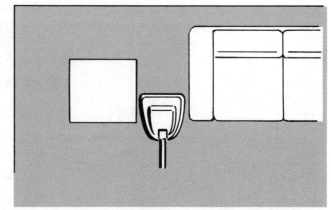

Don't arrange your furniture so that you have to move it every time you vacuum, left. Instead, put things at right angles with enough space for the dust mop or vacuum to fit between, as on the right. The room will look neater, too.

1. Vacuum up to the spot

2. Turn the vacuum off (so it won't run while you're moving the furniture)

3. Move the furniture out of the way (being careful not to nick it or hit the wall)

4. Go back to the vacuum and turn it back on

5. Vacuum the carpet where the furniture was

6. Stop the vacuum again

7. Move the furniture back where it was

8. Go back to the vacuum and turn it back on

9. Continue on

It makes much more sense to arrange the furniture at right angles. Then all you have to do is:

1. Vacuum up to the spot

2. Vacuum the spot

3. Continue on

Another reason furniture should be arranged at right angles is that this creates a crisp, clean line that makes a room look cleaner. Angles of all kinds in a room send your eye up, down, over, under, and around, giving the illusion of clutter.

If your furniture is poorly arranged, you work a lot harder. You're the one who must spend time moving all that furniture. You get tired faster, lose valuable time, and wear the vacuum out faster, turning it on and off more often. Having furniture sitting at angles triples your work.

Whenever possible, leave enough space between pieces of furniture and the walls for the vacuum to reach in. Little corners collect paper wads, popcorn hulls, pins, paperclips, and fuzz balls. If you can get to these corners on your main vacuuming sweep the whole job will be a lot easier. If you can't leave the space, you'll have to move the furniture and use a broom or attachment to clean these areas. You may want to put small pieces of furniture on wheels or casters so you can quickly roll them out of the way to vacuum under and around.

Buy Self-Maintaining Furniture

If a piece of furniture gets messed up whenever someone merely uses it, *it's not self-maintaining*. Someone has to come along and straighten things up. For instance, if every time

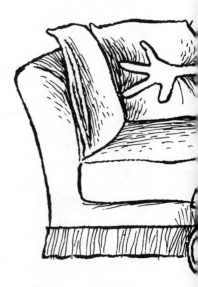

someone sits on the deep velvet chair it leaves a rump print, you'll spend your days brushing out rump prints. In all the furniture you buy, you should look for self-maintaining features that will help you enforce the discipline of structure.

Self-maintenance takes many forms. A picnic table with attached benches is self-maintaining because you don't have to re-arrange the seats; a hanging lamp is self-maintaining because it holds its position.

When it comes to sofas, for example, buy the kind with attached or fitted pillows. Where do you think "throw pillows" got their name? Kids delight in tossing them and love to have pillow fights—we haven't seen too many of them rearranging the furniture when they're finished, either. If you like the "free pillow" look, it would be wise to attach the pillows permanently to the back of the sofa. Otherwise your attempts at keeping the couch in order will be nothing more than a pillow sham.

Make a Material Gain

You're at the furniture store, staring at dozens of couches in every style, color, and price range imaginable. You've got to find one that's just the right shade for your living room, that fits in with your decor, that doesn't cost three months' salary, and that will be delivered before your in-laws come to visit next week. You don't have the time to think about the fabric, right? Wrong! You don't have the time *not* to. You can't spare the time you'll waste if you choose the wrong one—the hours spent smoothing, fluffing, shampooing, mending, and finally replacing a material that just couldn't take it.

Here are some guidelines for finding fabulous fabrics:

- A tight, dense-weave fabric has more threads per square inch and thus is stronger. It will hold up better to pressure—stretching, sitting, and wear.

Heavy threads also endure more abuse, won't break or ravel as easily, and lend a little blemish-hiding texture to the fabric they're woven into.

- A medium, slightly nubby texture is best. A very smooth fabric will show every speck of dust. A very heavy texture will hold hair, lint, etc., and be hard to clean. Fabrics that have a heavy nap will need to be constantly brushed or smoothed to look right. A medium texture can be scrubbed so spots come up without leaving a ring. Little bits of lint, threads, etc., will blend right in. Medium textures will also show wrinkles and creases much less readily than smooth fabrics.

- Treated fabric will resist stains and accidental spills. The newer the fabric, the more likely it is that a stain-resisting treatment such as Scotchgard is on it. The treatment does wear off over time and with cleaning, so upholstery should be re-treated

Don't buy a sofa you'll have to defend.

125

each time it is deep-cleaned. The fabric should also be color-fast to resist fading and color bleeding.

- Color and pattern are important. When you select a color for your upholstery, consider this question: Will lint show? As always, most dark colors (black, navy, royal blue, burgundy) show every piece of lint or strand of hair. Dark colors in general are harder to maintain than lighter ones. Patterns and prints hide a lot of little things that will show up immediately on solid-colored furniture. Prints are much easier to keep clean, and they don't show wear as soon.

Synthetic or synthetic-blend fabrics (nylon, Dacron, rayon, polyester) are far superior to natural. They will resist stains because they don't absorb moisture so readily and they wear much longer. The synthetics are resistant to moisture, mildew, rot, and many solvents, and are extremely strong.

Sofas and carpets will wear much longer if they're synthetic or synthetic blend. Natural fibers are more comfortable against the body—which is why we all favor them for clothing, sheets, pillow cases, etc.—but wherever a synthetic won't detract from your comfort, it will serve much longer and need cleaning less often.

The Lazy Way Out

Don't try to hide stained or worn upholstery under slipcovers. They're always wrinkled or in some state of disarray. Why not just buy furniture covered with an attractive, durable, cleanable fabric, then re-cover it as necessary?

Forget clear plastic covers. If you want plastic furniture, buy it.

Otherwise, save the plastic wrap for leftovers.

"Doilies" should have been named "oilies." (In fact, your grandmother may have called them *antimacassars*, a term coined in the late 1800s because doilies were often used to protect upholstery from the popular Macassar hair oil.) They are slippery son-of-a-guns, and very efficient dirt and dust collectors. "Pretty" is a lot better on a wall than on the back of a chair or under a lamp or vase. Hang your doilies up in a frame if you have to have them.

More Material Matters

Leather, aside from being an American institution, is a very durable and comfortable furniture material—but it must be maintained properly for long life. Clean leather with saddle soap and "feed" it with conditioner occasionally to help it maintain its suppleness.

Vinyl (or Naugahyde), which can be a leather lookalike, is quite durable and very cleanable in the better grades. It costs less than leather, but it doesn't have leather's natural beauty and it doesn't "breathe"—so you perspire and get "sticky" sitting on it.

Wood is another natural material that's hard to knock. Real, furniture-grade hardwood is beautiful and durable. Hard woods like cherry, maple, or oak are best. Avoid soft woods like pine, fir, spruce, and hemlock. If you can dent it with your thumbnail, it's too soft!

Real wood veneer offers much of the beauty and cleaning ease of solid wood and is a bit easier on the wallet. For families with small children or other heavy-use situations, simulated wood plastic laminates also make a lot of sense for tabletops, etc.

Cane or wicker furniture can be

pretty, but it doesn't hold up well to hard use and isn't good for families with children. It has charm and mood, as well as 900,000 surfaces to catch dirt and cobwebs. It's also susceptible to mildew and hard to disinfect. Rattan furniture is quite durable, but the plant-fiber wrapping can't take much wear and tear. Leather wrapping is much more resistant to damage.

How to Make Order out of Bedlam

Beds rate right up there on the list of maintenance-makers because making them is a *daily* task. Minimize the effort and the bed is more likely to get made every day.

First, eliminate some of the layers. A comforter can provide as much warmth as several blankets and can double as a bedspread, leaving you with just the comforter and sheets to straighten and tuck instead of as many as four layers on the average bed.

You should also make sure the bed is the right size. The wider a bed, the harder it is to make, since you can't reach across it easily and must take several extra steps every time you walk around it. The extra sleeping space may be worth that bit of extra work for many, but it's something you should take into consideration when buying a bed. As for height, beds that are about five inches above the knee are easiest on your back when you're bending over them.

Water beds, those symbols of the '60s that have become almost as common as VCRs, can be maintenance-savers. They can be a hassle to move, but my wife and I find ours takes less than half as long to make each morning—all you do is tuck the covers in around the edge (and most use standard size sheets now). The few minor problems we have had with leakage have been easily remedied—just be sure to use a waterproof liner to contain leaks—and the comfort is unbeatable. The tendency of water beds to have built-in drawers underneath is a good concept to adapt to conventional beds, too.

Side Tables

You probably think you couldn't live without those his-and-her bedside tables that are piled to the ceiling with half-read books, tissue boxes, the alarm clock, and your reading glasses, but think again. Build in a headboard with room enough for the few items you really need by the bed or try a suspended table that swivels over the bed and get rid of those quaint antique dust-catchers that the dog knocks over every time he tries to get in bed with you.

Headboards

Headboards often add an awkward set of little chores to bedroom cleaning. They need to be dusted and/or polished themselves, and they're hard to clean, dust, or vacuum behind and under. Stuff falls behind and under them and it's hard to retrieve it. A wall-mounted headboard solves this problem. It fits tight to the wall, so nothing can fall behind it. The bed slides out easily for periodic cleaning. Or you can make part of the wall serve as the headboard. You do this by applying a different color wallcovering, paint, or laminate to the wall right over the bed, in the shape of a headboard or even all the way up to the ceiling for dramatic effect. Motels often do this; it eliminates a piece of furniture to tend and gives the room a decorator touch.

The Good, the Bad, and the Unneeded

Now that you've learned that furniture can be either ally or enemy, use this checklist to figure out if you're winning the war for maintenance freedom.

Features of high-maintenance furniture:

Carvings or engravings

Fretwork

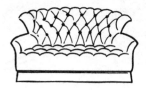

Tufting

Elaborate hardware

Exposed legs

Loose pillows

Solid colors

Extremely light or dark colors

Extremely heavy textures

Wicker and cane

Cross bars on lower legs

Cotton or natural fibers

Features of low-maintenance furniture:

Printed or patterned material

Subtle textures

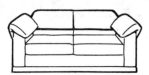

Attached cushions

Medium tone hardwood

Straight legs

Rounded edges

Antique or distressed finish for wood or metal

Beveled edges

Glass or Formica table tops

Simple, clean lines

Synthetic fabric

Flush to the floor

Chapter 14

Let There Be Low-Maintenance Light

Even though light itself is one of the cleanest, brightest aspects of the home, the fixtures that provide that light are among the highest maintenance items. Because of the heat they generate and the static they create, hair, lint, dust, oily fumes, and insects are attracted to them. And the fact that we have these dust and dirt magnets in every room makes their upkeep that much harder. To make matters worse, there are thousands of forms and designs of light fixtures to choose from.

In the Beginning

We humans have managed through the ages to take the simplicity out of everything. We've complicated eating, bathing, clothes, sex, and even dying. But our most dastardly deed is what we did to light. We so reverently believed it when God said, "Let there be light" that we misinterpreted it and ended up with "Let there be light fixtures."

Decorating our homes with light is a great idea, but that doesn't mean *light fixtures*. After thirty years of cleaning people's homes and offices I have one question: Where on earth did they get some of those abominable creations called lamps? I've seen lights sticking out of stuffed quails, Old Crow bottles, miniature trains, basketballs, wagon wheels, and mannequin bosoms, all, to say the least, impractical and extremely difficult to clean. Those with gargoyle bases, ornate stems, and unidentifiable shades are sources of confusion and worry from the day of purchase.

Don't get hung up on light fixtures. Bear in mind that when you're buying fixtures you're buying *light*—not furniture, not art objects, not collectibles, not memorabilia, not status symbols. If you want to decorate,

do it with your wallcoverings and drapes. Make sure your light sources are as inconspicuous and self-maintaining as possible.

Chandeliers, for example, look great in castles and light-fixture stores, but after thirty years of cleaning them in homes and hotel lobbies, the only thrill they give me now is watching Errol Flynn swing on them in old pirate movies. Anyone who has spent six hours disassembling a crystal chandelier, individually cleaning each prism, then putting the whole thing back together will have to agree.

You can't hang chandeliers high enough in a house with standard

8-foot ceilings—you need 10-foot ceilings at least, or better yet, 14 foot. Ninety-eight percent of the attention they get in the average low-ceilinged home is when you either bump your head or try to clean dust and grease off them.

And since a chandelier is usually the focal point of a room, everyone who comes in will know whether or not you've cleaned it in the last month. (They're so hard to clean you usually get around to it only when you notice the lights dimming.)

Some light isn't worth the maintenance, or the risks it requires.

129

Blinded by the Light

Some of the most common forms of light fixtures are also some of the worst maintenance-makers, but because everybody else has them we don't realize that they're a mistake. Among these are table lamps, floor lamps, flat bowl ceiling lights, and some types of wall-hung lights. So before you consider what to look for in lighting, here's what to look *out* for.

Table Lamps

Most table lamps don't have enough wattage or are so poorly designed that you have to install additional fixtures in order to see. In some homes you have to turn on five different lamps to be able to halfway see what you're doing. One genuine *light* should be all you need to do the job. Ever notice how many lamps you find at garage sales—cheap, too? It's easy to understand why:

1. Many are made of odd materials or in complex designs that are hard to dust or clean.

2. Their shades get dirty and stained (and most are uncleanable, which is why we always leave them in the cellophane wrapper—*ugly*).

3. Many have to be moved before you can clean them or clean around them.

4. Many are top-heavy or awkward, so they're easily knocked over.

5. Their cords create an unsightly, dangerous snarl.

Most ceiling lights are great dirt-catchers. The bowl light on the left is a nightmare to keep clean; an enclosed light with a smooth surface, such as the one on the right, is much better.

Ceiling Lights

Don't install or keep those old flat-bowl lights set in the center of the ceiling. They collect grease and bugs and present the perfect challenge for a spitball contest. And their hot bulbs can scorch the Sheetrock on your ceiling.

An enclosed ceiling light attracts less floating dust, although some bugs can still get in because they live in the ceiling insulation and crawl down. Enclosed lights will at least keep the majority of them out. A globe with smooth simple surface helps, too.

Floor Lamps

Floor lamps, in or out of style, are dangerous and hard to clean around. Floor lamps are top-heavy, the bottom is always dusty, their trailing cords obstruct the vacuum and trip exploring children. They use up valuable space, and their shades are always getting mangled because the lamps topple over so easily.

Wall-Mounted Lights

When I first experimented with maintenance-free lighting, I figured wall-hung lights would be a good idea. I installed four twin-bulb beauties and they looked great—the only trouble was we couldn't see. Most of the light was directed at the walls. The solution? Either a miner's hat or more fixtures. I kept adding more

and when our light-fixture count reached sixty-nine, our electricity bill was beyond belief. And guess what, we still couldn't see.

Wall-mounted lamps don't need much cleaning or maintenance but always seem to provide 20 percent less light than overhead ceiling units. Most of them are a lot more decorative than functional. Wall-mounted lights are better than table lamps, and they can work well for closeup task light next to beds or over desks, but they won't suffice for general lighting purposes.

Light Diffusers

Light diffusers or lenses—the part of the fixture that softens the light and keeps you from squinting at a bare bulb—can work for or against you, depending on their shape. To help solve the dust-and-bug problem, here are a few examples of shapes that allow bugs and settling dust to fall out easily. They'll fall on the floor and you'll simply clean them up in the course of your routine vacuuming or dust mopping.

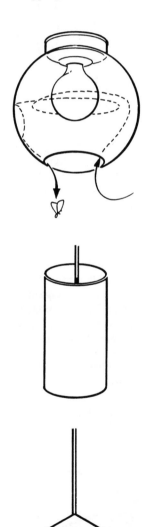

Lampshades

Shades can also help or hinder your efforts to achieve low-maintenance lighting—it all depends on how they're made and what they're made of.

Helps

Smooth surface

Glass or plastic

Earthtone colors

Milk glass

Hindrances

Etched or embossed surface

Cloth or pleated

Dark colors or white

Prism glass

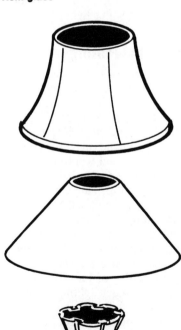

The Right Lights

Now that you've seen the light about overdone and overrated fixtures, you're probably wondering what kind of lights *are* good for your home. Hanging, fluorescent, and recessed or built-in fixtures provide good lighting and need little maintenance.

Hanging Lamps

Instead of a table lamp sitting on an end table near your sofa, install a hanging light. It's better because:

1. It never has to be moved to clean around.

2. It's easier to turn off and on.

3. You don't have to worry about knocking it over or bumping it off the table, breaking the lamp or the bulb or causing a fire.

4. It's easier to replace a bulb in a hanging light than in a table lamp with a shade, and because a bulb filament is designed to hang down, bulbs will last longer.

Cloth, creased, or extra wide shades will get dirty faster and are harder to clean than smooth glass or plastic ones.

131

Wrong   **Right**

Fluorescent Lights

Fluorescent lighting offers many benefits that have little to do with upkeep: it's more energy-efficient than incandescent light and provides a fuller spectrum of light (including infrared rays), so it's better for houseplants.

But fluorescent lights have a lot of maintenance bonuses, too. Fluorescent tubes last a good bit longer than incandescent bulbs, so you don't have to change them as often. They don't get as hot, either, so they attract less dust and grease. Plus, most fluorescent units are designed so that the dust and bugs can't get up inside them.

Four-foot fluorescents are by far the best; longer ones shatter too easily and longer or shorter ones are hard to find as well as much more expensive.

When using fluorescent lighting in the bathroom, where fully natural coloring is important for applying makeup, etc., ask for a "natural color" tube. These are more expensive but they'll assure that you appear in the mirror in "liv-ing color." You can also buy tubes specifically designed for makeup mirrors, which give off a somewhat softer light. Ask at your lighting store.

Built-In Lighting

Built-in lighting— ceilings of light, recessed lights, and boxed fluorescents—is the most maintenance-free form of light and should be the only thing you consider for kitchens, family rooms, playrooms, and workrooms.

Look down your hall—is it kind of dark and dismal? Check out your kitchen and bathroom—do the ceilings and light fixtures both look dingy and dirty? Make a ceiling of light instead of Sheetrock or cottage cheese texture. Build an entire ceiling of Plexiglas and then put fluorescent lighting behind it. The room will be lighter, safer, easier to maintain. You'll also cut down on the number of small lighting sources you'll need.

A ceiling of light requires no painting, yet looks crisp and sharp. And if it needs cleaning, a quick swipe of a squeegee on an extension pole is all it needs.

Don't buy frosted glass for a ceiling of light. Ask for "translucent Plexiglas" at a lighting or glass store and they will cut it to fit your specifications. A good Plexiglas light lens is smooth on both sides so it will always present a smooth surface you can wipe off easily.

Concealed fluorescent lights are also hard to beat. They use indirect light (hidden fluorescents behind the object or area you want to light) and won't go out of style or clash with any decor.

Yet another type of lighting that is easy to clean is the "eyeball" or recessed type. Recessed lights come in a number of shapes, sizes, and styles. And the light can be directed anywhere in the room.

A single overhead fixture lights only a small area just beneath it—the rest of the room is dim and has to be lit with lamps. A ceiling with fluorescent lights beneath Plexiglas panels not only provides an easy-to-clean surface, but also lights the entire room well and eliminates the need for all those lamps.

Track lighting is similar to the "eyeball" lights in concept, but the exposed fixtures hang down from the ceiling and collect dust, so they're higher maintenance.

Task Lighting

Why light up the whole bedroom when a little reading light will do? Put a good, strong light where you need it—over the desk, kitchen counter, or sewing station—then you won't have to light up the neighborhood to knead a loaf of bread or sew on a button.

While fluorescent lighting is excellent for entire rooms, incandescent lights are perhaps better for task lighting.

Task Lighting

It's Just a Bulb

Be careful about acquiring a lot of lamps and fixtures with non-standard bases (the part the bulb fits into). If you have one light fixture that takes standard Edison-base bulbs, another with a candelabra base, one where only special long, skinny tubes will fit, none of your bulbs will be interchangeable. You'll end up having to buy and keep on hand five or six different kinds of bulbs where only two or three should suffice. Here again, the principle of keeping things compatible comes into play.

The Touch Test

You love those intricate designs and etchings and textures in light-fixture glass? They're pretty, but run your hand over the design. Is it rough or smooth? The rough ones will catch dust and grease and you'll be scrubbing that fixture with a toothbrush to keep it from looking gray all the time (but the dirt will still be down in the pores of the design).

Make sure light fixture surfaces are smooth to the touch, so dirt won't cling. When shopping for light fixtures, bring along a cleaning cloth and do a mock cleaning job on the display light to see how it will actually be to maintain. Feel the surface—make sure it's smooth!

The touch test will help convince you that light fixtures are a good place to be conservative. Light fixtures are one of the most dirt-catching parts of a house and because they *do* light up, they're noticed by all. Take the time to choose the right designs and save yourself hours of cleaning and worry.

Daylight is Free

Costing nothing and taking no time to clean, daylight can cut down your need for artificial light, and thus on your lighting maintenance chores. Here are some things you can do to extend the natural lighting in your home.

1 Incorporate mirrors and other reflective surfaces into your decorating to bounce light off one surface to another.

2 When painting, use light colors and reflective, semi-gloss enamel paints on the walls to make the most of the light you get.

3 Whenever possible, extend windows all the way up to the ceiling.

4 Install skylights when possible. Properly mounted skylights are very low maintenance. I've had mine for thirty years; I've never had to wash the outside and the inside needs to be cleaned only once in a while.

Lighting Rated for Maintenance Ease

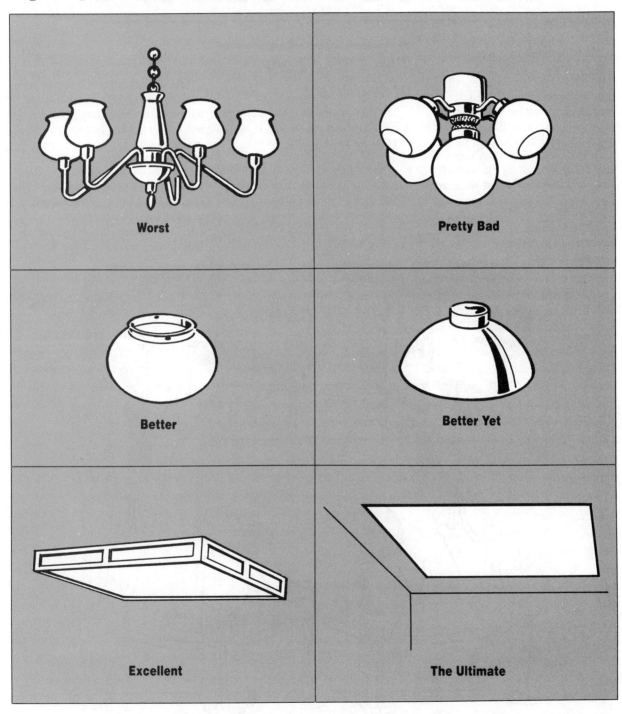

Worst

Pretty Bad

Better

Better Yet

Excellent

The Ultimate

Chapter 15

Floors to Adore

It's hard to think of a question I've been asked more than "Which is the best—carpet, tile, or a hardwood floor?" People seem bewildered by the questions of what flooring to use, where to use what, and how to care for a floor once it's down. But you can stop being floored by floors—all you need to know is that there are three basic types of flooring and the benefits of each. After that you'll be well on your way to floors you can adore.

The Three Types of Flooring

The first distinction you need to draw is whether a flooring is hard or soft. Soft flooring is carpet, rugs, and AstroTurf—everything else, including tile, wood, and vinyl, is considered hard flooring. While these two groupings may sound rather broad, they are important. When you think of some flooring as soft, it'll become clear that you want it in areas where cushioning falls or muffling sound is important—on stairs and in bedrooms, for instance. You'll want hard floors where they'll get hard use—the kitchen, bathroom, and utility room.

Once you've got a handle on the two main groupings, you can break hard flooring down into two smaller categories: resilient and nonresilient. Nonresilient flooring such as ceramic tile or concrete is harder than resilient, such as vinyl.

KITCHANUS
SHEET VINYL
FLOORICUS

Soft flooring is the most popular flooring in homes today, and for good reason:

- It's warm, appealing, and available in a rainbow of colors.

- The everyday "mess" on a carpet can be quickly cleaned up with a vacuum and most of today's carpets can be easily shampooed when necessary.

- Carpet has an insulating effect which can reduce heating and air conditioning costs.

- It's also safe, because it helps prevent slips and cushions falls.

- It absorbs noise, making the room more quiet and restful.

- Carpeting is almost like part of the furniture—you can sit or even lie on it comfortably. In high-abuse areas, however, carpet's advantages fade. In the face of frequent spills, hard wear, strong sun, or a blizzard of animal hair, carpet is a miserable failure as a flooring. **Never carpet any room where you have a high volume of use or activity, or a lot of standing or eating.** If you do, figure on replacing it before long. If a peanut butter sandwich falls to the floor, it takes thirty seconds to clean it off a hard surface and ten minutes to scrub it out of a carpet—and you can never quite get it all out.

Odors linger in soft flooring—as do spills, which are easily removed from a hard-surface floor. Carpet also will show "cow trails" in concentrated high-use areas, so in hallways and entrances (and even beneath mats) a hard surface is better. In areas of strong sunlight, hard flooring resists fading better.

Carpet or Hard Floor?

Here's a guide to help you make a good decision.

Definitely Hard Floor

garage

patio

utility room

entryways

storage areas

kitchen

bathroom

porch

All of these areas will be heavily used, abused, flooded, spilled on, lingered on, played on, stomped on, sprayed on, leaked on, exposed to extremes of weather. A hard surface will endure all this and can be cleaned up quickly.

Could Go Either Way

dining room

recreation room

child's room

sewing room

halls

This is the zone of uncertainty and personal preference—your location (rural or urban area), traffic and use patterns, lifestyle, and budget can be the final deciding factors here. The extra elegance of a carpeted formal dining room may be worth extra cleanup to you. And

the consequences of either choice here won't be too drastic.

Unconditionally Carpet

living room

bedrooms

bedroom halls

stairs

den or study

nursery

family room

In these areas carpet is usually the most comfortable, as well as the easiest to clean. These are areas where looks, comfort, safety, and sound absorption are important. And stairs—even to and from the attic and basement—are best carpeted to keep dirt and abuse down, unless they happen to be directly adjacent to and from the outdoors or in an extreme dirt-tracking area such as a beachhouse or farmhouse.

A Compromise?

Whatever you do, don't "compromise" by using both soft and hard flooring. Mixing the two will double your work when it comes to care and cleaning.

Consider wall-to-wall carpet vs. the area rug. Wall-to-wall carpet you only have to vacuum; with an area rug, you can have three different surfaces to contend with—rug, fringe, and hardwood floor. More time and equipment are needed to maintain it, not to mention that the wall-to-wall carpet simply *looks* less cluttered.

Flooring Rated from Best to Worst
Nonresilient Hard Flooring

1. *Ceramic tile*—If you want a long-wearing, low-maintenance floor with a strong glossy finish, the best thing to use is

Ceramic Tile

glazed ceramic tile. Ceramic tile wears forever and if you are careful to choose large tiles and medium-tone grout, it'll be very low-maintenance. About all you'll have to worry about is a piece cracking, and tiles can be replaced.

2. *Concrete*—There's no better choice for shop and garage floors or patios. A smooth strong surface with no joints or grout lines to worry about, concrete is easy to sweep and mop as long as it's been sealed.

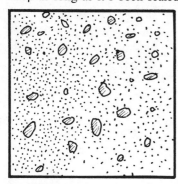

Concrete

All *interior* concrete floor surfaces should be sealed. (See page 83.)

3. *Terrazzo*—A hard, beautiful floor made with chips of stone imbedded in a colored concrete-like matrix, terrazzo is

Terrazzo

used for many commercial floors that get hard wear. It's a good hard-surface flooring for durability, maintainability, and beauty. It's expensive, but lasts forever. In some places it may be hard to find a contractor to install terrazzo in a home.

4. *Quarry tile*—Quarry tile is a porous earth tile which needs to be sealed after installation (until it's sealed, it's not a maintenance-free flooring). Be-

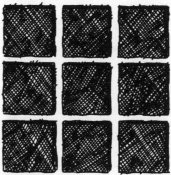

Quarry Tile

cause it's so rugged looking, most dirt doesn't show—for this reason it's good for kitchens and patios. Quarry tile

comes in a variety of colors and patterns—do you want a slick Hollywood shine or a matte-finish, earthy look? You can have either, depending on how you finish the tile. Used extensively in restaurant kitchens, quarry tile can be cleaned with aggressive chemicals without harm, and will last at least thirty to forty years.

5. *Natural stone floors*—The quarried stones commonly used for flooring listed from hardest to softest are: granite, slate, marble, onyx, and flagstone (sandstone). The harder ones,

Natural Stone

like granite and slate, are exceptionally long-wearing, while the softer stones will wear noticeably if not protected with a sealer and finish (wax). All require a finish to achieve a smooth, glossy surface.

6. *Brick floors*—Bricks are okay for patios, but we wouldn't rec-

Brick

ommend them for a kitchen, no matter how pretty they look in that home-decorating magazine photo. Because a brick floor is porous and has a rough surface, it is too hard to clean for a high-use area like a kitchen or entry. A better choice would be sheet vinyl in a simulated (but not textured!) brick pattern.

Resilient Hard Flooring

Resilient hard flooring, such as vinyl, offers a vast array of colors and patterns to decorate with. Resilient is a little easier on the feet than concrete or earth tile (especially when laid over a wood subfloor), and a dropped teacup has a fighting chance on it. Avoid the foam-backed "cushioned" vinyl for most home flooring, though—it's too easily torn when sliding heavy appliances in and out, and can be punctured by sharp objects.

1. Sheet vinyl—Is an excellent covering for wood or concrete floors. No-wax vinyl is a good floor, but despite its misleading

Sheet Vinyl

name, it does need to be waxed like any other floor. Over time, sand and grit tracked in and ground into a floor will abrade and dull *any* floor surface not protected by a floor finish. The clear-gloss top layer of no-wax flooring is thicker, and will wear longer than the top gloss of ordinary vinyl, but it's just a matter of time.

2. Vinyl tile—Good over wood or concrete floors and easy for do-it-yourselfers to install. A vinyl

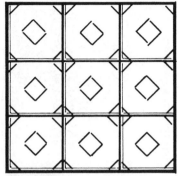

Vinyl Tile

tile floor is slightly harder to keep clean than a sheet vinyl floor because of the many little seams or joints. For the same reason, tile is more susceptible to water damage. It's easy, though, to remove and replace a damaged tile or two.

In vinyl tile or sheet vinyl, avoid deep "dimpled" and embossed designs. The "pits" is a good way to describe these styles. Wax and dirt build up in the indented areas, and no amount of scrubbing will get them out. Make sure the vinyl flooring you choose is smooth.

Quality counts here—buy the best and keep it waxed and you'll get your money's worth.

3. Hardwood floors—Can be very attractive and durable, but require careful selection of wood,

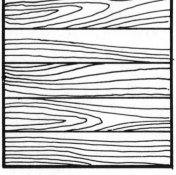

Hardwood

and may not be the best choice for a very high-traffic home. Select good hardwoods—oak, maple, etc. Avoid fir, pine, and other soft woods, which won't wear as well. Finish with a hard, membrane-type finish (like urethane) that will seal and protect the floor. Avoid penetrating-type finishes such as tung oil, danish oil, and paste wax. They don't protect as well, and require constant maintenance.

Keep floors clean—grit, sand, and gravel are very abrasive underfoot, and will do tremendous damage if not controlled. And be careful with water. Damp-mopping is okay, but flooding a wood floor can ruin it.

Parquet is pretty, but all those butt joints invite moisture damage and curling. Regular tongue-and-groove flooring is more practical.

4. Cork—Is a highly resilient floor, and can be beautiful, but it requires quite a bit more maintenance than other resilient floors and is more easily damaged. Not practical for high-use homes.

Cork

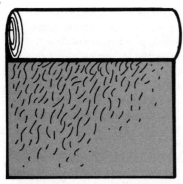

Linoleum

5. _Linoleum_—An old-style sheet flooring composed of cork, wood, and mineral chips bound together by hardened linseed oil, on a canvas backing. The forerunner of modern sheet flooring, linoleum is brittle and much more susceptible to chemical damage than today's vinyl.

Soft Flooring

1. _AstroTurf_—A polypropylene carpeting made to resemble grass, with a rubber or vinyl back. You should have mats of this material outside your en-

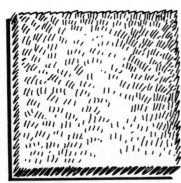

AstroTurf

tryways (see pages 77 and 103); it's also excellent for patios and exterior surfaces such as by the pool. It doesn't hold its new appearance long, but it's durable and sin-hiding.

2. _Commercial carpeting_—Dense, low-profile loop or cut-pile carpet used in many commercial

Commercial Carpeting

buildings. Not elegant and cozy, but it's hard to beat for all-around use and ease of maintenance. It's made of nylon, the best fiber for stain resistance and ease of cleaning in any type of carpeting.

3. _Shag_—Sculptured shag (multi-level pile) in a "tweed" or multi-hued earth tone is the

Shag

most effective dirt hider in the world and doesn't show traffic wear. Long-loop and level-cut shags are not low-maintenance.

4. _"Plush"_—Or level-cut pile carpeting looks elegant but especially in extremely light or dark

solid colors tends to show traffic wear and stains more than a multilevel shag.

5. _Area rugs_—Orientals are decorative, but high-maintenance

Area Rugs

and expensive to clean. Other types of area rugs are less trouble than oriental, but you still have the problem of two types of floor surface to care for in one room.

6. _Indoor/Outdoor Carpet_—On its way out. Shows—and holds—the tiniest speck of dirt or lint—by no means a maintenance plus.

Indoor/Outdoor Carpet

What Color Floor?

While you may have a favorite color in mind, give some thought as to how well that color will perform with your lifestyle. For our maintenance-free house in Hawaii, we took one look at the wonderful red dirt (and the potential stream of visiting grandkids) and decided the floors might as well be the same color as the dirt, because they'd get to be that color anyway, before long.

If you live in a thirty-story high-rise in the middle of the city and have to walk over miles of hall carpeting before you enter your abode, you might get away with a carpet of any color because you'll probably track most of the dirt off by the time you get home. But in a suburban house—and *especially* in a rural area, be sure to get a color that camouflages. It will take a lot of cleaning pressure off you.

The floor is one of those places in the house that *is* going to get dirty fast, so if you can hide the dirt, so much the better—you don't want to be dragging out the broom or vacuum twice a day! This means that when it comes to color, you don't want a floor that's very light or very dark.

A white floor will never look clean except for five minutes after it's mopped, before anyone walks on it. A very dark floor, on the other hand, is just like dark furniture and countertops—a few scraps of paper or dropped crumbs and the whole floor looks sloppy.

Carpet

The same goes for carpeting. A solid dark-colored carpet will show every speck of lint and you'll have to vacuum it constantly to keep it looking nice. A light-colored carpet will soil fast and you'll have worn patches where the carpet gets the heaviest use. Midtones are best for flooring of any kind.

Tweeds and pebbled textures help hide dirt, too. Patterns and designs disguise spots and stains best—use these carpets where frequent spills are likely to occur.

"Tone on tone" carpeting is good for hiding stains and traffic patterns. It looks like a solid color but there are ever-so-slight variations in shade that hide dirt and small dropped objects. It camouflages like a patterned carpet but it can be used with (low-maintenance) patterned fabric furniture, whereas patterned carpet generally can't.

Other carpet considerations:

- Resistance to abrasive wear

- Resistance to crushing and matting of the tufts or fibers

- Resistance to stains

- Moisture absorption

- Resistance to fading from sunlight

- Ease of cleaning

- Sound and impact absorption

- Flammability

- Appearance

Nylon carpeting is the most resistant to abrasive wear. It's also the easiest to clean and resists stains well—it's overall the best choice for homes. One of the better types of nylon carpet fiber is Antron.

Other synthetics (polypropylene, acrylics, polyesters) are not as good as nylon for general home use.

Wool has a luxurious appearance; good quality wool carpeting is also durable, resilient, and responds well to cleaning. But wool absorbs moisture more readily than synthetics, and so requires extra care in cleaning. It's more prone to damage by ammonia, bleach, strong detergents, and alkalies.

Cotton, because it stains easily and is difficult to clean, is not recommended for general home use.

The Look and Feel of Carpet

Now that we've considered the fibers a carpet is made from, let's take a look at its surface texture or pile. The simplest way to compare piles is to look at them in profile, as shown on page 142.

Level-Loop Pile

This is the most common pile. Its looped tufts—all the same height—make it very durable, but its flat, solid surface makes dirt and imperfections all the more noticeable.

Multilevel Loop Pile

Constructed the same way as level-loop pile, except that the pile height varies, providing a more interesting texture. The slightly staggered fibers don't show the use (or the footprints) like the level-loop pile does. Carpets of multilevel loop pile are frequently referred to as sculptured carpet.

Cut Pile

This is looped pile that has been cut on the tufting machine, leaving separate strands in place of loops. This technique provides a very attractive appearance when new, but cut pile is prone to flattening, matting, and fuzzing over time.

Level Loop

Multi-Level Loop

Shag

A carpet's pile or texture can make a big difference in how durable and cleanable it is. Tight, dense weaves wear the best.

Shag Carpeting

This carpeting has longer tufts and can be level-loop or multi-level. All shags are slightly more difficult to vacuum and shampoo than shorter-tufted carpeting, but they hide dirt and traffic patterns well.

Carpet tufts work better in a crowd. How closely together yarn tufts are placed is called density. Carpet density is expressed in terms of tufts per square inch—the denser, the more durable.

Tight weaves with densely packed tufts wear longest, and tend to keep soil on top where it's easily removed. Most commercial carpeting is like this.

Carpet Tiles

Some of the best commercial carpet can now be purchased in squares, like tile. Carpet tiles do have some advantages.

- Worn tiles from high-traffic areas can be rotated, swapped with good tiles from low-use areas, to keep the whole carpet more presentable.

- Damaged, stained, or hopelessly worn tiles can be replaced in minutes.

- You can easily install and change carpet tiles yourself.

I've maintained lots of high-use areas with carpet tile. Two companies, Interface and Miliken, have developed some good products. Interface has a tile for entrances that absorbs up to ten pounds of soil and seven quarts of fluid per square yard. It's used in many commercial buildings and it looks good. There's no reason carpet tile won't work as well in homes.

The disadvantages of carpet tile are:

- It's expensive

- The seams may show in lower-quality or improperly installed tile

- The corners of the tiles may curl up occasionally, or pull up or get torn up when moving heavy furniture around.

Soil Retardants

Treated carpeting repels soil and stains, so it can go much longer between cleanings. Almost all new carpeting has a soil retardant applied at the mill—that's why new carpet stays looking good so long. **We highly recommend that you treat your carpet with soil retardant after cleaning; it will repel wet spills and keep them from penetrating the outside of the fabric until they're cleaned up.** The best products have a fluorochemical base; silicone-based products don't resist oil stains well. Scotchgard or 3M brand carpet protector is good, as are other fluorochemical-based products. (Note: The aerosol can of Scotchgard you buy at the supermarket isn't a carpet protector—it's for upholstery and fabric. Buy *carpet* Scotchgard at a janitorial supply store.)

Where the Floor Meets the Wall

If you want to invent something that everyone wants, make a better baseboard. Vinyl baseboards come unglued and usually don't fit well around corners; wood baseboards get scratched, nicked, and gouged. And both wood and vinyl baseboards are hard to clean. A good-looking baseboard really complements attractive walls and floors, but a shabby-looking base can sabotage an otherwise neat room.

Since baseboards are just one more surface to collect dust (and damage), in our Hawaii house we're eliminating them entirely in the living room, hall, kitchen, bathroom, and utility area. We coved *all* the flooring in every room! Coving is simply installing the flooring so that it curves up the wall to cover the area where the baseboard is usually placed. **A coved baseboard can be easily cleaned with a dust mop, and it eliminates an extra surface to clean, as well as cracks and corners that collect grime.**

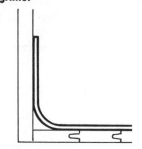

Coved Flooring

The second-best baseboard is factory-finished plastic-impregnated wood. A light-colored hardwood, stained and with a urethane finish, holds up pretty well. Painted softwood trim soon looks tacky and is a constant maintenance problem.

The third-best is a vinyl baseboard. It's fairly low maintenance, but has a tendency to come loose unless expertly installed.

Eliminate Floor Vents

They get stomped on and bent, Cheerios and popcorn kernels get stuck in them, and the air current blows up the wall, leaving a dark "fan" of blown-on soil. If you're planning a new home put vents in the wall instead, off the floor.

Floor Drains

One of the first things I hear when I mention a low-maintenance house is "Yeah . . . boy, I'd put a massive floor drain in the center of the house, and at the end of the day I'd turn on my high-pressure hose and blast all my troubles down the drain."

Our homes are not laboratories and dirt on hard floors is not our most critical maintenance problem, but floor drains do have their place in utility rooms, basements, or anywhere there's heavy water use and runoff. In fact, some building codes now require floor drains near the water heater, washer, etc.

A drain handles overflows so you won't end up with buckled floors, loose joints and tiles, and a rotting subfloor. But in garages, for example, simply sloping the floor slightly toward the door beats the engineering problems

and cost of installing a center floor drain.

Sweeping Grate

Here's another idea that'll make floor care easier. If your house is more than one story, you can install a sweeping grate in the upper floor so you can sweep dirt directly down to a trash bin below. Any room or garage or entry you must sweep often can use one—kitchens built above the basement are a likely place. Grates do save time in sweeping the floor because you don't have to use a dustpan and the grate is right there. Commercial buildings often use these for quick floor cleanup. Depending on your floor plan and your needs, one can be designed to fit what you use it for. If it might work for you, get a bid from your contractor and decide if the time saving is worth the cost.

Chapter 16

Where There's a Wall, There's a Way

(to Make It Easier to Clean)

Too long ago to remember, walls and ceilings served the simple purpose of sheltering us from the elements and no one worried much about cleaning them. From the Stone Age until now, we humans have pursued a course called "upgrading"—trying to make walls and ceilings better. We've gained structural strength, durability, insulation, and aesthetics. We've discovered a multitude of different building materials for walls and ceilings and new ways of constructing them. We've learned to decorate them, not just with colors and designs, but with wainscotting, molding, recesses, ledges. Unfortunately, upkeep has increased in direct proportion to the complexity of design.

At last count there were 6,221 choices of wall and ceiling materials. You've probably seen at least a few hundred yourself. Confusing as all this can get, it's a good thing we have so many choices here—because we spend the majority of our hours on earth inside these structures. Walls are the billboards of our homes—they stare us in the face at every turn and from every angle. You probably haven't given much thought to how much wear walls get, either. They're beaten on, gouged, decorated, written on, hung on, run into, leaned against—even climbed. So walls really *need* to be both attractive and maintenance-free.

Walls Are Not Forever

As permanent and "forever"as walls seem to be, we *can* change them, and for a modest amount of money and effort, at that. Don't use the excuse that you just bought the place, or your family's always had it this way, or you've just never thought about it—or whatever. **If the walls and ceiling entrap you physically or mentally, then** *change* **them.**

It's Your Wall— Make It Your Own

It's taken me twenty-nine years to do it, but I'm doing it. My maintenance-free house won't have an inch of Sheetrock in it and I won't miss it a bit. I hate Sheetrock. I dislike what it's made of, I despise hanging it, I hate taping it. I resent repairing it, and don't trust it for structural strength or fire protection. Its cheapness and convenience have a way of wooing people into submission— yet in everything I built, I realized I was gradually using less and less Sheetrock and more and more masonry, brick, hardwood, stone, and glass. And more and more I felt warmth and affection for my walls instead of resentment. **Sheetrock takes a lot of maintenance and care and it's far from a forever material.**

You may not be in a position right now to shed your Sheetrock or get rid of whatever the thorn in your side is. But we do want to stress that you can and must use materials that turn you on—what you like and feel good about and around, and what saves you time and money. It's your home—you should be able to enjoy and savor it forever.

The Art of Camouflage

"I'm going to paint all my walls black so you can't see any of the crayon writings and fingerprints," a woman shrieked from a seminar audience once. Everyone laughed—of course, because they'd secretly considered similar strategies.

If your wall is foil, light blue, or crisp gold, any mark, nick, or smudge will jump out at you as if it were magnified. Hiding those inevitable specks, marks, and little injuries is a wise and important thing to do, and it is *simple*. The ancient art of camouflage is well worth putting to work on your walls.

A woman who lives nearby covered the walls in the children's TV room with a jungle-pattern vinyl wallcovering. Assorted creatures peek out from behind the brush, and it's fascinating and forbidding. After four years with her six boys, it still looks nice and has required no maintenance. After all, who would write on a jungle (and if they did, who could tell the scribbles from the vines)?

How Many Walls?

Some walls *are* forever, if they support the structure of the house. I would move or remove a wall only as a last resort because of the cost and mess—but if you are building anew, build in as few walls as you can—instead, use "open planning." Divide rooms with storage units or furniture whenever possible and there'll be a lot less to clean. You'll enjoy openness more than you might imagine. Just look how well the open office and classroom concepts have been accepted! My wife and I left our kitchen, dining room, and fireplace areas open in one big 19x38-foot room, and it's been a pure joy to use.

The Stop-Sign Wall

The biggest obstacle to smooth, rapid progress is the contant appearance of stop signs. Just as stop signs on the road cause lost time, so do walls with too many "stops."

Multisurface Walls

Look at your walls now—how many different materials are there? One? (paint alone); two? (paint and wallcovering); three? (paint, wallcovering, glass); four? (paint, wallcovering, glass, and paneling). Do we need to go on to mention leather, brass, wood, tile, carpet, etc.? The record for a room, to our knowledge, is ten (in one room, mind you). Two or

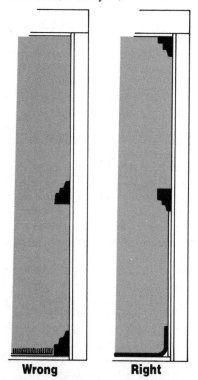

Wrong   Right

Fancy multilevel moldings and baseboards cause extra cleaning because they have so many surfaces to collect dust. Instead of baseboards, cove the flooring. Either put moldings near the ceiling where they can't get damaged and dust won't be easily noticed, or invert them so you have one surface to dust instead of four or five.

three wall surfaces in a room is a manageable number. Beyond that, multiple surfaces require multiple supplies, equipment, and know-how to make it all work.

Interruptions

Every interruption in a surface—a seam, crack, edge, or joint—is a maintenance headache. The less interruption to wall flow, the less time and money it takes to clean. Engraving or relief designs in a surface can enhance beauty, even be low maintenance, but designs that are too deep or in a bad location can literally be the "pits."

Also, notice the extra surfaces you create by adding ornate woodwork. All those extra surfaces have to be dusted and painted regularly. **If you simply can't live without those fancy multilevel moldings, invert them so that the edges face down (so they'll be easier to dust) and install them along the ceiling (where they can be enjoyed and not damaged). Instead of baseboards, extend the floor covering a few inches up the wall.**

Wallcovering

I grew up in a home where every year or so we "wallpapered"— a tortuous, tedious task whose results began to depreciate before the paste container was cleaned out. So stressful was this undertaking that it was considered the perfect activity for an engaged couple to do together to test the strength of their potential marriage!

Installation of wallcoverings hasn't gotten much easier since then, but there *is* some good news—the product itself has improved a lot. New, gorgeous, long-lasting, easy-to-clean materials now can be found among those

innumerable rolls. There are hundreds of types and thousands of designs that will make a wall look good for a long time. There are thicknesses, designs, and textures that will cover the roughest walls (old brick, cinder block, plaster, or cheap paneling) and still look spiffy.

Forget wall*paper*. It's the least expensive wallcovering but it's a high-maintenance item. True wallpaper is just that, *paper*. It's like gluing a piece of typing paper to the wall—it will absorb and hold every stain and it won't hold up to anything.

These days most wallcoverings, although they're often still called "wallpaper," are really vinyl, and vinyl is a good word in the maintenance vocabulary. Its plastic surface resists damage and it can't be penetrated by dirt, grease, water, etc. Vinyl can be easily cleaned with a sponge and any neutral detergent solution, then quickly buffed dry with a towel. It can even be scrubbed just like a countertop. Bear in mind, however, that there are different levels of quality. As a rule of thumb, if you tear a little piece of the paper, the easier it tears the thinner and less durable it is.

Fabric-backed vinyl is the most durable wallcovering. It has extra strength and durability and is especially good for re-covering and disguising irregular wall surfaces. Solid vinyl is the second best choice. A thick, vinyl-coated paper is also good, and a paper with a lighter vinyl coating is still better than true wall*paper*.

Patterns and designs in wallcovering help hide damage, dirt, and seams. Flocked (furry) and foil papers are elegant, but hard to repair and clean and a (#*@!) to hang properly. The surfaces are not at all durable.

That handsome, rich-looking

Wallpapering can put even the most tried and true do-it-yourselfers to the test.

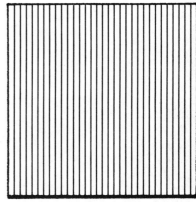

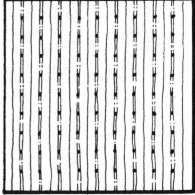

"burlap" or woven fabric you've seen on walls in offices or banks is actually a plastic material almost like vinyl but a little more resilient. It used to be available only commercially but it's now available for home use. It requires trimming and special glue to apply it, so installation might best be left to a professional, but once it's up, it'll last and last. It's not inexpensive but it's a rugged, forgiving, low-maintenance surface that tolerates and hides abuse and dirt. When you need a wallcovering for the toughest cases, zip down to the paint store and thumb through the "fabric" (it's called fabric though it is plastic) wallcovering book. You'll find one that warms your heart—and saves you a lot of time over the years.

Vinyl Floor Covering

If you're covering the floor with vinyl floor covering, go half-way up the wall with it, especially if the room gets very hard use.

- It's tough—won't mar, chip, or dent.

Very regular, precise, or geometric wallcovering patterns like the one at top will show spots only too well. A pattern that is less precise, like the one at center, is better and a free-flowing pattern, as at bottom, is best.

147

Carpet on the wall is soft, absorbent, safe, long-lasting, and quiet.

- It will endure children. Remember that the lower half of the wall is the part that's within scribbling, kicking, and pawing range of youngsters.

- Fingerprints won't show.

- It's scrubbable (can be quickly squeegeed off, too).

- Little ones (or grown ups) won't hurt themselves if they run into it.

- It's available in thousands of attractive designs.

- You can do it yourself (ask at your local DIY center—it's just like laying it on the floor).

Carpet

Some friends of mine have a houseful of little kids, mostly boys. From time to time they try to find a way to overcome the writing (and other kid-produced graffiti) on the wall. But within three or four months the walls have been destroyed—crayon, smears, chips, dents, rips, gouges, you name it—the walls need repairing *again*.

One day I went over there and as usual the walls looked like they'd been around longer than the pyramids. But suddenly I noticed one wall was perfect—not a ding or mark anywhere on it. I took a closer look. The wall looked like striped wallpaper, but it was carpet—tight short-weave carpet. It shrugged off all kinds of abuse and was safe for the kids, too, because it acted as a padding—they couldn't get hurt if they ran into it. It looked sharp, cut down the noise level of the room, and even provided some extra insulation. In fact, I can't think of one bad thing about it.

148

Carpet on the wall is not a new concept, but few do it! No wall is as practical or as plush as a carpeted wall. Since carpet is designed to withstand traffic and spills—particularly when stain repellent is applied at the factory—when it's used on walls it resists stains, is seldom defaced or damaged, and rarely needs cleaning. Just vacuum it once in a while and that's it. **Carpet's especially great for disguising "distressed" walls and for adding some warmth to those cold concrete basement walls.** (Be sure to use an adhesive especially for subgrade use in below-ground basements.)

You can use the same carpet on the wall as on your floor—some people change the wall carpet for variety, but it doesn't matter either way for maintenance. Short cut-pile carpeting in a nylon material is the hardiest.

Anyone can install carpet on the walls. Unlike floor carpet, wall carpet doesn't need padding under it and is usually attached with carpet adhesive. The carpet installer or your carpet store will know what glue works on what surface—it will vary with wall surfaces.

Wood

Why should home remodelers and new home builders consider hardwood wall paneling over other wallcovering materials?

1. *Beauty:* Made by nature and fashioned by man, every hardwood wall panel is a unique cameo of beauty with different colors and grains. The natural grain and beauty of wood is art in itself—it doesn't need decorations plastered all over it. It's versatile, too—hardwood paneling can be dignified, rustic, spartan, or exotic.

2. *Durability:* With today's modern finishes, hardwood paneling can resist almost any kind of abuse, and will normally last the lifetime of the home.

3. *Maintenance:* Simple wiping with a damp cloth or sparing use of ordinary furniture polish is all the maintenance a paneled wall will ever require under normal use.

4. *Cost:* It's not much more expensive to install than many other conventional wall treatments, and considering its durability, it can be a real bargain.

Many types of solid wood planking and siding designed for exterior use make for striking interior wall treatments and are low if not zero maintenance. Rough-hewn cedar "channel" siding, ship-lap, tongue and groove, and others can be applied vertically, horizontally, or diagonally for striking, beautiful wood walls that can take it and not show it.

When choosing wood for the walls, you have quite a few choices. From best to worst, they are:

1. Solid wood planks

2. Plywood with a thick veneer of finer wood glued on

3. Plywood with a thinner slice of wood veneer

4. Vinyl imprinted with wood grain and glued onto wood

5. Sheetrock with a vinyl wood grain finish glued onto it

Numbers 1, 2, and 3 are the best bets as they are made from real wood—they can be repaired easily and will probably last longer and look better than imitation woods. Numbers 4 and 5 have different quality levels and a good quality with a good finish on it will probably hold up okay. Keep in mind that there are some truly bad choices available, so beware if the price is *too* good. Paneling under $10 a sheet probably isn't the best grade. Also be careful of really inexpensive vinyl-covered paneling.

In a nutshell, wood is a maintenance-freeing material in interiors as long as it is *sealed.* Wood walls without a seal will show all too clearly the slightest bit of grease or stain. If the stain goes down into the wood, you've had it. If the wood has a couple of coats of satin-finish polyurethane, the stain will be repelled and can easily be wiped off.

When choosing a color to stain unfinished wood, bear in mind that a medium to light tone is best; a dark stain will show most nicks.

Smooth, glossy surfaces wash and dust easiest, but show dents, nicks, and scratches more. Roughly hewn planks, barn boards, etc., show imperfections less but are more difficult to clean.

Wood is a good insulator and soft woods like rough-hewn cedar help muffle noise.

Masonry

When you build something you want it to last and last, not rot and require the rest of your life to protect and care for. From this point of view, no wall surface can match *masonry*.

That's why I've long wondered why people don't use more of it on their walls, exterior and interior. When I ask, the response generally is "I never thought of it" or "I didn't know you could" or "Isn't it expensive?"

One of the most common assumptions is that masonry walls would be too cold and forbidding for a home. Bear in mind that color has a lot to do with it. Most of the cold-feeling masonry is also a cold color such as gray, black, or stark white and then, yes, it can be cold. For warmth and comfort a brown or tan color is better. Brown is one of the warmest earth tones and a room with one wall painted brown as an accent is usually very cozy no matter what the size. The size of the blocks or bricks will also play a part in making a room cozy or cold. Keep them on the smaller side for interiors, so they are more in accord with interior proportions.

Block Walls

Masonry block, cinder block, and pumice blocks are often used in commercial buildings, but are sometimes overlooked for homes. Several types of decorative blocks that give a nice appearance to interior walls are also available.

Block walls are extremely durable and fireproof, and they can be very thermally efficient when filled with an insulative fill.

Once a block wall is laid, you can take another piece of block and rub it all over the new surface to knock off all the protruding little mortar drops. Then, with a roller, apply a coat of block filler. The block filler is nothing more than watered-down Sheetrock mud. It fills the tiny pores and holes in the surface of the block and the mortar. It doesn't change the looks of the surface much, but it leaves it smoother and ready for painting.

Add a little of the paint you'll be using on the walls to the block filler, so the wall will be easier to paint. If the wall is nicked or gouged, it will still be the same color underneath as it was on the surface.

Or you can trowel a masonry wall with Sheetrock mud and texture in a light, skip-trowel Spanish design. This is easy and fun, costs very little and looks elegant. easy and fun, costs very little and looks elegant.

Brick Walls

There are literally hundreds of choices of bricks—from the slickest, smoothest, most modern to the old castle type. Just check out the types at a brickyard or lumber store and you suit your fancy.

Bricks' surface is often textured (with brushstrokes or indentations, for example) for effect. They are decorative because they come in different colors and even multicolor. Once up, your wall is forever. It won't peel, warp, dent, fade, rot, burn, or get termites.

There are actually two types of bricks: the standard size that you see on the exterior of most brick homes and interior bricks that are scaled down in size to fit the proportions of interiors. The interior bricks are also smoother and have a finer and sometimes coated finish. This gives the room a less massive look.

Be sure to apply a couple of

coats of a satin transparent seal on interior brick. You can buy it at most paint stores and it will keep grease spots and stains from being absorbed into the surface.

Do give some thought to the mortaring. "Struck" or "raked" joints look better than flush, but they offer a variety of ledges for dust. Groove or concave joints often are good compromises.

In the old days, walls were often constructed of solid brick, but no more. The norm now is to construct the wall of wood framing, concrete, or concrete block and veneer it with the more costly brick. **A solid brick wall would be superior to a brick-veneered wood-frame wall in strength and durability, but a concrete or concrete block wall with brick veneer would be better yet.**

Simulated Brick Facing

Simulated brick facing looks like real brick indeed and basically does do the job of providing an attractive low-maintenance wall. It's easy to apply and is a good second choice to a real masonry surface. It's very realistic looking and offers more choices of quality and color. Dust scarcely shows and not much can depreciate the look of simulated brick. It's nearly as durable and fire-resistant as solid brick.

Earth Tile

Like other masonry surfaces, tile is unlimited not only in durability but also in beauty and variety. It's good for kitchens, bathrooms, and patios. It's attractive, easy to clean, and almost impossible to damage.

Ceramic tile is the best for walls because it has a baked-on glaze that is strong and scratch-resistant—it doesn't need wax or other finishes to look great. It's durable and easy to clean because the dirt can't penetrate its glossy surface. While

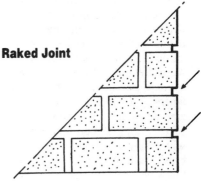

Flush Joint

Raked Joint

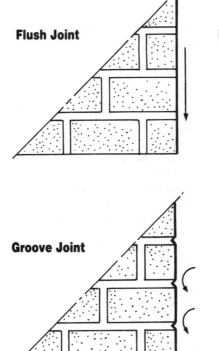

Groove Joint

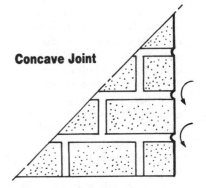

Concave Joint

there's some difference in grades of ceramic tile, only the most inexpensive is unsuitable. Make sure the tile is smooth to the touch, so it won't snag your cleaning cloth.

The precaution that does need to be taken with tile is the grout. If not sealed and colored, it can and will be a nuisance forever. To make sure tile is maintenance-free:

1. Keep the grout joints small and use large tiles, rather than small, whenever possible.

2. Color the mortar. Pure white is bad—but so are black and deep brown. A neutral color is best, any neutral color that blends with the color of the tile.

3. Seal the grout to prevent discoloration and to aid in cleaning.

You can have professionals install it or you can go at it yourself. There are books that give detailed instructions for laying tile, but it should only be attempted by experienced or indomitable do-it-yourselfers.

Rock

Nothing is more beautiful than a real rock wall. It is nature right in your room, offering solid permanence. It's indestructible and needs almost zero maintenance. An interior rock wall provides a point of interest in a room and doesn't require "decorating" like a plainer wall does. Rock offers total resistance to the meanest messes, and its rugged beauty overrules any scratch or blemish.

Stone walls don't require a lot of cleaning—just a periodic vacuuming to keep down the dust. The most important thing to do is to seal the stone when it's new, so it won't absorb stains and soil. Once every few years (more often if you smoke or use the fireplace a good deal) you will want to wash down the stone. This is especially true of fireplace facings, where you will get a certain amount of soot and smoke. For sealed stone, a good scrubbing with soapy water and a stiff brush, followed by rinsing, is all that's needed.

The only drawback to rock walls is the weight. Be sure you have the foundation and special footings to support the stone before you commit to it. You may want to attach anchors to the existing wall that will tie into the mortar of the stone to secure it. Anywhere that weight is a problem, use the lightweight imitation stones that can be attached with adhesive. Ask an expert to assess your situation before you begin installation.

If you decide on stone, you can buy it from a quarry or go out on a nearby hillside or mountain slide area and pick up a few loads of it (check with the landowner first, of course). Then build a wall any way you wish. You can do it— you *can!* Even if you've never picked up a pebble. Flat, slabby rocks are much easier to lay up than thick or round ones. You can lay them flat, on edge, sideways, upright—any way you want. Don't worry about coloring the mortar; getting a consistent color in mortar mix is a true art. When the wall is finished you can take a little brush and some heavy-bodied stain and make the mortar any color you want; once sealed the color will be as permanent as you want it to be.

Paint

Many people are so discouraged by the thoughts of preparing for and cleaning up after painting that they overlook it as one of the best, easiest, most practical maintenance-free measures of all. **A simple change of paint type and color in a room can reduce cleaning up to 50 percent! Fingerprints, marks, spills, splatters, dirt . . . all will easily clean off from good painted surfaces.**

When a wall won't clean up, looks bad, needs protection, or you just don't feel good about it, *paint it!* Surfaces with chipped, streaked, or dingy paint:

1. Depreciate fast.

2. Look bad.

3. Are extremely difficult to clean.

4. Do not reflect light, making a room dull and dreary.

Paint Types

Should you go with oil- or water-base paint? Don't let the fact that latex is called *water*-base lead you to think it's not as good as oil. The new latex paints are fantastic. Builders use clear latex water seal outside, inside, and on concrete factory floors that have to support forklifts and 5,000 other abuses. For new construction, latex enamel is hard to beat. Be careful in putting latex over an existing finish of oil-base enamel, though, without extensive surface preparation, you won't get a good bond. If in doubt, get someone who knows the difference to check it out for you. If the surface *has* been painted with an oil-base, the easiest solution is to sand lightly and then reapply oil-base enamel. If you insist on using latex over oil, the old surface must be thoroughly cleaned and deglossed, either with sandpaper or liquid deglosser. Even then, it's safest to prime the existing surface after deglossing with an alkyd enamel underbody.

Paints on both ends of the finish spectrum have maintenance problems. A flat finish shows body oils, chair scuffs, and tool marks, and when it's cleaned the paint streaks and some comes off. A ceiling is the only place I'd use flat paint, either oil or water-base.

A high-gloss finish reflects so much light that it highlights every adversity. Shininess radiates "clean and sharp," only if it's in smooth, perfect condition. Gloss shows *all* wall imperfections. Some people also find it too institutional for formal areas of the house. High-gloss paint is the easiest to clean, but the appearance trade-off usually isn't worth it.

Eggshell enamel has a low luster (about the gloss of an egg) and is a gorgeous, low-maintenance paint ideal for bedroom and living room walls. For kitchens, bathrooms, and maybe for woodwork, semi-gloss or satin finish is a better choice. They're both much easier and faster to clean than flat paint, yet still look luxurious.

Flat   Eggshell   Semigloss   Satin   High gloss

Principles of
Maintenance-Free
Painting

1 *Buy the best.* The cans, colors, labels, and claims may all look the same, but there is as much difference between good paint and cheap as there is between cardboard and wood. Good quality paint goes on faster, covers better, lasts 50 percent longer, is 100 percent easier to clean, and is generally only 30 percent more expensive—and we're talking about an expense you only have to incur about once every five years. Considering all the labor and expense involved in the preparation and the actual application, an additional five dollars per gallon for the better quality product is almost negligible—yet it will make all the difference. The top-of-the-line paints of the major brands are worth the bucks.

2 *What color?* Off-white and other neutral tones—almond is popular today—are the "cleanest" colors; light pastels and the real dark colors are worst. The intensity of a solid red, black, or orange wall magnifies the tiniest mark or scuff. Dark colors also can cause warping on outside surfaces because they draw the heat of the sun. Stark white is also hard to maintain.

Neutral colors are indeed neutral, completely indifferent to a few flyspecks and fingerprints. Use neutral colors on walls throughout the house and let your drapes, furniture, and carpets serve as accents. Woodwork and trim should be painted the same color as the walls. Use the same semigloss paint on walls and woodwork. Or, if you prefer an accent of a different color, use a natural stained wood sealed with a semigloss finish for the door frames and woodwork.

3 *One, two, or more?* Painting is done to preserve the surface, improve the looks, and facilitate cleaning. Most people paint to improve looks. That's not the most important reason, although it will be a natural by-product of painting done for surface preservation and maintainability. A good job of painting with periodic repainting could preserve a surface literally forever. So don't skip on coats. An unpainted surface will absorb most of the first coat, so two coats is the minimum. One more additional coat will fill the pores and surface irregularities and level the surface so the walls can be washed or wiped in seconds. And since over half of the work is in the preparing for and cleaning up after painting, an additional coat doesn't add much at all to the chore of painting—while it guarantees the results of all your efforts.

4 *Don't overpaint.* On the other hand, overpainted walls or woodwork (painted every two or three years) look globby and tacky and actually *create* maintenance problems—they chip more easily, for example. Good paint will last three to ten years inside.

Put on three good coats and leave it alone, except for touch-ups as necessary. Most repainting is done to change the color or to cover a couple of nicks. Both reasons can be eliminated. Use the best color when you paint in the first place, then you can just lightly feather the edges of any marks with fine sandpaper and touch them up.

To protect Sheetrock or plaster walls from chipping, install good doorstops and corner protectors. Corner protectors are made of clear acrylic or colored vinyl and fit along the corner of the wall to protect the bottom four feet or so from kicks and nicks. They're used extensively in commercial buildings and come in a number of colors.

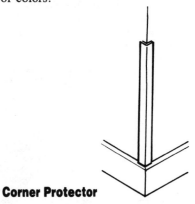

Corner Protector

Mirrors

Mirrors are low-maintenance—use them wherever you can. The more mirrors you have, the fewer light fixtures you'll need because mirrors reflect light and make your rooms brighter. **Mirrors use *your* movements and the furnishings and trimmings of the rest of the house to decorate.** One of the nicest motels I've ever stayed in had not a single wall decoration, yet the rooms were beautiful and comfortable. They did it with mirrors, which also minimized maintenance and damage to the unit.

We're not saying you can't get by without a mirror on every wall, but mirrors do beat paneling, paper, and paint on walls. All you have to do is squeegee a mirror off every month or so. Mirrors:

1. Enlarge the room.

2. Give an open, spacious feeling.

3. Reflect light from windows and other rooms for a brighter, lighter, cleaner-looking room.

4. Provide a strong, durable surface.

Ceilings—Let's Take Them from the Top

A lot of people treat their ceilings like an agnostic treats the idea of a supreme being—up there somewhere, but getting along just fine without too much interference from down here. But ceilings do need our help. They fall victim to cobwebs, smoke, dust, and leaks. They get dull, cracked, dingy. And because they are "up there," cleaning ceilings can be more intimidating than cleaning walls or even floors. Even so, a careful choice of materials and some cleaning know-how can make a believer out of you.

Sensible Ceilings

The first thing to consider in planning for cleanable ceilings is the height. **An eight-foot ceiling is standard, and a very workable height. It's easy to reach but keeps light fixtures, etc., out of the way of six-feet-five basketball players.** High cathedral-type ceilings are difficult to reach and are expensive in terms of heating or cooling costs. Believe me, the glory isn't worth the guts it takes to forever clean and service them.

Be as creative as you like with your ceiling, but use this checklist to assess your ceiling assets:

- Reachable/accessible
- Cleanable
- Resistant to abuse
- Concealing/forgiving

THE GREAT CEILING DIVERSION

SAFE LINE-OF-VISION. HANG ALL PICTURES BELOW THIS LEVEL

HIGH-POWERED LIGHTING. MOUNT ABOVE SAFE LINE-OF-VISION

DIT. DIT.

PASS OUT VISORS TO GUESTS BEFORE THEY ENTER

KEEP SMALL CHILDREN OUT OF THE SAME ROOM AS GUESTS.

ALWAYS KEEP YOUR CARPET LOOKING BRAND-NEW. COMMENT ON IT OFTEN.

Biggest Ceiling Problems

1. Installation casualties (from hanging and taking down swag lamps, plants, decorations, smoke detectors, etc.).

2. Stains from leaky roof or attic flaws

3. Cracks

4. Build-up of smoke from cooking and cigarettes, grease around vents and fans

Go to Great Paints for a Carefree Ceiling

A smooth-finished Sheetrock or plaster ceiling is quick to clean if painted with a good semigloss enamel. It tends to show streaks and blemishes more than a textured ceiling, though, so it will need cleaning more often.

When painting ceilings, I again prefer a satin-finish or an eggshell enamel instead of the old dead flat look, once the trademark of all ceilings. Or for better cleanability yet, semigloss. Don't go all the way to gloss—a glossy smooth ceiling magnifies imperfections like a mirror.

Another good way to cut up-keep time is to paint the ceiling off-white or another neutral color such as antique white, linen, and even the almond color.

Most people love a white ceiling, but pure white will show every speck of dirt. When choosing a "white" paint for the ceiling, bear in mind that an off-white will appear white against darker floor and furniture and wall decorations. What is "white" is relative and can fool the eye—

so you don't have to go for the whitest (and hardest to keep up) white. Pure white is too stark and bright—your room will look like a hospital operating room—and will show every drop of dirt.

Cut Down on Cottage Cheese for a Low-Maintenance Diet

I never do a seminar, lecture, or class but that the question comes up. "What can I do about my cottage-cheese ceiling?" I can give a fast, easy answer: get a different architect next time. Or if you installed one of these ceilings yourself, have your head examined. Cottage cheese is a maintenance nightmare.

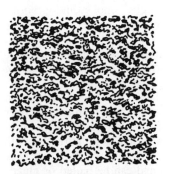

Cottage Cheese Ceiling

It's a nice soft texture that looks great when new, but is almost impossible to clean when it gets dirty. It's a sprayed-on mixture of texture mud and a lightweight filler such as Perlite. Sometimes shiny flecks are added to the material to create a "rhinestone" or "fleck" ceiling.

If you have either a cottage cheese ceiling or a fleck ceiling, your cleaning choices are limited. Try vacuuming with an extra-long hose and soft bristle attachment.

The Texture Treatment

A painted ceiling with a special texture mud applied is an almost maintenance-free ceiling (providing you don't go all the way to wolf-fang texture). The secret is to cover it with several good coats of enamel to fill the pits and round the sharp edges so you can wash or dry-sponge it in minutes. The texture also hides minor cracks and blemishes.

If you're stuck with Sheetrock ceilings, which 80 percent of you reading this are, a *light cleanable* texture is the best answer. The ceiling will look good and the texture will hide the dirt and fly tracks for a long time. Texture is a great solution for the ceilings in old homes where the seams and joints are showing. It hides a multitude of sins and leaves a low-maintenance surface. It's amazing what you can do with $25 worth of texture mud and one afternoon—and you *can* do it, too!

Just bear in mind that very deep textures or textures that have sharp edges are less easily cleaned than smoother ones. And don't get too carried away with texture in the kitchen or the bathroom. In the kitchen you have so much smoke and grease in the air that you should have a nice smooth surface to wipe. Bathroom humidity will shorten the life of any texture.

If your ceiling does have a deep texture, you can do something about it. Get a 2x4 or something equally aggressive and drag it across the ceiling surface and knock all of the wolf-fang long points off, until the tips present a somewhat even surface. Then roll on two or three coats of latex semigloss enamel—to fill in the pores and "canyons" at least to the extent that the ceiling can be dry-sponged or washed without

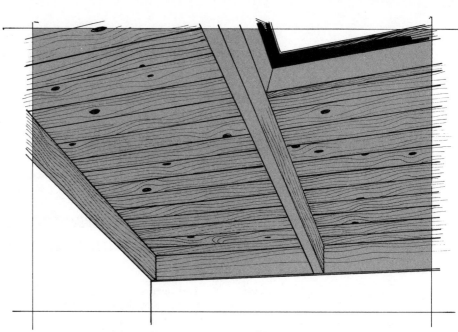

If you love soft woods that would be easily damaged in furniture or paneling, use it on the ceiling, where it will be both beautiful and safe.

snagging the sponge. That's the answer for an *overly* rough ceiling. Or try spray-painting it when it gets dirty.

The most common texture application is Perfatape mud, sprayed through a texture machine. You can use plaster and get a harder surface but it'll also be a more jagged surface which may be harder to clean (unless you make the surface *so* rough it doesn't need cleaning).

Charm Them from the Ceiling . . . With Wood

Once good old wood is installed up there above your head, it's basically there forever. The warmth and interest of wood are hard to beat, plus dirt will go unnoticed. In both our ranch and Sun Valley homes, we built ceilings of spruce decking that we stained a light cherry color and then coated with low-gloss polyurethane. They still look as good today as the day we installed them. Once someone lit a fire when the fireplace damper was closed and the room was covered with smoke and soot. A normal ceiling probably would have

had to be repainted, but in a few hours our wood ceiling was clean.

Wood is beautiful, warm looking, and maintenance-free forever if you give it a couple of coats of satin-finish (low-sheen) varnish or urethane-type finish. Wood does a very good job of disguising the cobwebs, smoke, and airborne grime that before you know it have you painting or washing a conventional ceiling again. It can also cover over a great many ceiling imperfections.

They make wood paneling now of every imaginable colored grain. Paneling or decking with false beams makes an attractive ceiling. These kinds of effects are beautiful and can be nailed or glued on in a few hours.

The wood you put on a ceiling can be a softer or darker wood than you would normally put on a wall. (Don't use too dark a wood, though, or you'll darken the room.) Not every wood is for the walls, as walls do take a lot of abuse. But if you have your heart set on a certain softwood, or an exotic expensive wood such as teak, you can dress up a room with it from the ceiling and not have to worry about it.

Covering ceilings in old homes is one of the smartest things you can

do with wood. It's quick, inexpensive, and hides all of the old earthquake cracks, water spots, and discolorations. (Stick a sheet of Cellotex under the paneling for sound absorption.)

Acoustical Tile

Acoustical tile is only so-so in appearance and hard to maintain. Age, smoke, water leaks, and light-bulb changing soil the tiles, and since they're generally glued or interlocked together, they're tough to replace. Besides, a carpeted floor does a better job of sound absorption.

Suspended Ceiling

Once a commercial design feature, the suspended ceiling is now being used in private homes. We love it and recommend its use whenever we can. You simply suspend a metal grid from the original ceiling and then you can hang soft fiber panels of all kinds and put a variety of types of recessed lighting in the gridwork. If you ruin a piece (or it gets too dirty to clean), it can be replaced inexpensively in minutes!

Chapter 17

Don't Forget the Doors

As Princess Di prepared to bring little Prince William home from the hospital, a representative of the British Broadcasting Company called me for any advice I might have for a healthy royal home-coming. I told them something every householder should heed—I said the *doorknobs* in Buckingham Palace probably hadn't been cleaned for decades. Just think of all the germ-handed people straight from toilet and towel duty who had handled those doorknobs—and all those responsible for feeding, bathing, and giving the pacifier to the baby would be "hob-knobbing" with

157

those germs. The person from the BBC gasped, and you will too when you realize that doors are a heavily used part of the house, yet are almost ignored when it comes to cleaning schedules and maintenance ease.

If you have any doubts about how much use your doors get, try spiffing them up and watch the reactions. Once my cleaning crews lightly sanded and painted all the doors and door casings in a Florida hospital. You couldn't believe how much better the whole place looked. Many of the staff and visitors thought we'd done a major remodeling job—just because of a little attention to the doors.

So if you, too, want your home fit for a king-to-be, you can no longer ignore the doors.

Get Rid of Unneeded Doors

This is not an act of home brutality, but rather an act of kindness to yourself. Doors are primarily intended to provide privacy and security; they also have a part in fire safety and act somewhat as sound barriers. If a door doesn't fulfill any of these functions, get rid of it. If you need to be convinced, going to buy a door will help motivate you to eliminate them. They range from $26 for a cheap hollow-core interior door to $1,226 for a solid wood front door. Next try to hang one—that nerve-racking and knuckle-burning experience will force you to take a second look at doors.

Look what office buildings have done. Some businesses have eliminated seventy doors per floor, in accord with the "open office" concept. And what needs to be more private, secure, or soundproofed than an office?

Most inside doors are open all the time anyway. Why have a door between the utility room and kitchen, or the living room and dining room if it's open all the time?

Closet doors are a national nuisance. Who is looking at your clothes in the bedroom, besides *you?* You have to use the door twice just to get a tie and something is always in the way of the door's swing or slide. Most bedroom closets have those squirrelly, floppy, roller-track-jumping sliding doors or doors with 4,000 separate little louvers to dust. Don't use the excuse that you'll get too much dust in a doorless closet. Most closet doors get left ajar a lot of the time anyway, and you can cut down on the dust that builds up on shelves by using wire shelving. Besides, any clothes that hang around long enough to get dusty aren't getting worn much and should be altered, stored alongside other seldom-used items, or given to your favorite charity. Eliminate closet doors whenever you can—you don't really need them.

When it comes to *bathroom* doors, notice how nice many newly designed airport and commercial building restrooms are. A simple extended partition provides plenty of privacy, looks sharp, and requires no more cleaning or maintenance than any other wall.

Most houses have one door for every 100 square feet of space. In our home, we cut this down to one door for every 300 square feet. It makes life easier from a maintenance standpoint—and it saves money, too.

It's the door that just hangs there, seldom used or needed, that often ends up being a high-maintenance item. If you can cut it out—do it! Or, if you think a door may not be necessary, but you don't want to commit to a final door detachment, just remove it for a week or two and test the results!

When you de-door, the closet door probably will be the easiest

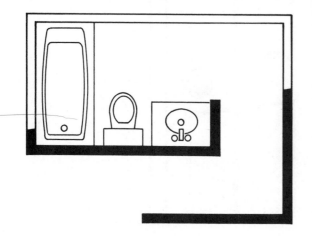

An extended partition eliminates the need for a bathroom door and requires very little upkeep.

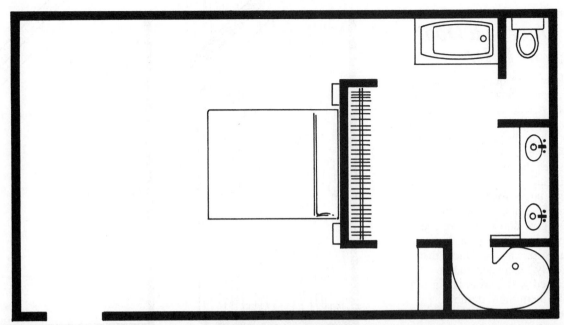

This floorplan of the master bedroom in our maintenance-free home shows how you can eliminate doors on the bathroom and closet. Partitions around the toilet provide privacy and the design keeps items in the closet out of view in the bedroom area.

to eliminate. (Of course having all of your junk now visible might set you back a few days while you hide it or haul it away.)

Before you cut *all* the doors out of your house or office, go through and look them over. Evaluate them in terms of

use

need

type or style

condition

If you find you're having withdrawal symptoms as you de-door, there's a compromise to going "all the way"—pocket doors. These are sliding doors that slip back into a pocket in the wall.

A pocket door fills the bill for those passageways where a swinging door takes up too much room, or where the door stands open most of the time but you *would* like to be able to close it once in a while. Getting a

seldom-used door out of the way like this keeps the door from getting beaten up, and eliminates the chance of a doorknob punching through the wall.

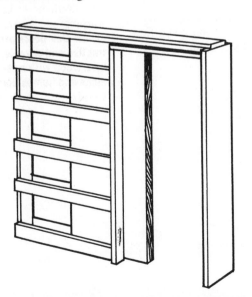

A pocket door can provide privacy when you need it without taking up a lot of space or getting in the way when you don't.

A Door Is a Door . . . or Is It?

Like most other building materials, doors come in all grades of quality, with the best ones being the most expensive. Just remember when choosing a door that it will have to take tons of abuse. Besides the everyday moving, swinging, and slamming, it's a prime target for fingerprints, scratches, nicks, and gouges. Always give doors an extra coat or two of varnish to protect them against this abuse. Doors that are severely mistreated can be sheathed with plastic laminate to make them more durable.

For exterior doors, choose a solid-core unit such as plain or carved wood, or a metal-sheathed door with a core of insulating foam. Hollow-core doors don't provide the strength and security needed for exterior use, and their insulating value is not as good, although they are used by builders on some less expensive homes. For interior doors, hollow-core doors may be all right. Just be sure you understand the differences before making a purchase or you could find yourself in a door jam.

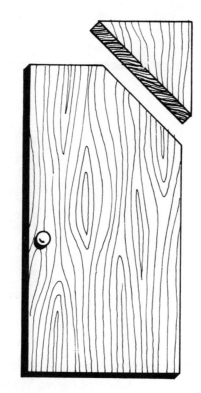

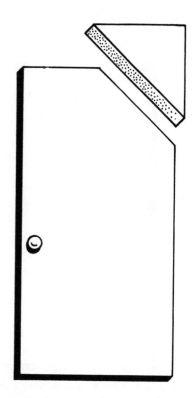

Solid-Core and Insulated Doors

Solid-core doors can be solid wood or particleboard covered with a veneer of real wood. Solid wood doors are best and can be smooth slab, paneled, or carved. They must be sealed and protected with urethane to keep them from warping and to make them easy to clean. **Oak doors are the most attractive and durable, since oak is a hard wood with a large grain so that nicks and bumps don't show.** Other woods used for doors are pine, birch, fir, and mahogany.

Smooth slab or paneled doors are much easier to care for than carved or other ornate doors, particularly for an exterior door. Remember, outside doors get twice as dirty as inside doors, so if they have a lot of little ledges and valleys, they will always be dirty. Besides, a flat surface shows off wood grain better.

An insulated door is a steel or hollow-core door with insulation inside the sheathing. It's the second choice for outside doors.

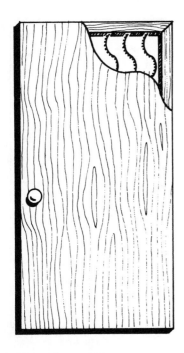

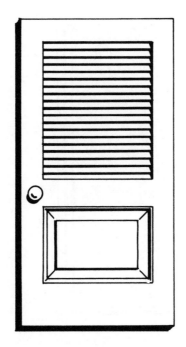

Hollow-Core Doors

Hollow-core doors are inexpensive but some are very flimsy and prone to damage. Cheap ones, usually made of wood or Masonite, are two thin pieces of sheathing bonded to a honeycomb core of corrugated cardboard. They are easily broken and warp or twist readily. **If you use hollow-core doors, spend the few extra bucks to get a good one with thicker sheathing and sturdy interior construction.** For the sheathing, birch is better than mahogany because it is harder. Oak is also one of the nicer and more popular surfaces. A stained and varnished surface is better than a painted one.

Louvered Doors

Louvered doors are a maintenance nightmare! Maintaining them is like cleaning a venetian blind with rigor mortis. If you need ventilation, maybe you can just leave the door off entirely. If you must have a louvered door, buy molded, case-hardened plastic, since it's slicker and more water-resistant than wood, and thus much easier to clean.

Windowed Doors

Avoid these wherever possible. The glass and framing get loose and they are vulnerable to "slam" breakage. It's also easier to rob a house with glass in the door—"what you see is what you get." This type of door also has two or more surfaces to clean instead of one, so you have to use at least two methods to clean it. Sometimes the value of being able to see out outweighs the maintenance complications of this style. Only you can make this decision, but strictly for security, a fisheye peephole in an exterior door makes more sense.

Stained glass is less of a problem than clear, as long as it is not extremely ornate; it doesn't show dirt or water spots as easily, so it can just be dusted and lightly wiped clean with the rest of the door.

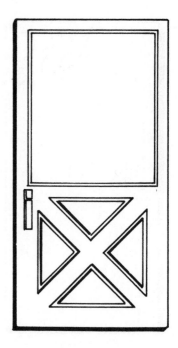

Sliding Glass Doors

Glass doors, such as those many people use as an entryway to the yard or deck, give a room a light, airy feeling and are a breeze to clean. They can be squeegeed squeaky clean as easily as a window and are a lot stronger than you might expect. **Most are 6'8", but try the 8' versions for even more light and maintenance savings.**

Storm Doors

Put your money into a good, solid, well-insulated front door instead of storm doors, and you'll be happier. A storm door is just one extra door to open and close, and to maintain. Despite their names, storm doors don't really fare very well in storms. Because they open outward, they can catch the wind like a sail and tear themselves apart banging against the side of the house. You don't really need them for ventilation—you no doubt have plenty of windows— and the "storm door" effect can actually work in reverse. With both the entry and storm door closed and in direct sunlight, heat can build up between the doors (especially if the entry door is dark-colored). This heat can melt plastic moldings and speed up deterioration of the finish on the entry door. Use a screen door if you really need the ventilation.

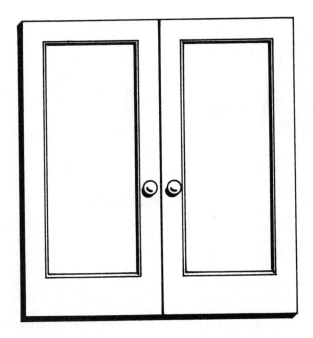

Double Front Doors

Double front doors may look good, but they're hard to keep in good working condition. If both doors swing open, it's hard to maintain proper alignment, so both are prone to damage. One door should be permanently shut so that the other door swings to it. Remember that double doors mean double knobs, double hinges and hardware, double refinishing and care—all for *one* entrance!

Commercial-Grade Doors

Many people are discovering a good alternative to solid wood doors. You won't believe how strong and carefree these are— nearly all new commercial buildings use them. They look exactly like finely finished wood but they are made of a vinyl-type material. The surface has tiny ridges and swirls that feel just like authentic wood grain. Ask your dealer about them—Stanley is a well-known company that makes them.

You know you have the right door when you can't nick or mar it, no matter how hard you try. With that strong synthetic finish, you'll never have to refinish it, and it can be easily cleaned with a cloth and spray bottle.

Other commercial doors you should consider are the new metal or vinyl-covered exterior doors.

More Ways to Cut Down on Door Chores

You don't want to paint doors—a painted door will soon collect (and *show*) dirt around the doorknob. Painted doors also chip and scuff and the paint wears off and they have to be repainted often. Stained and varnished doors are a better way to go and if you choose a medium shade (not too dark or too light), you will have the most maintenance-free doors. A stained finish hides fingerprints and will only have to be refinished maybe once in a decade.

Any doorway that sees a lot of transporting action should be at least three feet wide so that you don't damage the door when moving furniture, suitcases, and other large items through it. But don't make a doorway *too* wide, because the bigger the door, the more likely that it'll sag or hang crookedly in very short order. Bathroom doors can be narrower than most, since large objects like furniture are rarely moved through them. Thirty-two inches is wide enough for bathroom doors.

The tops of doors are big dust catchers and the cloth snags when you try to wipe them off. Very few people finish the top of the door, yet it only takes a couple of extra minutes and very little additional material to sand and varnish this area, too. Once it's smooth, the movement of the door will keep all the dust whisked off and it'll be a breeze to keep up!

Door Hardware

In a word, minimize it. "Smooth" and "quality" are the traits that low-maintenance hinges on. Avoid lion-claw lock plates

Wrong

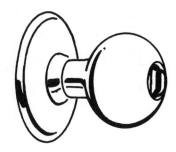

Right

and ancient castle ironwork—the more junk on a door, the more dirt and vandalism it will attract—and the more maintenance time it will claim. Let the beauty be in the wood itself.

For hardware, there is one finish that beats all—the brushed or antique finish. Most often a bronze or brass color, this finish helps hide fingerprints and dirt. It is *not* shiny, so you don't have to spend time polishing it.

Doorknobs

Common sense must be your guide through the many choices here. If *any* hardware in the house has to be functional first, it's the doorknob. From this point of view, there are two acceptable doorknob shapes:

Perfectly Round—These are the easiest shapes to clean because dust and dirt roll right off.

Lever—These have advantages for children, the elderly, and the handicapped because of their ease of operation. They are easy and fast to clean, too.

There also are two good choices for materials. A brushed brass knob coated with acrylic is a good choice for any door. Make sure it's smooth to the touch so that dirt will slide right off. For the kitchen or bath, ceramic or porcelain knobs are a nice low-maintenance alternative—the smooth baked-on surface (which is actually glass) cleans up fast and easy.

Kickplates

For those who kick before they push, or for doors in any garage or utility area, use rubber or plastic kickplates on the lower portion of the door. Don't use stainless steel or burnished aluminum—soft cushioned sheet vinyl flooring subdues noise and conceals scuffs and wear marks better.

Door Casings

The area right around the door—the "frame," or more precisely, the casing—is heavily abused by virtue of its location. As people pass by, often carrying groceries, suitcases, and large heavy objects like furniture, dings, scrapes, and dents are inevitable.

Painted casings are hard to keep nice because the paint chips and the smooth surface shows the dirt and nicks immediately. To minimize the problems, use a semi-gloss enamel in a neutral color that is slightly darker than the surrounding walls.

Stained wood casings are a much better choice. Because of wood's ability to blend in small imperfections with the grain, a stained casing can have a few nicks in it and still look presentable. **Choose *one* color stain and use it on all the woodwork throughout the house—you'll be much more likely to always know the color and have the stain available to touch up dents, etc.**

Chapter 18

The Ins and Outs of Windows

For thousands of years, the window was merely a hole in the wall through which light and air could enter the home (along with various forms of animal life). When the air became too cold (or the animal life too ambitious) for comfort, shutters were invented to cover the hole. We were still a long way away from the perfect window.

In our quest for a better window, we experimented with oiled paper, large sheets of mica, even loosely-woven cloth, but the ultimate material eluded us. And then . . . GLASS!! At last we were blessed with the raw material with which to build a better window, but we still haven't worked all the kinks out.

Some advanced and highly de-

sirable window treatments have evolved in recent years, but we still have some real losers from a window maintenance point of view. This section will help you better understand window construction and the options available, so you can make more liberating choices of "window treatments."

Window Styles Rated for Maintenance Ease

1. **Skylight**—The easiest "window" to maintain is a skylight, assuming it doesn't leak. A properly installed skylight is longer-lasting than a roof, but skylights in flat roofs present a leakage problem. A skylight lets in natural light and is naturally washed by rainfall so you never have to clean it. More natural light means fewer light fixtures to change, dust, and repair. While skylights don't eliminate the need for light fixtures, they do help out while the sun is up.

Skylight

2. **Single-pane**—The easiest true windows for maintenance are the large single-pane type. They can be squeegeed off quickly, have no moving parts, and no hardware to fiddle with.

Single-Pane

3. **Slider**—For windows that you can open and close, it's a toss-up between the casement type and the horizontal slider. The sliders are good because they usually come with an aluminum frame, which is a low-care material, and most of them can be cleaned entirely from the inside, without climbing up for second-story windows.

Slider

4. **Casement**—Modern casement windows are mostly wood-framed, which is an advantage in a lot of ways but does add to the maintenance considerations (see window frames, page 169). Most casements, like the horizontal sliders, can be

cleaned entirely from the inside. Steel-framed casements are not as desirable as wood.

Casement

5. **Double-hung**—These windows are standard in older homes, and almost always have wood frames that require painting. They must be cleaned from the outside, and there are two separate panes of glass to wash. It takes a certain amount of fiddling to keep them operating smoothly.

Double-Hung

6. Rotary—These windows aren't used a great deal. While there is only one pane of glass to clean, the operating hardware often doesn't work as well as it should, and leakage is sometimes a problem.

Rotary

7. Awning—These windows, usually with steel frames, are plagued with operating hardware problems. They have two or more panes to clean, and it must be done from the outside.

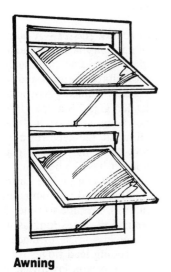

Awning

8. French, Victorian, or "lattice"—These windows are hard to clean by hand or squeegee; the tiny glass areas and all those corners really slow you down. The multiplication of the frame complicates maintenance because there is much more frame to sand, repaint, and glaze (or to rot and deteriorate). The quaintness of this style seems nonetheless to have a hypnotic hold on some of us. If you have a persistent liking for small panes, you can get a decorative plastic lattice unit that snaps on and off for ease of cleaning; there are also windows that have a decorative lattice sealed *between* two large glass panes. The surface you clean, both inside and out, is flat and smooth, yet it still gives the cozy, charming feeling of country-paned windows without all the work.

French

9. Jalousie windows—These are perfectly designed to accumulate dust and dirt—they are a maintenance nightmare! All those narrow little panes can't be cleaned with a squeegee, but must be washed by hand. They are opened with a crank, which often sticks, and sometimes causes one of the panes to break.

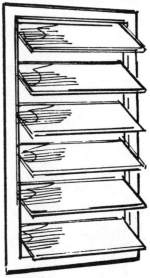

Jalousie

10. Multi-level (3-piece) Storm Windows—These are real losers, the highest-maintenance glass you could ever install. You have to take the storm windows off to clean them and then replace them. Mechanisms get sticky and break, so the windows fail to operate properly after a few years. Plus, you have all those separate pieces to clean, on both sides. Avoid hinged and take-apart units like the plague. In my thirty years as a professional painter and window cleaner, I've never found one that works like the brochures claim it should. If it's *insulation* you're after, get double-thickness or Thermopane windows.

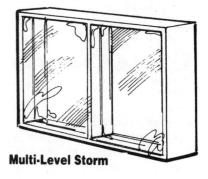

Multi-Level Storm

Window Materials

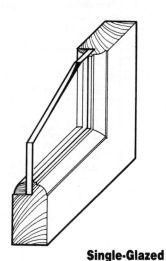

Single-Glazed

1. Single-glazed glass—This is the standard window in most homes: glass installed in a frame in a single thickness. Single-glazed glass is available in either single-strength (¹/₁₆" thick) or double-strength (¹/₈" thick).

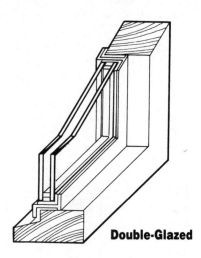

Double-Glazed

2. Double-glazed (or Thermopane)—Thermopane is a "sandwich" of two panes of glass with a layer of insulating air sealed in between. By itself, glass is a very poor insulator, but Thermopane cuts heat loss (or gain) in areas of temperature extremes, reducing utility bills. The double thickness of glass also almost totally eliminates condensation ("sweating") of interior panes in cold weather. Double-glazed glass is as easy to clean as single-glazed—since the inside surfaces are sealed off, it still has only two exposed surfaces.

3. Plate glass—³/₁₆" to ¼" thick or more, is the heavy-duty glass required for picture windows and other broad expanses of glass with no supporting internal framework.

4. Tinted glass—Any of the above glass types can be given a tint, such as smoked glass, bronze tint, or mirror glass. Although you see tinted glass mainly on commercial buildings and in automobiles, the reasons it is used commercially also apply to homes—to reduce fading from the sunlight, control heat loss, reduce air-conditioning costs, increase eye comfort and privacy. Beware the application of "solar film" to existing windows, however. These films are easily scratched and nicked, and tend to come loose around the edges after a while. They create more problems than they solve.

5. Obscure glass—This semi-opaque glass is installed with privacy in mind, usually in bathroom windows. It comes in many varieties, but avoid the sandblast (frosted) glass—the surface is too rough to clean easily. The smooth patterned type is best. If it feels rough to the touch (like fine sandpaper), it'll be hard to clean.

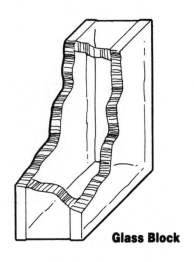

Glass Block

6. Glass block—Once used extensively in public buildings and slowly coming back into vogue, glass block is a good concept. It's quite durable and has insulating properties, but is difficult to replace if damaged because it's laid in mortar, like brick.

7. Specialty glasses—A number of specialty and decorative glasses are available, such as the colored Flemish and bottle glasses, stained glass, and leaded glass. Stained-glass windows are attractive and they eliminate the need for a window covering. Stained glass doesn't have to be shined clean—it can just be dusted or lightly wiped with ammonia solution from time to time. So stained glass, as long as it isn't extremely ornate or made with protruding lead ridges (or so expensive you lay awake nights wondering if it'll be stolen), is okay in a low-maintenance house.

8. *Plexiglas*—An acrylic plastic sheet, "Plexiglas" is very flexible and resistant to breakage, and is often installed as a "safety glass" where breakage presents a hazard. Although it works well in a "ceiling of light," Plexiglas scratches quite easily and is very difficult to keep in its clear, pristine state, so it's not so good as a window. Regular "Windex" type glass cleaner will cloud it, and special cleaning compounds and procedures are necessary to avoid damaging it.

Window Frames

1. *Anodized aluminum*—The first choice for a low-maintenance window frame material, it doesn't warp, crack, blister, peel, or rust, never needs painting, and the bronze and other colors available make it quite attractive.

2. *Standard aluminum*—This has all of the properties of anodized, except that the film of oxidation that naturally forms on the surface of aluminum tends to wipe off if rubbed, staining fingers and clothes with blackish smudge. It's also not available in colors, only in the "silver" natural aluminum color.

3. *Vinyl-clad wood*—While not as maintenance-free as aluminum, vinyl-clad wood does have advantages. Wood is a much better insulator than any metal frame, so it controls heat loss much better and doesn't "sweat" in cold weather. The vinyl skin on this type of frame protects the wood from weathering and should last for years and years with very little care.

For beauty, comfort, and durability, this window frame is a good choice.

4. *Steel*—As a window frame material, steel is not used as widely as it once was before the advent of anodized aluminum. Most steel frames require periodic painting to protect them from rust, but with good paint protection are very strong and will last forever.

5. *Painted wood*—The standard window frame material on many homes, it has the comfort and appearance advantages of vinyl-clad wood. Plus, the choice of colors available is almost infinite, and can be changed if you grow tired of a particular color scheme. The disadvantage is that periodic painting is required to protect the frame from weathering, whether you are tired of the color or not. "Lifetime" factory-painted finishes will hold up better than on-site applied paint, but *will* need attention eventually. (Wood frames stained with a solid color fall into this category, since the longevity of the coating is similar.)

6. *Varnished or stained wood*—The least desirable material from a maintenance standpoint, clear-stained or varnished wood breaks down from solar radiation much quicker than wood coated with paint or solid-color stain. If a natural wood-grain finish is your heart's desire, be prepared to refinish every three or four years.

Don't Let Yourself be Framed

Cleaning a window the right way—with a squeegee—is fast and easy; most of the maintenance of a window has to do with the frame. As we have seen, there are many different types of windows—from swing-outs to sliders to roll-outs—and there is a window that is best for each climate and area. In choosing from a maintenance standpoint the thing to remember again is simplicity. The simpler the window, the faster you can clean it and the less repairs it will need.

And don't design in trouble. Windows can be made in any size and shape you want. Most glass dealers have materials on hand that will enable them in a few hours to whip out a custom unit to fit what you want (instead of your having to adapt your design so that a standard unit will fit). The thing that you want to *avoid* is designing in hard-to-clean shapes and angles—triangle-shaped windows, and the like. **Remember: *The larger the uninterrupted expanse of glass, the better.* Small-paned windows are a pain because every edge touching the frame is a maintenance area. Acute angles are hard to clean!**

For truly maintenance-free windows, the ideal choice is tinted or bronzed Thermopane with brown anodized aluminum frames. These are available in fixed panes or horizontal sliders. For beauty and convenience, the vinyl-covered wood casement type windows are also very good. Be willing to pay for top-of-the-line, guaranteed windows. You'll get your money back ten times over.

Odd-shaped windows make cleaning a tricky task.

Solving the Common Window Woes

1 Replace small-pane windows with single-pane Thermopane units. Avoid frames with rough edges and ridges. You want smooth, flat, even frames on your windows.

2 Avoid cheap wood frames. Stick to vinyl-clad and factory finishes on wood or aluminum frames.

3 Don't paint window tracks—it makes windows stick and thus hard to open and close.

4 Buy only well-established name-brand windows. Good brands are well made and have good service and distribution.

5 Don't build in high, hard-to-reach windows, or windows with broad sills, odd-shaped frames, or acute angles—these all make for difficult cleaning.

Through a Glass Darkly?

Window cleaning is one of the few types of cleaning that's scheduled entirely by visual appraisal. Glass is a non-depreciating material; a window could go uncleaned for years and still not be damaged, but if it *looks* bad we've got to clean it. If windows face head on into direct sun, even quite clean ones will look bad and you'll wear out thirty squeegees in a lifetime. By putting a slight tint in the glass, or extending the eaves of the roof, or installing awnings—you'll reduce sun and rain exposure. Cleaning needs can be reduced even more by recessing windows back in from the outside wall surface, keeping the light from hitting the glass directly. (Protected windows can also cut air conditioning costs up to 25 percent.)

Screen It

In just about any geographic location there are a certain number of days each year when you'll want to leave the windows open. Lower air-conditioning bills aside, there's something soothing about a fresh breeze wafting through the open window, toying with the curtains. But unless you want to share your living space with all the tiny winged creatures, you need window screens.

Screening material is available in either metal or nylon fabric. While nylon mesh is not as resistant to punctures and tearing as metal mesh, it doesn't rust, is more elastic—more likely to spring back to its original shape when pushed on, instead of permanently bulging like the metal will. Nylon is also much easier to work with when replacing a screen or piece of screen. It can be cut with scissors or a knife, and easily stretches into the frame to form a flat, taut surface.

The best screens are those with aluminum frames held in the frame channel with spring clips. These can be easily popped out to be put in storage or be sprayed clean with a garden hose.

Cover-Ups

Choosing a window covering—drapes, curtains, or blinds—is like being asked which way you'd like to be tortured. They're all painful, your only choice is which hurts least. I was tempted to treat this topic the same as I did Chapter 5 of *Is There Life After Housework?*, "What to expect out of your husband and children" (which is nothing but blank pages). What's a good maintenance-free window covering? Nothing!

Any window covering has a built-in conflict: you want to be able to see out and let the light in, but you don't want passersby to see in. Because windows are a light source and a focal point, they attract fingerprints, noseprints, pets, and kids. The moisture accumulated from condensation on the window attracts airborne dirt and dust, much of which will roost on the window covering. And all that lovely sunlight rots and fades and deterio-

rates whatever you use to shield, shade, or secure your window.

It's a Catch-22: Glass is a low-maintenance material, and the natural light is nice, but liberal use of glass necessitates a profusion of window coverings that are mostly high-maintenance. These window coverings are mostly meant for privacy; if we can accomplish this with more private yards (landscaping, fences, etc.), we can "let it all hang out" and eliminate some of the nuisance of window coverings.

But for now at least, let's assume draperies, curtains, and other window coverings are here to stay. We need privacy and security and we love the sunlight to shine in during the day, so we must have window coverings. The trick is to make them as low-maintenance as we can.

Drapes and Curtains

The key thing to remember is to keep them simple—curtains controlled by side pulls (drawstrings) are good because they can be *pulled* open and closed and not have to be adjusted otherwise. If you have to hand-straighten drapes each day, they're taking more of your time than they should.

If curtains or drapes have a loose valance, make sure it's made of fabric too. If it's a hard

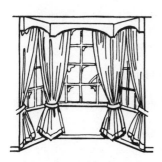 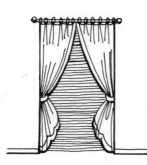  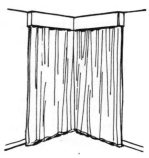

Tiebacks, complicated rods and hooks, and multi-tiered curtains, as shown on the first three windows, mean a lot more work. Draw drapes with a valance that goes all the way to the ceiling, as shown on the fourth window, are good.

valance, make sure it's washable, whether it's vinyl or painted wood.

You want drapes and curtains to go at least one foot below the window ledge so they won't lie on the sill, where moisture (and dirt) accumulate.

The top attachment area of drapes and curtains is the biggest maintenance problem because hardware breaks or jams or otherwise malfunctions as well as collects dust. Keep the hardware—rods, rings, etc.—simple and get good quality

The more complicated the drapes the more maintenance they will take—multi-tiered means more work. Keep them simple and functional. If you want to be fancy, get a floral or other printed fabric—it will be the best at hiding little imperfections and stains, too.

Drapery and Curtain Fabrics

There are literally hundreds of fabrics used in draperies and curtains. If you follow some basic principles, you can manage to choose low-maintenance window coverings from this array.

1. The fabric should be easy to launder—fabrics such as cotton/synthetic blends that will "wash and wear" (instead of needing ironing) are best for kitchens, baths, bedrooms, utility rooms, etc.

2. Be sure, on the other hand, that it's a *natural* fiber blend. The moisture that accumulates at windows and the constant exposure to the sun is hard on any fabric, but curtains made of natural fibers, including cotton, linen, wool, silk, ramie, and mohair, will retain their original shape better in the changing climate and moisture level of a window. Pure synthetics (nylon, acrylic, polyester, rayon, and olefin) will not "remember" how they are supposed to hang, they simply begin to sag with the moisture and stay that way.

3. Choose a moderately textured surface—a little variation in the surface will help hide fading, water spots, and dust so drapes won't require cleaning/removal so often. Prints in a drapery can also decorate a room, cutting down on the need for other "decorations."

4. Choose a neutral color—not too light or too dark. Dark brown, for example, will show dust and sun fading almost immediately. Trim your neutral color with a dark color for accent, if necessary. Or go with a print, which will also camouflage dust.

5. Choose a tight, durable weave—tapestry weaves or gauzes are so loosely woven they won't hold their shape. Just as in furniture fabrics and carpet—the more threads per inch, the greater the density and the stronger the fabric.

6. Heavier fabrics will serve as insulation, but avoid fabrics like corduroy or damask that hang heavy on the rod and are hard to draw. Corduroy and velvets will attract and hold lint and dust.

Some fabrics to avoid at the window:

Burlap

Damask

Brocade

Cotton net

Organdy

Tapestry

Velvet

Corduroy

Brocatello

Satin

Fabrics to use:

Tightly woven fabrics

Cotton chintz (it's actually glazed to resist dirt)

Textured fabrics

Gabardine

Polyester/cotton blends

Rayon/cotton blends

Nylon/cotton blends

Vinyl fabrics

Wool blends

Ramie blends

Linen blends

Silk blends

"Blind" Spots

In the maintenance-free vocabulary "modern" is normally a good word, but where blinds are concerned, modern is the worst. The modern form of blind known as the mini-blind *compounds* the problem. You have at least twice as many little ledges and surfaces to clean on these svelte little slats.

Blinds are not only a wretched cleaning job, they need cleaning much more often than drapes or curtains because the dust really shows on those smooth surfaces.

If you *must* have louvers, get the vertical ones. They won't collect dust as much. Smooth metal is best—avoid fabric-covered ones.

There is one form of blind that's acceptable. It's a mini-blind sealed inside two sheets of glass. You can adjust the slats from without, but the blind is totally enclosed within the glass and thus maintenance-free.

Interior shutters are high maintenance—they're right up there with venetian blinds in the difficulty of keeping them clean and in good repair.

Cloth and canvas shades are harder to clean than the vinyl-coated ones, especially if you can't use soap and water on them. Regular roller blinds (shades) aren't very decorative. Their spring-loaded rollers are temperamental and the fabric ones yellow and show soil over time.

Woven woods, however, are one of the best window coverings because they're simple, durable, and don't show dust readily. They roll up out of the way when not in use and don't require expensive dry cleaning. They are subject to fading, though, and since they have to be pulled up and down frequently, will eventually require some repair to cords, etc. (Make sure they have a finish, or everything that hits them will stick—more maintenance!)

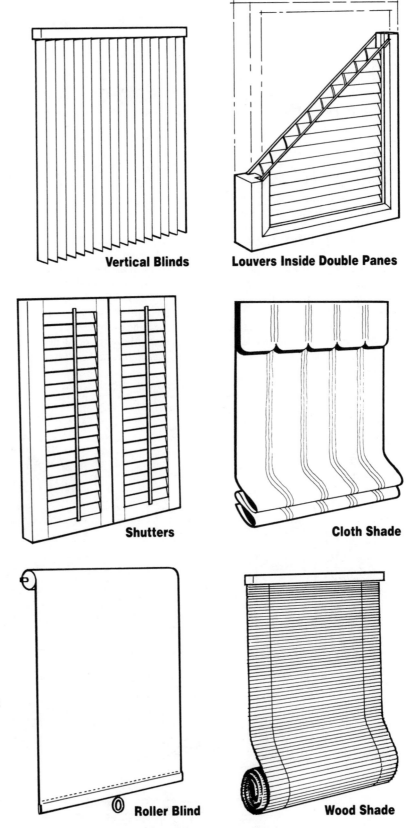

Vertical Blinds

Louvers Inside Double Panes

Shutters

Cloth Shade

Roller Blind

Wood Shade

Chapter 19

The Outside Story:

Eliminating Exterior Maintenance

The outside of the house not only has a lot of control over how much cleaning is done inside, it's what is seen first, and where many people spend the most money on repairs and restoration. It's as important to make the outside maintenance-free as the inside—maybe more. The inside basically suffers the use and abuse of humans; the outside, however, receives that plus the full force of the climate, wet and dry, hot and cold. It handles more birds and bees than any bedroom, it holds the dust-bearing breezes at bay, withstands the attacks of neighborhood baseballs, rocks flung from the mower, and the stain of dirt from the landscape. If your home's exterior handles all that well, you don't have to spend your life patching and piddling around to keep it fully functional and looking good.

Let's take a quick tour of the anatomy of the exterior.

Roof

Though a roof over our heads is the original and primary purpose of a house, the roof is the least and last thing ever to get attention. Most homeowners wait until it leaks before they replace or redo it. Yet everything on the inside and outside of a house depends on the roof to shed the elements effectively. Better and more varied roofing materials exist now than ever before, and many can be added without altering the existing structure. You can even bring light and heat into a house from the roof using solar panels and sky lights. Santa's reindeers shouldn't be the only ones who pay the roof any attention.

Rating the Roofings

1. Any kind of flat roof is maintenance suicide! Always use a pitched roof. A simple pitched roof gives the least trouble and is the least expensive to re-cover.

2. Slate or clay tile roofs are among the most attractive as well as the longest-lasting and most maintenance-free. They're also the most expensive.

3. Composition (asphalt) shingles on a pitched roof are the next best. Asphalt roof shingles can last up to thirty years. The more costly shingles are usually the better grade; get the ones with the longest guarantee. The method of application makes a lot of difference in how long a composition roof lasts—pay the extra money to get the best contractor, because a quality job is worth it.

4. Galvanized metal roofing is quite durable and trouble-free, but lacks elegance. Colored aluminum panels are more decorative, and never rust. In snow country, metal roofs are great because snow slides right off them.

5. Wood shakes or wood shingles crack and curl, need to be periodically oiled to preserve them, and usually require replacement within fifteen years. Aesthetics is their main attraction.

6. Roll roofing is not recommended for maintenance-free home roofs, because it usually isn't as durable as shingles, and has a "cheap" look.

Gutters

As for roof gutters, your best bet is a house without any gutters. To eliminate gutters the roof must have sufficient overhang so that water flowing off it won't pour into the soil adjacent to the foundation walls and then splash up on the side of the house or onto the sidewalks. So when you put a new roof on or build your dream house, extend the overhang and forget the gutters—they're just another thing to maintain. **If gutters are necessary for your design, make sure they're the self-cleaning kind, which have a covering to prevent leaves and other debris from clogging them.** Screens can easily be installed on existing open gutters to keep out leaves and twigs—a real labor-saver!

Eaves

Older-style, open eaves attract nesting birds and insects, take three times as long to paint as boxed-in eaves, are hard to seal up against moisture infiltration.

Boxed-in eaves cost only slightly more but reduce, if not eliminate, bird nests (and droppings) and reduce painting costs.

Be sure eaves are vented for a good air circulation or accumulated dampness will rot wood and blister paint. Keep boxed eaves caulked and screwed or nailed tight so that nothing but air can get in there!

And don't be tempted to leave eaves open for that rustic look on summer homes and cabins—box them in for easy maintenance. If you have an older home, with open eaves, a good maintenance-freeing improvement would be to enclose any open eaves.

Fascia Board

This is the board that runs along the edge of the eaves—behind the gutters, if you have them. It gets a constant bath from the roof runoff and constant exposure to the sun. No wonder it blisters, cracks, peels, and warps. The maintenance-freeing approach is to:

1. Keep water off by a further extension of the roof sheathing or a waterproof flashing.

2. Install a self-cleaning gutter.

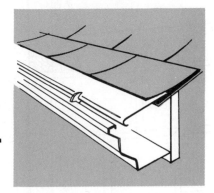

Self-Cleaning Gutter

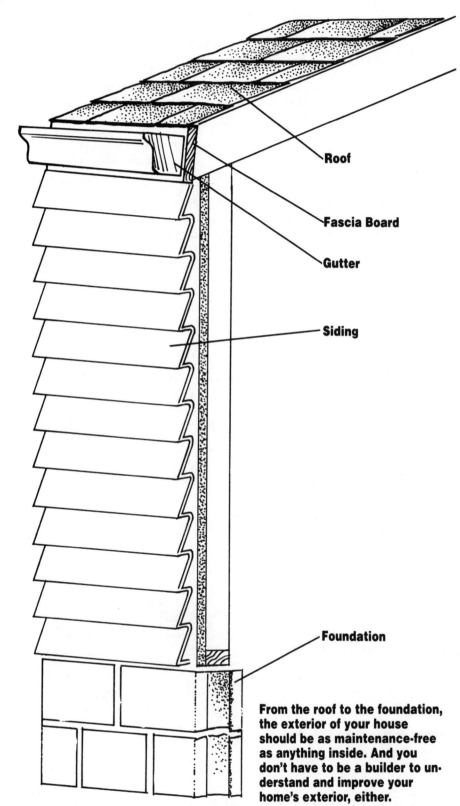

Roof

Fascia Board

Gutter

Siding

Foundation

From the roof to the foundation, the exterior of your house should be as maintenance-free as anything inside. And you don't have to be a builder to understand and improve your home's exterior, either.

Keep well painted so moisture can't penetrate wood and swell it, causing chipping.

We prefer latex paint—it has enough flex so it doesn't pop off when wood gets damp. A dark-colored fascia absorbs more sun, hence heats up and warps so the paint deteriorates sooner.

Another solution is to cover wood trim with aluminum or vinyl siding. And copper-covered fascia is forever!

The Outside Walls of Your House

What makes an easy-care house? An exterior with straight, simple lines will of course be easier to clean than one covered with ornamentation such as columns, porticos, cupolas, and gingerbread trim. A house with simple lines will also look cleaner because the lines don't zig and zag and jumble up the overall impression. In all design, inside and out, clean lines make things look cleaner.

True, the basic structure of a house can't usually be changed—a frame house is and will be a frame house, even as a masonry house will remain masonry. But there are things you can do to the outside walls that will quickly change the whole appearance of your house, as well as the amount of time and effort that needs to be applied to its care. Changing paint color was once about the only choice available, but today there are types of paint, coatings, siding, and facings tailored to fit any situation, any climate, and any aesthetic taste. You're *not* totally stuck with what you've got.

Siding makes up the bulk of your house's exterior. The siding is the "skin" of your home, and is the part that takes the most abuse from weather. **The siding of the average house needs attention every three to five years; you can extend that to eight to twenty years with the right type of siding material.**

Bear in mind that the lower one-third of your house takes two-thirds of the beating. It catches the splashing from eaves and lawn sprinklers, so the lower portion may need more frequent attention than the upper reaches.

Exterior Siding

Exterior siding is a little like clothes. Good quality siding, like good clothes, fits perfectly and looks good. If it seems to be tacked on or hangs awkwardly, the house, like you, will seem poorly dressed. Lots of siding is "added on" because the first surface failed or was high-maintenance. Be sure, if you add new siding, that you aren't adding another high-maintenance surface in your house. Late-late-show siding almost never looks as good on the model house on TV—especially the high-pressure, fly-by-night installation deals. Work with a reputable contractor who can help you select a good siding material, and see that it is installed correctly. In siding, as in clothes, there are good materials and bad, and climate has a voice in which is best for you.

Go look at sidings and talk to several people who already have the type you're considering—this is a simple precaution and will cost you nothing. Synthetic stone and wood products especially merit close examination before buying.

Scoring the Siding Choices

Wood shakes—Their rustic appearance hides a lot, but shakes are essentially a high-maintenance siding. They have to be treated regularly or they will curl, crack, peel, and rot.

Natural/stained wood—Durable if regularly (every three years or so) coated with stain. Natural wood grain is attractive and does hide defects. It requires more frequent recoating than painted wood, but the preparation time is minimal (no chipping, sanding, scraping). Dark colors deteriorate faster than lighter ones.

Natural Wood

Painted wood—This old standby requires recaulking and repainting every five years or so. Between paint jobs, though, it's very serviceable and comes in a vast array of styles. There are wood-sided homes that have been well maintained for literally centuries that still look terrific.

For ease of application and cleanup, and for durability, make sure you use a top-of-the-line latex house paint from one of the major manufacturers.

Aluminum siding—Much less trouble than painted wood, but not quite the miracle cure-all promised in brochures. It's noisy, cracking and popping as it expands and contracts, and it's susceptible to dents and scratches. It tends to get tacky looking, especially on the lower third of the house. Factory-applied paint is quite durable, but will eventually fade and chalk. Aluminum siding made with alloys and in thicker grades is as dent-resistant as steel, and probably the best metal siding, but it costs more than steel.

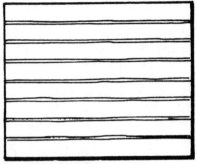

Aluminum Siding

Steel—Good steel siding doesn't dent as easily as aluminum; the original finish lasts up to thirty years, though it will fade a bit in that time.

Vinyl siding—Vinyl siding can be made to look amazingly like wood and you will *never* have to paint it. Because vinyl siding is softer and more flexible, it's quieter and less susceptible to dents and scrapes than aluminum. It's tough to repair if damaged, and will get brittle after a year or two in the sun, but overall, it's quite durable.

Brick—You never paint it. It still looks good if chipped or scraped. It won't burn. It doesn't rot. It doesn't warp or show wear and actually becomes more attractive with age; it only needs a little patching up on the mortar every ten years or so. It even increases the value of a house, and because it's fire resistant, it's cheaper to insure. What more can we say—brick is almost the perfect siding.

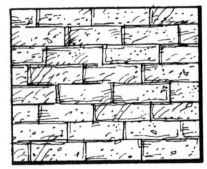

Brick

Stone—For twenty years on the desert farm where I grew up, we labored in the sun picking up and hauling those dreadful lava rocks. Now, thirty-five years later, I pay good money to have them put on the side of my house—why?

You know why! Stone is maintenance-free. It looks utterly natural, and shrugs off abuse. It hides every type of mark and you never have to paint it. Weather keeps it clean naturally and a little dirt only makes it look better. Rock and stone fit the criteria of an easy-care material perfectly.

Stone

Stucco—A textured masonry finish for exterior walls. It's not as desirable as brick or stone because it has to be painted to look good. Also, cracks develop over time, which have to be painted, and dirt can lodge (and stay) in highly textured stuccos. Its advantages are that it doesn't need repainting as often as wood siding, it's fireproof, and is not susceptible to rot or water damage.

Stucco

Masonry block—Very serviceable, but not as attractive as brick or natural stone. Decorative concrete block, such as that used for many shopping centers, may be too commercial looking for homes, but is good for fences and planters.

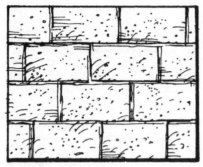

Masonry Block

What Color for the Outside of Your House?

Once again, stay with a neutral color; dark colors show the dirt. White or light colors should last at least twenty years on factory-finished siding, but the bright colors will begin to fade in just a few years. The metal sidings with baked-on finish will hold their color better than vinyl. Vinyl is good because the entire thickness of the paneling is the same color so injuries won't show—the color can never get scratched or chipped or peeled off.

Windows

We covered windows in Chapter 18, but because they're generally the most troublesome and time-consuming part of a house exterior, they're worth another word or two here.

Wood window frames not protected by a factory finish are the first and foremost of exterior elements to deteriorate.

Painted wood windowsills—especially dark-colored ones—deteriorate the fastest. Sills are at just the right angle to fare the worst from the weather. **Windowsills can be covered with a no-maintenance material such as brick, aluminum, concrete, cultured marble, or vinyl to prevent water damage and rotting. Always slant the sill down four degrees or more so water will roll right off.**

Shutters

Shutters should have stayed in the story books. All you Cape Cod cottage owners are probably hissing at me now, but shutters are seldom used for protection, as was their original purpose. Now they are for accent, decoration, aesthetic balance—and they also provide a breeding ground for the insect and bird fraternity, a proving ground for wood preservatives, and a grand exam of painting skill. Since they are now a focal point of the house, they must be continually cleaned and painted. If you have classy low-maintenance windows, however, you won't need a shutter to give your house character.

Foundation

For an exposed foundation, keep the natural color—painting it will only necessitate constant repainting. A semismooth texture is the best; it's rough enough to hide imperfections and not so rough it can collect dirt and bugs in fissures.

Cracks and leaks are the eternal headaches of basement walls. You can't fix them from inside, notwithstanding the trinket kits they sell at the hardware store—they're a waste of money. **A heavy asphalt coating on the foundation and good drainage is the answer to the wet-basement problem.** Don't hope, pray, and attack it with self-seal or go cry on your neighbor's shoulder—dig up the ground around it and fix it right. Once you've dug deeply enough to expose the foundation, really cover the foundation with asphalt coating. I'd even cove the corners with mortar for good drainage.

Slant the earth away from the foundation so that water and snow don't accumulate around the house and leak down alongside the foundation. Good drainage is a must for a maintenance-free foundation. In wet areas, a gravel sump or clay drain tiles may be necessary.

Also be sure to set up your *yard* for good drainage. It's just as important to have the water drain off the entire yard as it is to have it drain away from the foundation. When grading your yard, don't leave low spots where water will puddle and make soggy places that you can't mow, that breed mosquitos, and that manufacture mud.

Yardwork

Having an outside that will take care of itself extends beyond the outside of the house itself, though the lawn, shrubs, and fences need attention too.

After you finish a day of clipping and snipping, digging and planting, weeding and watering to keep things looking good around your place, get in the car and drive to as wild an area as you can. Walk into the fields, among the hillsides and among the trees and sit down for a few minutes and look at the job nature does of keeping things maintenance-free—things harmonize, balance, look good, and take care of themselves. Modern advances have managed to compound the workload, with all the scientific machines and sprays now on the market. You can take a tiny patch of nature around your house and spend more time and money on it than on all of Idaho's giant primitive area. The lawn once could be cut in an hour with the old push mower. Then someone invented power mowers that would do the job in ten minutes. So people planted bigger and more complicated landscapes and now it takes three hours to mow the lawn. If you love gardening and landscaping— if there's nothing you like better than wielding a hedge clipper or feeling the dirt between your toes—all the hours you'll spend outdoors will be worth it. If not, it might as well be a prison yard you're laboring in.

The Green, Green Grass of Home

A big yard is nice to look at, play in, and offers privacy, but the upkeep isn't worth it if you try to maintain a yard the "conventional" way. Keep the yard, but cut the toil with some maintenance-free design—it might even make the yard more fun to be in. (For ideas on using your yard for recreation see pages 74-75.)

The prestige of neatly manicured grass—our modern lawns— dates from the days of the old English manors where the Lord's sheep and cattle kept the rolling green short and neat with nipping lips and sharp hoofs. (They also served as mobile fertilizer spreaders.) Today we pour commercial fertilizer on the grass, then curse it for growing so fast and complain about the lack of room in the garage, which is filled to the rafters with chemicals and equipment.

If you want to cut down on lawn maintenance time, it's important to choose grasses that are well suited to your area. They'll need a lot less care—less watering and weeding and nursing along over time.

Try, too, to plant *slow-growing grass*. Grass that grows more slowly won't have to be cut as often. Your local nursery or county agricultural agent will know what slower-growing varieties are most likely to thrive where you live.

Limit Grass Lawn Areas

Grass lawns are the most time-consuming of all ground coverings. If you're going to water and mow the grass, you want to be sure you're using it for more than show. You should check into and consider replacing some of your unused lawn area with plants that are native to your region. Check "weed ordinances," though. Some communities do have restrictions as to how high your grass can grow, which may prevent you from letting areas of your property grow wild. But natural meadow, woodland, prairie, or desert is no less attractive or inviting than grass—and it's more varied and interesting at any time of the year.

What part of the lawn do you really *use*? The part that you walk on, lay on, run, and play on. If you go out into your yard to relax, you aren't likely to lie right next to the fence or the house—you'll probably go out somewhere in the middle of your yard or under a tree. That's where your grass should be. You don't need it in and around the bushes, other plants, and foliage—you just have to trim it there and pull the lawn mower in and out trying to maneuver around things. In these areas it makes more sense to put

Plant grass only where you really need it—not next to trees or fences that are hard to mow around.

180

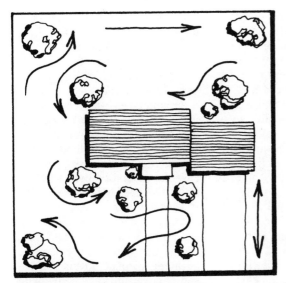
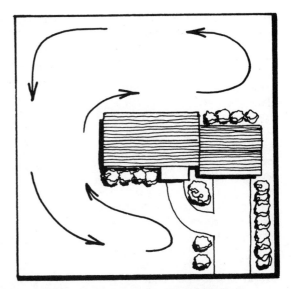

Look at all the maneuvering you have to do to mow the lawn on the left—in and out around all those bushes. The lawn on the right can be mowed in one continuous motion and offers the same plush green look.

down a ground cover or mulch that doesn't require as much care and manicuring as lawn. **Then plant grass in the middle of your yard in a circular arrangement so you can mow in a continuous path instead of back and forth. It'll cut your lawn care time in half.**

Plant your lawn in a pattern that's easy to mow. Grass looks bad when it's interrupted, cubed, islanded.

Eliminate Edging

Lawn edges are like baseboards inside a house—they're a pain to take care of, and they never look good. Yes, you can buy a power edger, but edging a lawn is still a time-consuming job. Plus it's just one more expensive tool to store and insure and have the neighbors borrow and break. From now on, whenever you build anything new, add three inches of lip to the footings or foundation when you're pouring the concrete, You can do the same thing along sidewalks and fences too. It not only saves

mower maneuvering, it looks sharp, too.

Another way of putting in an edge for quick mowing is cement lawn edgers. These are sold as individual blocks, or they can be poured in concrete. (Talk to your cement contractor.)

Put metal or concrete edging around trees so you won't have to trim grass around them—you can mow right up to the edge.

Cement lawn edgers make mowing around bushes and plants much less difficult. They come in individual blocks or can be poured by a cement contractor.

Rock the Hills

Well-laid rocks or masonry looks nice on a hill and you never have to lift a hand to maintain it. The rain will clean it and moss it. You can do it yourself, too. Buy natural stone from a quarry or stone mason, or from a farm or road construction site. Some land-owners will even give you the stone.

Use a concrete or stone border for your rock work, not wood (even cedar and redwood rot eventually). If you want a base for the rocks to sit on, a few bucks' worth of ready-mix concrete will do it. Always spread a heavy piece of black plastic on the ground first to kill the weeds and prevent them from growing up through the rocks. Sand, gravel, pebbles, small rocks, or cinders will fill in the cracks.

Don't Let Dirt Loose

Though we're urging you to re-think how much of your yard you really want to devote to lawn, do be sure all the bare earth in your yard is planted. The more loose dirt you have in your yard, the dirtier the inside of your house will be. Have you noticed how dirty you or your kids get on a camping trip as compared to an ordinary day around home? If there's a lot of loose dirt around, people pick it up. Loose dirt gets tracked in, it blows in, it comes in on toys and tools, etc. It clings to feet and paws and animal fur and when it gets wet, will stick to anything. **If all of the yard surrounding the house for a distance of at least twenty feet is covered with grass or ground cover, it will keep dirt pickup down. Get control of dirt on the outside of your house and you'll have the inside battle half won.**

Designer Ground Cover

"Ground cover" is the general term for low-growing plants that cover the bare ground as an alternative to grass. Ground covers do the same things grass does—keep soil moisture in and loose dirt from flying around—but with much less maintenance on your part. There are hundreds of kinds of ground cover—it creeps, squats in a rosette, is evergreen, flowering, has large leaf, or small leaf. You can achieve any kind of effect you like with it. **Use ground cover for decoration, not a lot of plants that need to be manicured to stay looking nice.**

Many ground covers never need cutting back—they maintain themselves. Others need only periodic trimming. Ground covers enable you to cover hills and banks with no-mow greenery, create a front or side yard you can plant and forget, and let you have "something green" in areas where it's tough to grow grass—under trees, for example. Then except for an occasional watering, if needed, it can be left alone.

Ground covers aren't only plants—many mulches also fall under the category of ground cover. Here are just a few of the great many options available:

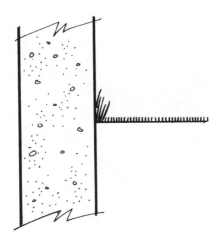
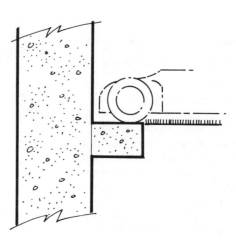

Trimming grass along the walls, sidewalks, and fences is a painstaking task. You can eliminate it by pouring a lip around the foundation so that grass doesn't grow all the way up to the wall and a lawn mower can take care of all the "trimming."

- Cinders

- Rocks

- Bark

- Pachysandra

- Asian jasmine

- Loop grass

- Wild or domestic strawberries

- Low sprawling evergreens

- Ivy

- Ferns

One note of caution: If you choose rocks, bark, or cinders as a ground cover, remember not to get it too fine. The finer it is, the more likely it'll get spread out and kicked onto the sidewalk and then tracked into your house.

And don't succumb to the temp-tation of letting ground cover be-come "house cover." Ivy crawling up the walls may look quaint, but it's a real maintenance nightmare. Ivy on brick is marginally okay, if you just have to have it, but *never* let it cover painted siding. The trapped moisture will deteriorate the siding, and removing those charming vines at repainting time is a real job.

Trimming Back on Trimming and Pruning

For every part of your property try to choose trees, shrubs, and vines that maintain themselves. Some plants grow shoots and branches that constantly need pruning; others have very little ex-tra growth. Avoid plants that re-quire constant cutting back and trimming.

Don't overplant or plant things too close together. If they're given sufficient room to grow, plants will be healthier and require less shaping and thinning out.

When it comes to the time-honored practice of clipping shrubs and trees into balls, rectan-gles and heaven forbid, even more complicated shapes, *forget it!* Out-door art like this is best left to the Disneyland Gardens.

It's usually a lost cause to try to make something into what it's not. Why sculpture bushes into unnatu-ral shapes? It's a lot of work and doesn't make them any more at-tractive. Bushes and hedges all have their own God-given shape and beauty and trying to make them into geometric shapes defeats the whole point of having a tree or plant in the yard.

Tree and Shrub Savvy

1. Select trees that won't have a great deal of limb loss. Your local nursery is a good re-source here, or the county ag-ricultural agent.

2. Select trees that won't pose a huge clean-up problem in the fall. Some trees are inherently messy, particularly those with plentiful pods, fruits, cones, or nuts. Any kind of pod or fruit that falls on the ground is a problem, unless of course you had the foresight to plant such trees over ground you don't manicure. You have to rake or clean them up and the next day there are a bunch more. If the fruit isn't edible, I wouldn't want it in my yard. (Even edible fruit that doesn't get harvested is a maintenance problem.)

3. Also avoid planting shrubs where they will pose a clean-up problem in the fall. Certain shrubs tend to catch leaves falling from nearby trees and are difficult to clean out. And some shrubs, too, have fruit or other fallout that must be dealt with. Also, be sure to plant shrubs far enough away from the house so that they don't interfere with access for window cleaning, painting, and other maintenance tasks.

4. Choose hardy plants, trees, and shrubs that won't require special protection from cold or from pests and disease. Whenever possible, choose plants that grow naturally in your area for your yard; Mother Nature was the original low-maintenance gardener. Your local horticultural society, garden club, county agent, or nursery is a good source of information on plants and the conditions they require.

How to Minimize Watering

Design your lawn so that the outdoor hard surfaces (the sidewalk, patio, and driveway) and roof shed rain water where water is needed—it works! You won't have to water as often. Also, use ground covers and mulches (such as wood chips or grass clippings) to help retain moisture in the soil around shrubs, etc. If you live in a dry region, choose drought-resistant plants, trees, and shrubs, and reduce grass lawn surface.

There's also something you can do with a lawn to cut down watering right from the beginning. If you are planting a new grass lawn, once it's established, let it go dry a while. Let it get to the point that the grass is still basically green but beginning to fade. A few stalks will be turning brown, but most of them will still be green, just wilting slightly. Then deep-water it again. The reason you do this is to get the roots to go down deep for moisture. A deeply rooted lawn will draw water from below instead of needing you to water it all the time.

It's best to water a lawn deeply at long intervals rather than a little bit every day or so; this, too, encourages a deeply rooted, drought-resistant lawn. An automatic underground sprinkler system controlled by a time clock is a definite plus for cutting yard time, if you can afford it.

Good Fences Make Good Sense

The quest for greater privacy has inspired many people to go "fence shopping." The day of the wide open spaces has ended, the only open space most people have now is a 75x100-foot yard that they aren't anxious to share—so they fence it.

With a few exceptions, a fence won't keep anything or anybody out if they really want to get over it or under it or even through it. A pompous structure suggesting something valuable is behind it may actually encourage thieves and vandals. Unless you have a very specific purpose in mind, such as keeping a certain animal out or perhaps sound from a highway, fences ought to be polite, pleasant markers of your boundaries, saying "Please remember this belongs to me," not "KEEP OUT!"

The Right Fence Can Keep Your Yard for You

Choose the fence style you need for whatever you want to keep in—or out. A chain-link fence will help keep leaves and debris from blowing into your yard; a rail fence won't keep groundhogs out of your garden. Make a list of your practical and aesthetic needs in a fence and then run down this fence checklist:

Strength

Durability

Susceptibility to rot, decay

Security

Safety

Upkeep requirements

Ease of repair

Installation cost

Appearance

I love the look of wood fences, but wood does have some distinct limitations when it comes to fencing. It warps, too much sun dries it, too much rain rots it, too much snow sags it, and it burns. Also, wood usually needs stain or paint to beautify or preserve it, and this is a maintenance headache.

In an impetuous moment once, I built a wood corral fence (like I'd seen in the cowboy movies) around my ranch outbuildings, using pine posts and large spikes to fasten the poles onto the posts. It looked official cowboy, all right. But the cost of putting it up was exorbitant, and in three years the posts rotted in the ground, the wind and weather loosened the nails, and the rails fell off when anyone leaned on them.

Today you ought to look at the versatility of masonry fences. There is no end to the fence styles you can create with masonry. In Los Angeles I saw over forty miles of block fence. It was beautiful, strong, water repellant, weather proof, and a great screen for pri-

vacy and sound. The cost of masonry fences is about $8-$10 a running foot. Around the average yard, a masonry fence costs about $1,500, but once it's in, you're finished with it forever.

You can also blend features right into a masonry fence for uses like concealing the garbage can, storing yard tools, mounting lights, swings, etc.

You can choose between brick, stucco, rock, and decorative block. A DIY or masonry store should have a pile of brochures on fences.

A Quick Rating of Residential Fencing

1. Masonry (decorative concrete block, rock, brick, poured concrete, etc.) comes in two general categories: solid masonry and masonry posts with other materials used as rails. A solid masonry fence isn't cheap to install, but once it's in, it's forever.

2. Chain link is not the most attractive fence in the world, but low-maintenance as long as it's galvanized.

3. Wrought iron is a good strong fence but it must be painted regularly or it will rust.

4. The many types of wood fence fall into two general types: board fences and post and rail fences. Wooden posts have to be treated with preservative and all above-ground structures have to be kept painted or stained or they will deteriorate and rot.

5. Hedges have to be watered, fertilized, and weeded, and have to be clipped at least monthly.

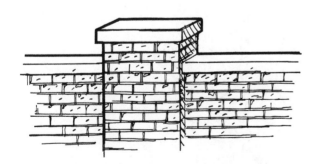 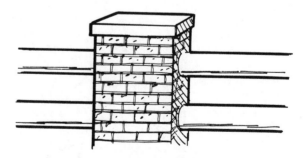

Masonry makes a sturdy and self-maintaining fence. If you build a solid masonry fence, as shown at left, you can also build in hideaways for the garbage cans or anything else you store outside. Another good choice is a fence of masonry posts with metal, concrete, or wood rails, right.

Chapter 20

You Can Do It Yourself

Think again about all the ideas you've had for making your home easier to care for, to use, to enjoy. For years now men and women from all walks of life have been approaching me to share their ideas for cutting housework time. Many of these ideas are good, some brilliant. Yet 99 percent of the time when I ask if they have put them into practice, they say no. They lack confidence: they tell me they're too timid, too busy, too old, or too young to try something like that. "It's too late to make my place maintenance-free." Or "I can't afford it."

That's all nonsense. Colonel Sanders was sixty-three years old when he started his chicken empire, fast-food tycoon Ray Kroc was fifty-one when he founded McDonald's. I know fourteen-year-old kids who can build houses, paint, plumb, wire, and pour cement.

Are you going to surrender all your needs, dreams, desires, and opportunities to lack of confidence?

You may still remember the last thing you made; it may go all the way back to sixth grade when you built two bookends, drove in the nails yourself, too! They were beauties, weren't they? But somewhere along the line you may have lost the nerve to try your hand at building or repairs. Maybe you tried something once and failed, and it left you wondering if you really could do it. Now when you see tools, blueprints, and building materials, you say, "If I were only as skilled and clever as all those hammer-wielding builders. . . ."

You're Not Alone

We're trying to tell you that *you*, man or woman, banker or forklift operator, weakling or weight-lifter, are not beyond doing some good building, remodeling, or designing. Every do-it-yourselfer went through the same thing many of you are going through right now. "I could never do it." "I'm not smart enough or strong enough." "When I get finished the electricity will probably come out the water faucet and water out the electrical outlet." To further shatter your confidence you hear builders talking among themselves. "Hey, Stubs, when you tilt up the bearing wall, make sure the plate butts on that joint where the joists overlap." "Do you think the ten penny galvanized will bond this T1-11 through the sheathing?" And they go on to use lots more of those seemingly forbidding building words. When I used to hear them, I would skulk out of the way like a back-alley dog, utterly convinced that I could never presume to build or remodel anything as massive as a house. Builders were like gods to me, and I looked on construction with awe, from a dis-

tance. But as my little cleaning business grew, many clients, living in the same fear of touching anything "contractorish," would ask me to do little repair jobs while I was cleaning their house. Being a hungry college kid who wanted to provide as full a service as possible, I ran to the hardware store or to friends and asked questions. First I repaired a hole in a Sheetrock wall, then I refinished a cupboard, and later a wooden floor—and, amazingly, each of these projects looked good. It wasn't hard or complicated at all. Soon I was beginning to break through the barrier from "fix it" to "build it."

Construction Instruction

My initiation into construction came when my church bought four acres adjoining my house and began building a chapel. All the church members were asked to volunteer some help with the project. The very first week of construction, I ventured out to the general foreman, a big hairy-armed fellow. "Hey, brother, give me a reading on this elevation," he yelled at me. He gestured to a surveyor's transit. My legs turned to rubber, but I did what he said and within a few minutes I realized it required nothing any more complicated than all those little tenths and lines I learned about in the fourth grade.

The foreman kept saying we were laying out the "footing lines," but I didn't know a footing line from a fishing line. I helped and watched as they dug a trench for the footings (which I found out were what the foundation sits on), then put in forms to hold the cement and reinforcing bars to strengthen it. By the time they had poured the footings and foundation, I was a construction junkie.

I was getting up at 4 A.M. before my first college class at 8 and

learning to build. I found that most of the stuff was easy to understand or used skills I already had—getting the confidence that *I* could do it was the only hard part.

Once I gained the confidence, it was all a breeze. Everything made sense, there wasn't anything too complicated, not even the finishing work. Once I learned to be careful and to measure twice and cut once, instead of measuring once and cutting twice, even that was easy. In nine months the chapel was finished, and I knew I could build and I never forgot it.

Being able to do some of your own work is an important economic consideration too. Service is expensive, and often the serviceperson's charges for labor and travel time are a lot more than the cost of any parts or materials involved. **If doing it yourself allows you to spend $100 for a project instead of $250, you'll have the same end result, plus a feeling of satisfaction and confidence . . . because *you* did it!**

You Can Do It Better *Yourself*

Making improvements to your home yourself isn't just fun and cheaper—often you will do a better job than someone you hire. (Because it's your own place and you *care* about it.) We're not saying you should do *all* your own work—there are things you never would or could do. I'm just saying that you can, and will, enjoy not only the doing but the result—the finished product—for years and years after. Even more so because *you* did it.

Once you start doing your own repair, remodeling, and building work, it won't be long before you begin to notice the workmanship—the joints, installations, and finish work—in big, fancy, and famous hotels and restaurants. Suddenly you'll realize (and what a thrill it will be) that your work is better. Your confidence will soar. It's like owning a Mercedes, doing your own moving, or having a hernia, you hardly give good workmanship a thought until you experience it yourself . . . then suddenly you notice it everywhere. You'll love being a knowledgeable remodeler and builder.

Ask and Ye Shall Receive

So you've built up your confidence and you're ready to start building something else. Where can you go for some help? Fortunately, DIY or "Do-It-Yourself" centers have blossomed all over in recent years. These stores not only offer every conceivable supply you need—all the latest angles in materials and design—but also have them attractively displayed and stand ready to answer all your questions. After all, it's in their best interest to make you a full-fledged do-it-yourselfer.

The clerks in most DIY and hardware stores can answer your questions or refer you to someone who can. As part of their service, they can tell you what size joist or rafter you need, how thick to make the floor, or how many coats of paint or varnish something needs. They have wiring, plumbing, tiling, and building manuals of all kinds, even some books of code requirements. You can get directions (often illustrated) for almost anything.

Write and Ask

Most companies that produce construction supplies and materials not only have consumer reps who can be very helpful, but the companies themselves will be delighted to send piles of information on their products and the things that can be done with them.

Talk to a Few People

Talk to not only the DIY dealers but also to builders, contactors, and tradespeople you come in contact with. All have had experience and may well think of something you haven't. **Check with friends**

who have done what you're thinking of doing—they're likely to have lots of advice. Ask them how they like the project now that it's finished and if it is indeed saving them time and trouble.

Visit Construction Sites

Spend a few spare afternoons or days off scouting around construction or remodeling sites; just watch and ask questions. Owners and craftsmen alike love to talk about what they're doing and to show off a little—they can help you enormously.

Do all this *before* you start a *project* so you can decide if it's worth the time and money for you to take it on. If you don't have the tools or the time, or it involves skills that truly do take a long time to master, it might be cheaper and wiser to have it done by a professional.

When the clerk asks you, "Is the flashing for a plumbing vent or a gas flue?" It's not wrong to say, "It's for the big pipe that goes up through the roof from right behind the toilet." Contractor jargon isn't a prerequisite to doing a good job—any more than you need to read music to sing well. I built two entire houses and never even learned the official nail sizes. After you've figured out and identified your needs and requirements, you can probably come up with a better description than the official one anyway.

Don't Be Intimidated by What Others Think

Here, at last, is a chance to use *your* ideas to meet your needs, suit your purposes, promote your interests, save yourself time, and further your own creations, so your home will truly be an extension of you and serve you—instead of vice versa. Don't let others tell you it can't be done, or that you should do it the way everyone else does.

Start now, collect information, make sketches, start to plan. It's educational and stimulating, and you'll be surprised what a good engineer you are.

When you're planning, you can have a professional home designer analyze your house to see how it can be made low-maintenance. The cost is usually a consultation fee by the hour (see the Source List).

Building Codes and Licenses

You don't need a lot of licenses to do minor repair work on your own house. But for any major remodeling or construction, ask your local building and zoning authority what you

need. Remember—construction codes are for your own good. They are the rules experts have decided on to make sure systems work, to keep people from getting electrocuted and houses from burning down. The local authorities will give you a list of do's and don'ts—read them and you'll be able to comply very easily.

I was a little defensive about codes and zoning myself at first. I went to a few meetings and ranted and raved with the worst of them until I finally realized that the codes work for the good of all. To wire my home in Sun Valley, for example, I had to get a permit. The permit simply informed the state electrical board that a house was going up and that I was wiring it. Every contractor gets a permit, too. This lets the officials drop in and make periodic inspections to see if everything is okay. When I was about halfway finished with my house, an inspector showed up and asked to look around. In the pump room he stopped and examined some light fixtures I'd installed in the basement ceiling. He, being an electrician and a forty-year veteran at that, said, "Those are old fixtures." He was right—though they were still in nice crisp boxes, I'd bought them from a guy who had them left over from a building twenty years ago. They were unused, but outdated. "These things were taken off the market because they burned a lot of houses down," he said, and showed me how to put them in so the fixture wouldn't heat and burn. "They're actually good fixtures," he said, "but you need about four washers' worth of space here. That will separate them from the wood and completely eliminate any chance of fire." Inspectors not only perform an important service, but most of them are actually nice people.

Some Words of Wisdom

Do-it-yourself is not a question of *can you*, it's more like *do you want to* and *will you enjoy it*. I'm convinced that you can do the majority (if not all) the maintenance-free adjustment work on your home with the easy-to-use tools, materials, and the DIY stores we have almost everywhere right at our elbow. So the question is: **Do you have the time and the interest, or is it really economical for you to do the job?** Major electrical or plumbing changes, for example, might not be the wisest thing to tackle first. When I was still a novice in these areas, I got a permit and designed and wired my new home (the water didn't come out of the electrical outlet, either). However, when I finally called in a twenty-year electrical veteran to finish up one of my projects, he installed and wired in my current so quickly I couldn't open the parts packages fast enough to keep ahead. He charged $20 an hour, but he was *much*, much cheaper (and better) than me.

Nothing is out of your reach if you want to do it, but try to be realistic about a few things.

- Do I really have the time to do it myself (or will it take more time than I have available)?

- Do I have the right tools for the job (or can they justifiably be bought)?

- What is my (and my family's/partner's) patience level?

- Do I have the expertise, or do I know where to find the help I need?

Side by side with "you can do it" is always "you can get it" (a broken toe or neck, a wrenched shoulder, etc.), too. The two extra caution areas are:

1. *Electricity*—It's fast and deadly. A good place to get help if you have any doubts about your ability.

2. *Heights*—Gravity isn't selective. Slip or fall from a high area, and you lose. Many people can't handle height well—hire a pro if it bothers you.

Getting Outside Help

When you do choose to hire a professional—whether because you want to do part of the work and hire out part, or because you prefer to have a contractor do everything—you'll need to know how to get help from and to deal intelligently with a contractor. Here are some tips:

Select a Good Builder

Some builders are human snails who can stretch a three-week job into two months. Others are crude craftsmen, and still others are promoters who invest all their energy and handiwork in selling the job to you. It's important that they be competent as well as convincing. A few minutes checking references can save years of regret.

Ask builders:

☑ **How long have they been in business?**

☑ **Are they bonded and insured (get a copy of the insurance certificate)?**

☑ **Are they in debt over their head (do they have the credit to do your job)? Call a couple of their suppliers. If they ask for money up front to buy materials, they're probably strung out financially.**

☑ **What are the names and telephone numbers (or addresses) of the last four jobs they did? Call or visit previous customers to see if they were satisfied.**

☑ **Be careful about hiring the local high-school shop teacher or your cousin or your unemployed brother-in-law. They might be putterers, not finishers.**

Know What You Want

Too many people call builders or carpenters over and end up asking them to come up with all the suggestions. Especially when you're creating your own maintenance-free house, you don't want this to be the case. Have a written plan or sketch of what you want them to do and hand it to them and *then* ask, "Any suggestions?" Then they can and will help, just don't ask them to do all the planning. Tell them your *main* objective is to have an easy-to-clean house and be sure they understand. They may know a lot more about construction than you do, but only you know what you want and need.

Follow Up on Them

They'll do a better job if they know you are watching.

Get Everything in Writing

Leave nothing to chance or word of mouth. Have the contractor give you a written bid stating the full price, exactly what services are included for that, what length of time it will take, and how and when you'll pay. Payment for small jobs generally comes at the end. Large-scale remodeling can be set up in graduated payments as the job progresses. For a new home (or new addition), it's customary to pay 25 percent when the foundation work is in, 25 percent when the roof is on and the house is sealed, 40 percent when the project is completely finished, and the rest when it's inspected and accepted. Never pay all up front—and always reserve the right to pay the balance when the job is *complete* right down to the last doorknob. It's great motivation for them to get the job done fast and well.

Extra, Extra

Bear in mind that often, in fact most of the time, if you ask a contractor to do something out of the ordinary it will cost more.

Kitchen cabinets are a good example of this. Most cabinets are prefabricated—the pieces are all cut in bulk to a certain height and depth. If you want something different, a large manufacturer may have to break down an entire assembly line to do it. Look around. It's usually the small-time cabinet-makers who are willing to do the non-standard. Because their overhead is lower and they're not committed to elaborate machinery, it may not cost you much more than a standard style. If you can't find a cheaper way to get the job done, you will have to weigh the value. A major change in the kitchen, for example, because of its constant use, is probably worth the investment. You have to deal with the irritation of a wrong-sized or wrongly equipped kitchen at least three times every day. In other parts of the house it's up to you to decide what importance you place on the alterations.

When you're building, changes that make a house maintenance-free can cost *less* than conventional methods and materials. They can also cost very little to add to a house, especially if you keep it simple and do it yourself. It's not uncommon to get bids from a contractor of $3,000 or $4,000 to do some remodeling in the basement, whereas you could do it yourself for about $650 in materials. About 60 percent of remodeling and building costs is labor, so if you do it yourself, you'll cut the need for capital right at the start. Then if you watch for sales and discounts on the materials, you can save another 20 percent.

Step 1. Measure and plan

Step 2. Find or make a design to match the rest of the structure

Step 3. Undo what's there now, rip it out

Step 4. Clean up and haul away the mess

Step 5. Deal with the unexpected structural defects

Step 6. Find materials

Step 7. Build it

Remodeling

Step 1. Measure and plan

Step 2. Order materials

Step 3. Build it

Building from Scratch

Ready, Set . . .

We're determined to convince you that you can go to work immediately on your maintenance-free pursuits. A cracked, flaking, finger-painted wall could be covered with three sheets of good, hard, beautiful maintenance-free oak paneling for under $50, no more than the cost of a night out on the town or tickets to the big game. (You can spend that night or afternoon putting up the paneling.) And while you're planning and dreaming about the big stuff, go ahead and start on the small stuff, using your spare time and money. You'll be amazed at how many things you can change.

If you really want to dive in further, you have some other resources you may not have considered. Instead of buying a new car and taking on those $300-a-month payments, remember that for $10,000, the cost of upgrading to a fancier, shinier (but not necessarily more functional) car, you could perform a maintenance-free miracle in your home. And I promise you'd get ten times more good out of the home improvements than you would from a lot of exotic extras in an automobile.

Much maintenance-free building is relatively inexpensive and can be accomplished over a period of time. **Whether the project is major or minor, be sure to take the time to *plan* and think things through. Many a failure is in the impatience; don't get in a big hurry and leap into a project.** And think twice before you drain your equity by getting a second mortgage to remodel. Those finance charges often mount up into thousands of dollars. Instead of paying finance charges, use that money to cut tons of maintenance problems out of your house—a little at a time.

Remodeling

Before you dive into major remodeling, be aware that it often entails more than building from scratch. Some contractors estimate 45 percent more time on a remodeling job over what it would take to build it new.

Finding the Financing

How many great ideas have been abandoned and how many opportunities have been missed because of the immediate impulse to say "I can't afford it"? As soon as you begin to plan the change, somehow the question of finance throws a bucket of cold water on your idea and ZAP, the dream is dead. Oddly, money to be spent on something "around the house" is the first to be questioned, challenged, or siphoned off to something else, because it's only for improvements *we* would see and enjoy and use every day of our lives. Pride or "show" expenditures that are done for reputation or prestige will get the nod a lot faster. We're convinced that the only tough thing about making your house maintenance-free and your life at home better is developing the guts and determination to make the decision to *do* it.

Once that decision is firmly made, the rest is simply answering the mechanical and procedural questions of how you are going to do it.

There are "bottom-line" questions you will want to consider, like how will your plan affect your home's resale value? If you don't plan to stay in your home for a long time, there are many maintenance-free design changes that wouldn't make good economic sense (lowering the countertop height, for instance). To increase resale value, a design change should hold appeal for a broad range of potential buyers.

Building something almost anyone would appreciate into a home that you may sell, or something you really want into a home that will undoubtedly be your lifetime dwelling can make your investment a good one.

You may not be able to recoup all the money you spend making a house more maintenance-free. You will have to decide how important a change is to you personally—how much it enhances your life by freeing you up for other things, and how much of a concern the resale value is.

Financing Unconventional Ideas

Banks and lending institutions do have guidelines and rules, but if you look and talk long enough, you'll find someone willing to go along with your idea and you'll be on your way. Hang in there!

Bankers aren't likely to understand or be sympathetic to your idea if you just tell them about it or try to describe it. The best approach is to make it as visual for them as possible. *Show* them— with sketches, drawings, photographs, or even a scale model. Clearly outline the advantages and disadvantages in list form, show them exactly how much it will save you in time, effort, and worry, as well as in repair and upkeep costs. If you can, mention others who have done this successfully.

In other words, show them that you've thought it out carefully. A detailed plan will usually make the difference—it will make them feel secure enough to advance the money for it.

One Step at a Time

Now that you're thoroughly versed in all the ways you can make your house help out with the house-work, you may be asking your-self, "Where do I begin?" To help you sort it all out, we've tak-en a typical three-bedroom home through four stages of maintenance-free redesign. We'll begin with alterations that cost very little and can be taken with you if you move, and we'll end up with major alterations that in-clude structural changes to the house. You'll find that no matter how much you have to spend, there are ways to cut down on cleaning—and our suggestions are only the beginning.

Step One: I Want to Take It With Me When I Move

Don't put off making your life easier simply because you rent your home, plan to move soon, or just don't have much money right now. There are plenty of improve-ments you can make that don't cost much and are portable.

1. Mat the entryways

2. Arrange the furniture at right angles

3. Suspend small appliances

4. Add wire shelving in bath-rooms, laundry room, kitchen

5. Concentrate plants in one area (here, in the dining room)

6. Replace layers of bedclothes with one comforter

7. Declutter throughout

8. Simplify wall decor

9. Suspend garbage cans

10. Install brackets or clips to hold shower curtain in place

11. Replace burner pans with Teflon-coated pans

12. Buy plastic storage bins for the kids' rooms

13. Hang tools on garage or shop walls

14. Use liquid soap instead of bars

15. Separate live and dead storage

Master Bathroom · Master Bedroom · Dining Room · Kitchen · Laundry Room · Bathroom · Bedroom · Bedroom · Living Room · Garage

Step Two: I Don't Want to Put a Lot of Money Into the Place

You don't have to make major structural changes to enjoy the benefits of an easier-to-clean home. These small projects—many of which you can do yourself—are all things that you can do without major expense. Do one or two as money becomes available and before you know it you'll find yourself with more and more free time on your hands.

1. Install vinyl sheet flooring in entryways, bathrooms

2. Suspend lighting

3. Build in beds and other furniture wherever possible

4. Extend kitchen cabinets above the refrigerator

5. Install closet organizers

6. Seal the garage floor

7. Paint walls with semigloss enamel in neutral tones

8. Replace ornate hardware with simple hardware (doorknobs, faucets, handles)

9. Install a full-length mirror in the bathrooms

10. Put modular furniture in the kids' rooms

11. Replace elaborate drapes and window coverings

12. Install soap dispensers in the bathrooms

13. Create a control center in the bathroom or kitchen

14. Make children's closet rods adjustable

15. Store cleaning supplies where they're needed

Step Three: I'm Doing Some Remodeling

When you're doing remodeling, you can take some giant steps toward a maintenance-free existence. Just make sure you spend your money wisely—by improving your most heavily used areas, not those that are just for show. You'll find that guests are much more impressed by a clean, comfortable home that they're not afraid to use than by an elaborate, showy room that's too delicate to touch.

1. Install sheet vinyl throughout the work areas

2. Extend the kitchen wall to separate the living and dining rooms

3. Extend kitchen counters to create a U-shaped kitchen

4. Add a linen closet near the bedrooms and baths

5. Install three-sided tub enclosures

6. Remove doors from closets

7. Install a table with suspended chairs

8. Move furnace from the laundry room to the garage

9. Add a wall in the laundry room to create a family room

10. Move back door so that laundry room functions as both a mud room and a buffer to reduce energy losses

11. Build kitchen cabinets all the way to the ceiling

12. Buy low-maintenance appliances

13. Finish the attic, basement, and garage

14. Add a basketball court, sandbox, or other outside play area

15. Install a drinking fountain

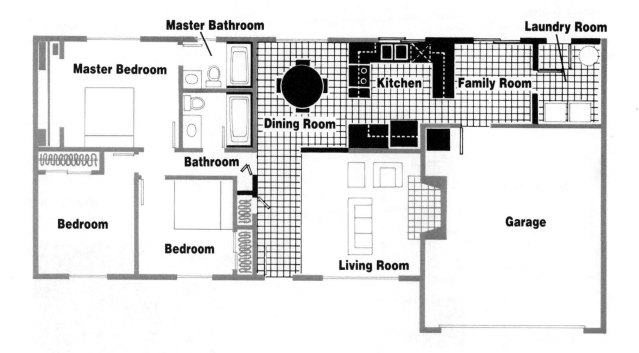

Step Four: I'm Adding On or Building New

Now's the time to have everything your way! In everything you do, remember to use materials that don't require a lot of care, choose colors and fabrics that camouflage dirt, look for smooth surfaces, and build in or suspend whatever you can. In addition, look for specific changes that improve traffic flow, increase storage, give you more room. In this house, that means:

1. Add a walk-in closet to the master bath so all grooming and dressing supplies are stored together

2. Leave only a small closet for bedclothes in the master bedroom, creating more space

3. Lengthen the vanity in the master bath

4. Suspend the toilet in the children's bathroom

5. Add sliding glass doors in dining room

6. Expand the kitchen and family rooms

7. Redesign the kitchen with a full pantry

8. Create a second linen closet in hall

9. Install a central vacuum system

10. Replace leaky or hard-to-clean windows

11. Open up the counter between kitchen and dining room so cook can hand food through

12. Cover the entryways

13. Cove all floorings

14. Plant shrubs, trees in an easy-mow pattern

15. Add sidewalks

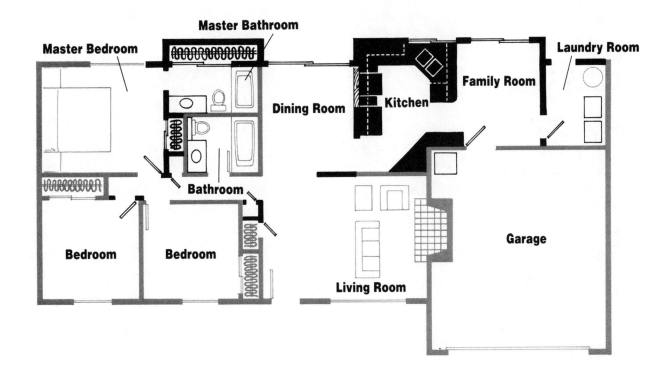

Where Did You Get That?

When you're not doing things the way everyone else does them, you can run into trouble finding the materials and equipment you're looking for. Don't let that deter you from your goal! To save you some time hunting down names, addresses, and contacts, here are some of ours that can help you find what you need.

American Carpet Institute
350 Fifth Avenue
New York, NY 10001

American Standard
(suspended toilets)
100 Ross Road
Pittsburgh, PA 15219

Asphalt & Vinyl Asbestos Tile
Institute
101 Park Avenue
New York, NY 10017

Building Stone Institute
420 Lexington Avenue
New York, NY 10017

The Carpet & Rug Institute
208 West Cuyler Street
Dalton, GA 30720

Hoover Institute
101 East Maple Street
North Canton, OH 44720

Housework, Inc.
(low-maintenance cleaning
supplies and equipment)
P.O. Box 39
Pocatello, ID 83201

Marble Institute of America
1984 Chain Bridge Road
McLean, VA 22101

National Oak Flooring
Manufacturers Association
814 Sterick Building
Memphis, TN 38103

National Pest Control Association
250 W. Jersey Street
Elizabeth, NJ 07207

National Terrazzo & Mosaic Association, Inc.
716 Church Street
Alexandria, VA 22314

Nutone (central vacuums, recessed
and suspended dispensers)
Madison and Red Bank Roads
Cincinnati, OH 45227

Swan Corp. (shell showers)
408 Olive Street
St. Louis, MO 63102

System I (design consultation)
Maintenance-Free Division
P.O. Box 1682
Pocatello, ID 83201

Wallpaper Council, Inc.
969 Third Avenue
New York, NY 10022

Index